*Marlene Sorosky's*

# YEAR-ROUND
# ❀ HOLIDAY
# COOKBOOK

# *Marlene Sorosky's*

# YEAR-ROUND ❋ HOLIDAY COOKBOOK

*Photographs by Robert R. Stein*

HARPER & ROW, PUBLISHERS, New York

Cambridge, Philadelphia, San Francisco,
London, Mexico City, São Paulo, Sydney

1817

FIRST EDITION

Food stylist: Marlene Sorosky

Designer: Charlotte Staub

---

Library of Congress Cataloging in Publication Data

Sorosky, Marlene.
   Marlene Sorosky's year-round holiday cookbook.

   Includes index.
   1. Entertaining. I. Title.
TX731.S663 1982     641.5'68     82-47533
ISBN 0-06-015045-9            AACR2

---

82 83 84 85 86 10 9 8 7 6 5 4 3 2 1

*This book is lovingly dedicated to two exceptional persons:*

*To Julia Child, for universally furthering cooking as an art and generously opening the door for all cooking enthusiasts to follow. For her warm encouragement and interest in both me and my career and for the wonderful insights and confidence I have gained by working with her. I thank her for her zest for life and for caring, not only for me, but for the world.*

*To Danny Kaye, who is not a professional cook, but who is truly the most professional nonprofessional I know. His philosophies of life and mankind are enthusiastically poured into his cooking, and his creativity has overflowed into mine. He always makes me reach for greater heights, and I thank him for being such a special friend.*

# ACKNOWLEDGMENTS

*A very special thank you to the following people, whose contributions enhanced my book:*

*To Ann Bernstein, for her assistance in my classes since I started teaching twelve years ago, and for her help in food styling and wine selection.*

*To Randy Fuhrman, a top Los Angeles caterer, whose creative ideas helped formulate this book.*

*To Janice Wald Henderson, who, by assisting in the writing of this book, helped convey my thoughts and feelings into expressive words.*

*To Angela Wilson, Maddie Katz, Carol Halperin, Danny Fendel, and their families, for devotedly testing and tasting recipes with great enthusiasm.*

# INTRODUCTION

*The pleasures of life pass all too quickly, and the best way to capture time's passages is with holidays and celebrations. Of course it's impossible to remember every minute of our lives, but I'm sure you can recall nostalgically many celebrations in your life, even as far back as childhood. That's exactly why holidays and celebrations become so important in our lives—each special one becomes a cherished memory that we hold on to forever. Indeed, we tend to live our lives from occasion to occasion, from holiday to holiday, with much anticipation.*

*If I had my way, I would have the merriment of holidays never end. I'd stretch the moments around the dinner table into many hours. But in order truly to enjoy celebrations also as the hostess, it helps to take shortcuts that will reduce the workload in the kitchen. Having had four children in six short years, and a professional husband who loved to entertain, I soon became convinced that it is only by pre-preparation, freezing, and the judicious use of some packaged mixes that I could relax, have fun, and really be a carefree hostess.*

*Though I never employ a shortcut that will compromise the flavor of what I am cooking, I do try to simplify recipes, and I believe that is why the cooking classes I teach have been so successful. I always encourage that extra effort to make each dish unique and beautiful—with a dramatic garnish or a creative flourish, with something that will bring a smile. Isn't that what it's all about?*

*I have no single philosophy of cooking or entertaining, only a philosophy of life, which is translated into my recipes. If one enjoys giving, one will get tremendous satisfaction through entertaining. I love giving to others, bringing them into my home, and sharing with them. If this book helps you to entertain your family and those you love with warmth and joy, then I have given a little of my home, and my love, to you.*

❋ *indicates that the recipe can be prepared ahead and can be refrigerated at this point*

❀ *indicates that the recipe can be prepared ahead and frozen at this point*

# CONTENTS

**1**

**HERALDING
THE NEW YEAR**

*New Year's Eve Midnight Supper* 3
*New Year's Day "Soup Bowl"* 11

**2**

**A LITTLE
WINTER WHIMSY**

*Valentine's Day Dinner* 22
*St. Patrick's Day Party* 31

**3**

**SPRING
FEASTS**

*Easter Gala Buffet* 43
*Passover Seder* 61

**4**

**A FAMILY
AFFAIR**

*Mother's Day Breakfast in Bed* 75
*Father's Day Seafood Supper* 83
*Anniversary Dinner* 95

**5**

**SPECIAL
CELEBRATIONS**

*Saluting the Graduate* 108
*Baby Shower Brunch* 121
*Sweet Sixteen Luncheon* 133
*Wedding Reception* 143

**6**

**PATRIOTIC
PARTIES**

*Fourth of July Barbecue* 171
*Labor Day Picnic* 184
*Election Returns Lap Party* 193

**7**

**FALL
FARE**

*Treats for Halloween* 201
*A Bountiful Thanksgiving* 209
*Day-After-Thanksgiving Dinner* 226

**8**

**SEASON'S
GREETINGS**

*A Christmas Banquet* 232
*Holiday Open House* 247
*Cookies for Carolers* 273
*Hanukkah Candle Lighting Party* 281
*Gifts from the Kitchen* 291

*Index* 297

# 1
# HERALDING THE NEW YEAR

# New Year's Eve Midnight Supper

MENU

CONFETTI CHEESE SPREAD
TUNA PÂTÉ
BLINI CUPS WITH CAVIAR
HAM BISCUITS
CASSIS CHAMPAGNE WITH
RASPBERRY CUBES
❀

MADEIRA CHICKEN AND SHRIMP
SPINACH GRATIN
ORANGE-GLAZED CARROTS
❀

VANILLA MOUSSE WITH
BUTTERSCOTCH-RUM SAUCE
❀

WINE RECOMMENDATION:
A YOUNG, LIGHT, FRESH AND FRUITY
RED WINE SUCH AS A GAMAY
OR GAMAY BEAUJOLAIS

*New Year's Eve is a celebration with built-in excitement—a time for well-wishing, toasts, and good cheer. A New Year's Eve supper is the combination of two parties in one, a cocktail party and a dinner party. I serve more hors d'oeuvres than usual to help "tease" everybody's appetite and prolong the dinner hour for a late midnight supper. These hors d'oeuvres recipes expand easily to accommodate the size of your crowd. The Blini Cups with Caviar and the Ham Biscuits are served hot from trays, and the Tuna Pâté and Confetti Cream Cheese Spread are help-yourself hors d'oeuvres.*

*At the end of the hectic holiday season, it's a pleasure to entertain with food that can be prepared ahead. The Spinach Gratin—seasoned spinach layered between thick, cheesy béchamel—and the Madeira Chicken and Shrimp freeze beautifully. Although the elegant Vanilla Mousse won't freeze, it can be refrigerated up to two days ahead. All serve 8 to 10.*

*So out with the horns, the hats and bubbling champagne. Let's lift a glass to the coming New Year.*

*Blini Cups with Caviar surround Ham Biscuits on a silver platter. Cassis Champagne with Raspberry Cubes is served in tall champagne glasses.*

## Confetti Cheese Spread

Four cheeses combine to make a rich and creamy spread.

7 ounces Edam cheese
8 ounces Brie, at room temperature
8 ounces cream cheese, at room temperature
1½ ounces blue cheese
0.6-ounce package dry Italian salad seasoning mix
½ cup chopped parsley
Pimiento for garnish (optional)
Parsley for garnish (optional)
Crackers

Remove rind from Edam; shred cheese. Combine cheeses, salad dressing mix, and chopped parsley in mixing bowl; mix until blended. Or, process half at a time in food processor fitted with the metal blade. Place in a crock and refrigerate at least 4 hours before serving.

❄ May be refrigerated up to 4 days.

❁ May be frozen.

Before serving, decorate with parsley and pimiento if desired.

Makes 2 cups, about 8 servings

## Tuna Pâté

This pâté is much lighter than most. It's especially smooth, and its flavor is enhanced by a mellow hint of brandy and the slight crunchiness of pistachio nuts.

6½-ounce can tuna packed in oil
3 tablespoons brandy or cognac
¼ teaspoon freshly ground pepper
¼ teaspoon dried dill
8 ounces cream cheese, at room temperature
2 hard-boiled eggs
¼ cup chopped pistachio nuts
Crackers or bread rounds

In food processor with metal blade or in blender, process undrained tuna, brandy, pepper, and dill until blended. Add cream cheese and eggs and mix until smooth. Stir in pistachio nuts. Spoon into a crock or serving dish.

❄ May be refrigerated for 1 week.

Serve with crackers or bread rounds.

Makes 2½ cups, about 8 servings

## *Blini Cups with Caviar*

Some of the clamor at your New Year's Eve party may be over this luxurious version of Russian pancakes and caviar. The blinis are shaped into miniature cups that taste a bit like one of my favorite foods, crusty deep-fried potato skins. They'll fall slightly as they bake, making a perfect indentation for a swirl of caviar.

BLINI CUPS
- **1 pint small-curd cottage cheese**
- **1 tablespoon sour cream**
- **1 teaspoon vanilla extract**
- **½ teaspoon sugar**
- **3 tablespoons butter or margarine, melted**
- **3 eggs**
- **½ cup buttermilk biscuit mix**

FILLING
- **½ pint (1 cup) sour cream**
- **4 to 6 ounces red or black caviar, lumpfish or whitefish roe**
- **½ cup finely chopped onion (optional)**

Make blini cups: In food processor with metal blade or with electric mixer mix together cottage cheese, sour cream, vanilla, sugar, and butter or margarine until blended. Add eggs one at a time. Mix in biscuit mix and beat until blended.

Preheat oven to 350°. Spoon batter into greased nonstick or Pam-sprayed 1½-inch miniature muffin cups, filling each three-fourths full. Bake for 35 to 40 minutes or until tops are golden brown. Remove from oven, go around edges of cups with a small knife, and remove to rack to cool.

May be stored at room temperature in airtight container for 2 days.

❄ May be frozen. Do not defrost before reheating.

Before serving, preheat oven to 350°. Place cups on cookie sheets and bake for 10 to 15 minutes or until hot and crisp.

Place sour cream, caviar, and onion (if you like) in small bowls. Let guests help themselves by topping blini cups with sour cream, caviar, and onions if desired.

Makes about 36 cups

## Ham Biscuits

These bite-size biscuits are crisp on the outside and soft, buttery, and dense on the inside. A generous helping of ham is mixed into the pastry, adding to the texture and flavor.

1¼ cups all-purpose flour
 1 tablespoon baking powder
 ½ teaspoon salt
 ¼ pound (1 stick) cold butter, cut into 8 pieces
 2 tablespoons shortening
 6 ounces finely chopped ham (about 1¼ cups)
 ¼ cup finely chopped green onions
 ½ cup grated Parmesan cheese
 ⅓ cup milk
 3 tablespoons mayonnaise
 3 tablespoons prepared mustard

In food processor with metal blade or in mixing bowl, mix flour, baking powder, and salt. Add butter and shortening and mix just until size of coarse meal. Add ham, green onions, and Parmesan cheese. Mix until blended. Add milk and mix until dough holds together.

Shape dough into 1-inch balls. Place on greased baking sheets. With a wet finger, press an indentation into the center of each ball. Bake at 375° for 10 minutes. Remove from oven and with handle of wooden spoon press indentations again. Put back in oven and bake an additional 10 minutes or until golden.

❀ May be frozen.

Before serving, defrost and reheat at 375° for 5 to 10 minutes or until heated through.

In a small bowl, mix mayonnaise and mustard. Fill center of indentations with mixture and bake at 375° for 3 to 5 minutes.

Makes 42 biscuits

# Spinach Gratin

This rich, cheesy casserole cuts into easy-to-serve squares. A great dish to make ahead, take to a friend's dinner party, and put in the oven when you get there.

CHEESE SAUCE
4 cups (1 quart) milk
7 tablespoons butter or margarine
1 cup all-purpose flour
8 large eggs, at room temperature
1 teaspoon salt
¼ teaspoon white pepper
¼ teaspoon ground nutmeg
2⅔ cups shredded Swiss cheese (about 11 ounces)

SPINACH FILLING
3 tablespoons butter or margarine
¼ cup finely chopped onion
2 tablespoons all-purpose flour
½ cup half-and-half
Two 10-ounce packages frozen chopped spinach, thawed, drained, and squeezed dry
Salt and pepper

Make the cheese sauce: Bring milk to a boil; set aside. In large saucepan, melt 7 tablespoons butter or margarine. Stir in flour and cook, stirring over low heat, for 2 minutes or until frothy. Remove from heat and slowly whisk in the hot milk. Return to heat and cook, whisking constantly over moderate heat, until mixture comes to a boil. Remove from heat. Using electric hand beater, add eggs one at a time, beating well after each addition. Add salt, pepper, and nutmeg. Do not be concerned if the sauce is slightly lumpy; it will smooth out in the end. Stir in 2 cups of the cheese. Place a piece of waxed paper directly on sauce to prevent skin from forming.

Make the spinach filling: In medium skillet, melt 3 tablespoons butter or margarine. Sauté onion until soft and beginning to brown, about 8 minutes. Sprinkle flour over and cook, stirring, until flour is incorporated, about 2 minutes. Add the half-and-half and cook over moderate heat, stirring constantly, until sauce comes to a boil. Stir in spinach. Season to taste with salt and pepper.

Grease a 9-by-13-inch casserole. Spread half the cheese sauce in casserole. Spread spinach filling over sauce; it will mix with cheese sauce slightly. Cover with remaining cheese sauce. Sprinkle top with remaining ⅔ cup cheese.

❋ May be refrigerated, covered, for 2 days.

❊ May be frozen for 1 month. Defrost in refrigerator overnight.

Before serving, bring to room temperature. Bake uncovered at 400° for 25 to 30 minutes or until top is golden and casserole is bubbling.

Serves 12 to 16

*Variation:* Two 10-ounce packages frozen chopped broccoli, cooked, drained, and finely chopped, may be substituted for the spinach.

## Madeira Chicken and Shrimp

If you like coq au vin, you're going to love this easy, yet impressive rendition with an added splash of vinegar and Madeira. This is perfect party fare because it reheats splendidly and stays moist and flavorful on a buffet. The addition of shrimp is optional, but they add an elegant and dramatic touch.

Two to three 4-pound broiler fryers,
   cut up, or 16 to 20 pieces of
   chicken on the bone (such as
   breasts and thighs)
   Salt and pepper
2 tablespoons butter or margarine
2 to 3 tablespoons vegetable oil
16 to 20 whole mushrooms
16-ounce bag frozen whole onions,
   thawed and drained on paper
   towels
2 tablespoons sugar
4 cloves garlic, crushed
1 cup beef broth
¾ cup red wine vinegar
½ cup dry Madeira wine
1 teaspoon dried tarragon
1 teaspoon dried thyme
1 tablespoon plus 1 teaspoon
   tomato paste
¾-ounce package brown gravy mix
16 to 20 medium shrimp, shelled
   with tail left on and deveined
   Parsley for garnish

Dry chicken well and sprinkle with salt and pepper. In a large, heavy saucepan, melt 2 tablespoons butter or margarine and oil. Over moderately high heat, sauté chicken pieces a few at a time until brown on all sides. As they are browned, remove them to an ovenproof casserole. Sauté whole mushrooms in same saucepan until lightly browned. Remove and add to chicken. Add onions to saucepan, sprinkle with sugar, and sauté over moderate heat, stirring until glazed and lightly browned. If too dry, add an additional tablespoon of oil. Stir in garlic, beef broth, vinegar, Madeira, tarragon, thyme, tomato paste, and brown gravy mix. Bring to a boil, stirring constantly, scraping up any brown bits that stick to the bottom of the pan. Pour sauce over chicken and mushrooms in casserole. Cover and bake at 350° for 45 minutes.

❊ May be refrigerated up to 2 days.

❅ May be frozen.

If serving immediately, add shrimp, cover, and continue to bake an additional 15 minutes. If preparing ahead, bring to room temperature; bake covered at 350° for 25 minutes or until heated through. Add shrimp, cover, and bake 15 minutes longer, or until shrimp turn pink. With slotted spoon, remove chicken, shrimp, onions, and mushrooms to serving platter. Spoon over desired amount of sauce. Garnish with parsley.

Serves 8 to 10

## Orange-Glazed Carrots

A friend had me over for dinner one evening. I tasted her carrots and exclaimed, "These are absolutely delicious!" She said, "Marlene, it's your recipe!" She had substituted frozen carrots for fresh, which I had never done, believing they would turn out soggy. Thanks to her experimentation, I learned that they are delicious either way. These carrots have more of an orange flavor than a sweet one and are a lovely side dish to a roast chicken.

2 **pounds fresh or frozen baby carrots or large carrots cut into 2-inch lengths and 1 inch wide**
4 **tablespoons (½ stick) butter or margarine**
¼ **cup chicken broth**
¼ **teaspoon salt**
1 **cup orange marmalade**
  **Freshly ground pepper**
2 **tablespoons Grand Marnier (optional)**
2 **tablespoons chopped parsley**

Peel and trim carrots if necessary. In a heavy saucepan, bring the butter or margarine, broth, and salt to a boil. Add the carrots and cook covered over moderate heat for 10 to 20 minutes or until barely tender.

Uncover and stir in the marmalade. Cook, stirring, over low heat until liquid has reduced to a glaze. Season to taste with additional salt and pepper. Add Grand Marnier, if desired.

❋ May be refrigerated overnight.

Before serving, reheat gently, stirring carrots until heated through. Garnish with chopped parsley.

Serves 8

## Cassis Champagne with Raspberry Cubes

Because you add black-currant liqueur to this festive punch, you may use a less expensive champagne. The raspberry jewel ice cubes are the crowning touch for any celebration.

1 **to two 10-ounce packages frozen raspberries in syrup, defrosted and strained to remove seeds**
½ **to 1 cup water**
**Two 4/5-quart bottles champagne, chilled**
½ **cup crème de cassis, chilled**

Make raspberry ice cubes by placing raspberries and their syrup in a bowl. Gently stir in ½ cup water per package of raspberries. With a spoon, divide raspberries among plastic ice cube containers. Fill with raspberry liquid. Freeze until firm. Pop out of trays and freeze in plastic bags until ready to use.

Punch may be assembled in punch bowl or directly in champagne glasses. Place approximately 1 tablespoon crème de cassis in bottom of each glass. Fill glass with champagne. Place one raspberry ice cube in each glass. Or, combine all ingredients in punch bowl.

Serves 8

## Vanilla Mousse with Butterscotch-Rum Sauce

You can use any mold for this sensational dessert, but the more fluted the mold, the prettier it will be. Technically this is not a mousse—it's more like a creamy, dreamy pudding.

MOUSSE
- 3 envelopes unflavored gelatin
- 1 cup sugar
- ½ teaspoon salt
- 4 cups (1 quart) milk
- 2 tablespoons vanilla extract
- 4 cups (2 pints) whipping cream

BUTTERSCOTCH-RUM SAUCE
- ⅔ cup light corn syrup
- 4 tablespoons (½ stick) unsalted butter
- 1¼ cups light, or golden, brown sugar, firmly packed
- 2 tablespoons dark rum
- ⅓ cup milk or half-and-half

In a medium saucepan, stir gelatin, sugar, and salt. Slowly stir in milk. Cook over medium heat, stirring frequently, until gelatin is dissolved and mixture *just* comes to a boil. Remove from heat, pour into a bowl, and stir in vanilla. Place bowl in a larger bowl filled with ice water and stir until mixture cools and begins to thicken.

In a large bowl, beat cream until it forms soft peaks. Fold cream into cooled gelatin mixture. Lightly grease a 12-cup mold and fill with vanilla mousse. Cover top with plastic wrap. Refrigerate until set, a minimum of 3 hours.

❉ May be refrigerated up to 2 days.

Make butterscotch-rum sauce: In a medium saucepan combine the corn syrup, butter, brown sugar, and rum. Bring the mixture to a boil over medium-high heat. Insert a candy thermometer and boil until mixture reaches 236° or forms a soft ball. Immediately remove the saucepan from the heat and slowly pour in the milk or half-and-half, stirring rapidly.

❉ Sauce may be refrigerated up to 1 month.

Reheat sauce over low heat. If it becomes too thick, it may be thinned down with additional rum, milk, or cream.

Run a small knife around edge of mold, dip in warm water, and unmold onto large platter. Before serving, drizzle warm sauce (not hot, or it may melt the mousse) over the top, letting it drip down the sides. Pass remaining sauce.

Serves 10 to 12

# New Year's Day "Soup Bowl"

## MENU

Country Minestrone
Seafood Bisque
Mushroom Barley Soup
Tomato and Scallop Chowder

Honey Wheat Bread
Beer Rye Bread
Onion Poppy Seed Bread

Fresh Whipped Butter
Amaretto Butter
Herb Butter

Toffee Trifle Bowl

Beverage Recommendation:
bloody marys or beer

New Year's Day has become synonymous with football games, and my theory is, if you can't beat them, join them. So why not invite some friends over for your own "soup bowl" buffet? Soups always make entertaining a breeze because they can be prepared far in advance and go from freezer to table with little effort.

Here are four of my favorite soups to pick and choose from. They are accompanied by three wonderful breads.

Be patient as your bread rises and wait until the dough doubles in volume, even if it takes longer than stated in the recipe. The cooler the kitchen the longer it will take. Denser breads, such as the Beer Rye Bread, take longer to rise than lighter ones. A great place to let bread rise is on a cookie sheet over a large soup pot filled with several inches of simmering water. (Cover the cookie sheet with a folded towel and place the bowl with the dough on top of the sheet.) My students, who like this method, say it's fast and fail-safe. I never refrigerate bread because I find refrigeration dries it out. If you freeze bread and reheat it, it will taste just like freshly baked.

Each of the soups in this menu serves 6 to 8.

## Country Minestrone

This soup, no matter what you add to or subtract from it, is always superb, and it freezes beautifully. To make it a hearty main-dish soup, place a slice of Italian bread in each soup bowl, top with Parmesan cheese, and ladle the soup over it. Delicious!

4 tablespoons olive oil
1 large onion, coarsely chopped
1 stalk celery, coarsely chopped
2 large carrots, peeled and chopped
4 large cloves garlic, crushed
¼ cup chopped parsley
2 zucchini, diced
½ small head green cabbage, chopped (about ¾ pound)
16-ounce can whole tomatoes, undrained and chopped
¾ cup chopped fresh spinach
4 cups beef broth
1 potato, peeled and diced
½ cup elbow macaroni
Salt and pepper to taste
½ to 1 cup freshly grated Parmesan cheese
Additional Parmesan cheese for serving

Heat olive oil in soup pot. Sauté onion, celery, carrots, garlic, and parsley over moderate heat for 10 minutes, until soft but not brown. Add zucchini, cabbage, tomatoes with their juice, and spinach. Cover and simmer for 10 minutes. Add broth, potato, and macaroni. Simmer uncovered for 20 minutes or until potatoes and cabbage are tender. Season with salt and pepper.

❀ May be refrigerated up to 4 days.

❀ May be frozen.

Reheat before serving and stir in Parmesan cheese to taste. Stir until melted and adjust seasonings. Pass additional cheese.

Serves 8

## Seafood Bisque

The base of this bisque is so rich that you can use canned seafood instead of fresh or frozen and it will still be superlative. A glass of cool white wine, a tossed green leafy salad, and a steaming bowl of this creamy chunky soup—utter contentment.

4½-ounce can shrimp
6½-ounce can minced clams
6-ounce package frozen crabmeat, defrosted, or 7½-ounce can king crab
4 strips bacon, diced

Drain shrimp and clams, reserving liquid. Shred crab with hands, and add to seafood; set aside. Sauté bacon in soup pot until crisp; add garlic, seafood liquid, wine, salt, pepper, and thyme. Bring to a boil, add potatoes, cover, and simmer 20 minutes or until potatoes are tender. Add

1 clove garlic, crushed
1 cup dry white wine or imported
    dry vermouth
1½ teaspoons salt
⅛ teaspoon pepper
½ teaspoon dried thyme
2 cups diced potatoes
16-ounce can creamed corn
½ cup chopped green onion
2 tablespoons chopped parsley
2 cups milk, at room temperature
1 cup half-and-half, at room
    temperature

creamed corn, green onion, and parsley.

Stir in milk and half-and-half. Bring to a boil, whisking constantly. Add reserved seafood and cook until heated through. Season to taste.

❋ May be refrigerated overnight.

❋ May be frozen up to two weeks.

Before serving, reheat slowly until hot. If too thick, thin with additional milk.

Serves 8

## Mushroom Barley Soup

A slightly thickened old-fashioned soup that is light and creamy and beautifully balanced in taste and texture. Dried mushrooms are sold by the quarter-ounce or half-ounce and are a real flavor booster—much more pungent than fresh mushrooms.

¾ ounce dried mushrooms
3 tablespoons butter or margarine
1 large leek, white part only,
    chopped (about ¾ cup)
2 stalks celery, chopped (about 1
    cup)
1 onion, chopped
4 cups chicken broth
⅓ cup pearl barley
¼ cup chopped parsley
1 bay leaf
½ teaspoon dried thyme
½ teaspoon salt
    Freshly ground pepper to taste
1 potato, peeled and diced (about 1½
    cups)
1 cup whipping cream or half-and-
    half

Soak mushrooms in hot water to cover for 30 minutes. Drain and squeeze dry. Cut off tough stems and chop mushrooms into small pieces. Set aside. In medium soup pot, melt butter or margarine. Sauté leek, celery, and onion over low heat, stirring occasionally, until soft but not brown, about 20 minutes. Add chicken broth and barley, and bring to a boil. Stir in parsley, bay leaf, thyme, salt, and pepper. Cover and simmer for 1 hour, stirring occasionally. Add diced potato and dried mushrooms. Cover and simmer 30 minutes longer. Remove bay leaf.

Stir in cream or half-and-half and correct seasonings.

❋ May be refrigerated up to 2 days.

❋ May be frozen.

Reheat before serving.

Serves 6

## Tomato and Scallop Chowder

This tomato-based soup is robust without overpowering the delicate flavor of tender scallops. The key is to add the scallops at the last moment just to heat them through, as they will simmer in the savory broth while the soup is being served.

6 slices bacon, diced
1 large onion, sliced (about 1 cup)
1 small green pepper, sliced into thin strips (about 1 cup)
2 carrots, thinly sliced (about 1 cup)
1 tablespoon chopped parsley
1-pound 12-ounce can tomatoes, undrained and chopped
7½-ounce bottle clam juice
½ teaspoon salt
1 bay leaf
2 teaspoons bottled steak sauce
¾ teaspoon dried thyme
1½ cups chicken broth
2 medium potatoes, peeled and diced (about 2½ cups)
Freshly ground pepper
1 pound scallops, cut into bite-size pieces

In medium soup pot, sauté bacon until almost crisp. Add onion, green pepper, carrots, and parsley; cook over low heat about 10 minutes, stirring occasionally. Add tomatoes with their juice, clam juice, salt, bay leaf, steak sauce, thyme, and chicken broth. Bring to a boil. Simmer covered for 30 minutes. Add potatoes, cover, and simmer 30 minutes longer, or until potatoes are tender. Remove bay leaf.

❄ May be refrigerated up to 2 days.

❅ May be frozen.

Reheat before serving. Season to taste with salt and pepper. Stir in scallops and cook for 2 to 3 minutes or until scallops are cooked through. Do not overcook or scallops will become tough.

Serves 6 to 8

## Honey Wheat Bread

The taste of honey highlights the wheat flavor of this golden-brown bread.

1 package active dry yeast
½ cup warm water (100° to 115°)
1 teaspoon salt
¾ cup whole wheat flour
1½ to 2 cups all-purpose flour
1 egg, at room temperature
3 tablespoons honey
2 tablespoons butter, at room
   temperature

Sprinkle yeast over ¼ cup warm water and stir until dissolved. Set aside. Place salt, whole wheat flour, and 1½ cups all-purpose flour into mixing bowl or food processor fitted with metal blade. Add egg, honey, butter, ¼ cup warm water, and yeast mixture. Mix or process until dough forms a ball. Knead until smooth and elastic, adding more flour as needed. Dough may be kneaded in food processor with metal knife for 1½ to 2 minutes, by hand on floured board, or in mixing bowl with dough hook. Shape dough into a ball and place in greased bowl, turning to coat all surfaces. Cover with buttered plastic wrap and a damp towel and let rise in a warm place until double in bulk, about 1 to 1½ hours.

Punch dough down and knead lightly. Place dough in a buttered 9-by-5-by-2-inch loaf pan. Cover and let rise until double in bulk, 45 minutes to 1 hour. Bake at 375° for 25 to 30 minutes or until bread is nicely browned. Remove from pan and cool on rack.

❋ May be frozen. Do not refrigerate.

Makes 1 loaf

*Tip:* To measure honey, oil a measuring cup or spoon with vegetable oil. Honey will slip right out.

*Onion Poppy Seed Bread is cut into large slices and served with Fresh Whipped Butter.*

## Onion Poppy Seed Bread

If you're going to bake bread, make one that you won't be able to buy. The minute you taste this bread, you'll know it's homemade. It is divided in two sections, rolled around the filling, then baked in the shape of a ring. The onion and poppy seed mixture will be prettily marbled throughout.

DOUGH
- **1 package active dry yeast**
- **¼ cup warm water (100° to 115°)**
- **¼ pound (1 stick) butter or margarine, melted**
- **1 cup milk**
- **4 to 4½ cups all-purpose flour**
- **¼ cup sugar**
- **2 teaspoons salt**
- **1 egg**

In large mixing bowl, dissolve yeast in warm water. In small saucepan heat butter and milk until lukewarm. Add to yeast mixture with 2 cups flour, sugar, salt, and 1 egg. Beat at medium speed for 2 minutes, scraping down sides occasionally. Mix in 2 cups additional flour. Dough should be fairly stiff. If it is too soft, add a little more flour. Knead on floured board or with dough hook, adding more flour as needed, until smooth and elastic, about 8 to 10 minutes. Shape dough in a ball, place in a greased bowl, and turn to grease all surfaces. Cover with buttered plastic wrap and a damp towel and let rise in a warm place until double in bulk, about 1 hour.

ONION POPPY SEED FILLING

**1 medium onion, chopped (1 cup)**
**4 tablespoons (½ stick) butter or**
  **margarine, melted**
**3 tablespoons poppy seeds**
**¼ teaspoon salt**

TOPPING

**1 egg, lightly beaten**
**1 tablespoon poppy seeds**
**1 tablespoon chopped onion**

Meanwhile make onion poppy seed filling by mixing all the filling ingredients in a small bowl. Set aside.

Punch dough down. On lightly floured board, roll dough into a rectangle 15 inches by 10 inches. Cut dough in half lengthwise, forming 2 rectangles 15 inches by 5 inches. Spread half of onion poppy seed filling on each strip, leaving a ½-inch border all around. Fold 15-inch edge over from top to bottom. Pinch seams to seal, and twist into a long rope. Repeat with remaining dough. Twist the ends of both ropes together to shape a large ring. Place loaf on lightly greased baking sheet. Cover and let rise in warm place until double in bulk, 45 minutes to 1 hour.

Preheat oven to 350°. Brush dough with lightly beaten egg. Sprinkle with poppy seeds and onion. Bake for 40 minutes or until golden brown and bread sounds hollow on bottom when tapped with fingers. Cool on wire rack.

❀ May be frozen. Do not refrigerate.

Makes 1 loaf

*Place the filling down the center of two strips of dough and enclose by folding the strips of dough top to bottom and crimping the edges to seal. Turn dough so that crimped edge is underneath.*

## Beer Rye Bread

This Old World–style bread is earthy, healthful, tangy, moist, dense, and crusty with a rich chestnut-brown shading.

2 packages active dry yeast
¼ cup warm water (100° to 115°)
2 cups beer
4 tablespoons (½ stick) butter or margarine
⅓ cup molasses
½ cup wheat germ
1 tablespoon grated orange rind
3 tablespoons caraway seeds
2 teaspoons salt
2 cups rye flour
4 to 5 cups all-purpose flour
Cornmeal
1 egg mixed with 1 tablespoon water for glaze

Sprinkle yeast over warm water, stirring until dissolved. Set aside. In a saucepan, heat beer, butter or margarine, and molasses until lukewarm. Transfer beer mixture to a mixing bowl and add wheat germ, grated orange rind, 1 tablespoon caraway seeds, salt, and yeast mixture. Blend well. Beat in rye flour and enough of the all-purpose flour to make a stiff dough. Knead on floured board or with dough hook until smooth and elastic, adding more flour as needed, about 10 minutes. Shape dough into a ball and place in a greased bowl, turning to coat all surfaces. Cover with buttered plastic wrap and a damp towel and let rise in a warm place until double in bulk, about 1½ to 2 hours.

Punch dough down and knead lightly; cover and let rest for 10 minutes. Form into 2 round loaves. Grease baking sheet and lightly sprinkle it with cornmeal. Cover dough and let rise until doubled, about 1 hour. Brush with egg glaze and bake at 350° for 25 minutes. Remove from oven, brush again with glaze, and sprinkle with 2 tablespoons caraway seeds. Bake 15 to 20 minutes longer or until loaves sound hollow when tapped on bottom. Remove from pan to racks and cool.

❀ May be frozen. Do not refrigerate.

Makes 2 loaves

## Fresh Whipped Butter

Whipping air into butter makes it easier to spread and much creamier. Make it just before serving for the fluffiest results.

½ **pound (2 sticks) unsalted butter, at room temperature**

Place butter in mixing bowl and beat until it turns very fluffy and light, about 8 to 10 minutes. May be held at room temperature up to 4 hours.

Makes 1½ cups

## Herb Butter

Herb butter is wonderful on store-bought bread and it's even better on homemade.

¼ **pound (1 stick) unsalted butter, at room temperature**
1 **tablespoon lemon juice**
1 **small clove garlic, crushed**
1 **tablespoon chopped parsley**
¼ **teaspoon dried thyme**
¼ **teaspoon dried tarragon**
¼ **teaspoon dried basil**
¼ **teaspoon caraway seeds**
¼ **teaspoon salt**

In small bowl or food processor with metal blade, mix all ingredients together. Refrigerate until ready to serve.

❋ May be refrigerated several days.
❊ May be frozen.

Remove from refrigerator 30 minutes before serving.

Makes ½ cup

## Amaretto Butter

You can both smell and taste the perfumed scent of sweet almond essence in this fluffy fresh butter. It's especially fragrant on the Beer Rye and the Honey Wheat breads (see preceding recipes).

¼ **pound (1 stick) unsalted butter, at room temperature**
1 **tablespoon honey**
2 **tablespoons Amaretto liqueur**
¼ **teaspoon almond extract**

In mixing bowl, mix butter and honey until well blended. Add Amaretto and almond extract, blending until incorporated.

❋ May be refrigerated several days.
❊ May be frozen.

Makes about ⅔ cup

## Toffee Trifle Bowl

No, this is not really a trifle. A trifle is cake doused with liqueur and layered with custard and fruit. On the third layer, instead of fruit, I use chocolate-and-almond-coated English toffee. It's got a sensational coffee-toffee flavor. I guarantee, no one's going to complain.

5⅝-ounce package vanilla instant pudding

3 cups half-and-half

6 cups angel food cake cut into 1½-inch pieces (about 1 pound)

¾ cup Kahlúa

1 pint (2 cups) whipping cream

2 tablespoons instant coffee, powder or granules

2 tablespoons sugar

1 teaspoon vanilla extract

½ pound English toffee, broken into 1-inch pieces and coarsely crushed

12 coffee candy beans (optional)

Prepare pudding as package directs, substituting half-and-half for the milk. Sprinkle cake with Kahlúa and let set 5 minutes. Mix pudding and cake together; set aside. Pour whipping cream and coffee into mixing bowl. Let stand 1 minute. Beat until mixture begins to thicken; add sugar and vanilla. Continue beating until mixture forms soft peaks. Set aside approximately 1½ cups whipped cream for garnish.

In an attractive 2-quart (8-cup) serving bowl, layer half the cake-pudding mixture, half the coffee-flavored whipped cream, and half the English toffee. Repeat with remaining pudding and cream. Dollop the reserved cream around outer edge of bowl, or pipe rosettes through a pastry bag using a large star tip. Sprinkle remaining English toffee over top. Place a coffee candy bean on each rosette, if desired.

Serves 8 to 10

# 2
# A LITTLE
# WINTER
# WHIMSY

# Valentine's Day Dinner

## MENU

Strawberry Banana Daiquiris
Seasoned Nuts

❧

Cream of Pimiento Soup
Curry or Garlic Toast Hearts

❧

Salmon Wellington
Broccoli Bouquets

❧

Poached Pears in
Raspberry Sauce

❧

Wine Recommendation:
A fresh, fruity, aromatic
white wine such as
Johannesburg Riesling

Hearts and flowers—and a touch of pink—are the theme for this intimate candlelight dinner: pimiento hearts float atop creamy pimiento soup, crisp garlic toast is cut into hearts, and fresh broccoli is tied into "bouquets." Pink salmon fillets topped with chopped, sautéed vegetables and then baked in a flaky pastry dough make a spectacular entrée. Pears poached in a crimson red raspberry sauce are a refreshingly light dessert.

Set your table for romance by adding red velvet hearts to an elegant fresh flower centerpiece and setting a long-stemmed red rose by each woman's place.

This menu is designed for 8 but can be easily altered to make a romantic dinner for 2.

22

## Strawberry Banana Daiquiris

This slightly sweet, frothy, and fruity drink is so rich that it takes the place of an appetizer.

**6-ounce can frozen daiquiri mix**
**1¼ cups light rum**
**Two 10-ounce packages frozen strawberries in syrup, partially frozen**
**2 ripe bananas**
**Ice cubes**

Place half the daiquiri mix, half the rum, 1 package of strawberries, and 1 banana in blender. Fill to within 1 inch of top with ice cubes. Blend. Add additional ice cubes and continue blending until mixture is thick and smooth. Repeat with remaining ingredients.

Makes twelve 6-ounce servings

## Seasoned Nuts

You can vary the type of nuts and also the seasoning according to your whim. They're great for any party as well as for a Valentine's Day dinner.

**12-ounce can (2 cups) mixed nuts**
**4 tablespoons (½ stick) unsalted butter, melted**
**2 tablespoons vegetable oil**
**2 teaspoons barbecue seasoning mix**

Rub nuts between hands to remove any excess skins. Preheat oven to 350°. Spread the nuts evenly in a baking dish or jelly-roll pan. Lightly dribble the butter and oil over all. Roast at 350° for 15 to 20 minutes, shaking the pan several times to coat all the nuts evenly. Turn the nuts out onto paper towels. Place barbecue seasoning in plastic bag. Add nuts and shake to coat them with the seasoning. Empty into bowl, shaking bag to remove all seasoning.

May be stored airtight for several months.
❋ May be frozen.

Makes 2 cups

*Variations:* For garlic-seasoned nuts, add ¾ teaspoon garlic powder and 2 teaspoons coarse salt to 2 cups nuts. For curried nuts, add 1 teaspoon curry powder to 2 cups nuts.

## Cream of Pimiento Soup

*A pale delicate orange hue and a mellow velvety taste characterize this soup.*

6 tablespoons butter or margarine
2 medium onions, chopped (about 2 cups)
Six 4-ounce jars diced pimiento, drained
3 tablespoons all-purpose flour
4½ cups chicken broth
2 teaspoons sugar
2 cups whipping cream, at room temperature
2 cups shredded sharp Cheddar cheese (about 8 ounces)
1 teaspoon dry mustard
½ to 1 teaspoon salt (depending on chicken broth)
⅛ teaspoon white pepper
¼ teaspoon Tabasco sauce
Sour cream (optional)
1 whole pimiento (optional)

Melt butter or margarine in soup pot. Sauté onion and diced pimiento over low heat until very soft, but not brown, about 30 minutes. Purée in food processor with metal blade or, for a smoother texture, purée in blender. Return to saucepan and gradually whisk in the flour. Add chicken broth and sugar. Cook over low heat, stirring occasionally, until mixture thickens and boils, about 10 minutes. Add cream, cheese, mustard, salt, pepper, and Tabasco. Stir until heated through.

❋ May be refrigerated up to 2 days.
❊ May be frozen.

Before serving, reheat until hot. Do not boil. Adjust seasonings. If desired, garnish each serving with a dollop of sour cream and a pimiento heart cut out with an aspic cutter.

Serves 8

## Curry or Garlic Toast Hearts

*Everyone loves garlic bread, and a heart-shaped rendition is positively romantic. Curry is the most misunderstood blend of spices in my classes. After the students try it, they really like it.*

4 slices good-quality white or egg bread

CURRY BUTTER
4 tablespoons butter
½ to ¾ teaspoon curry powder

GARLIC BUTTER
4 tablespoons butter
1 clove garlic, crushed
1 tablespoon finely chopped parsley
Salt to taste

Remove crusts from bread and cut into hearts, using a 2-inch heart-shaped cookie cutter. You should get 3 to 4 hearts per slice.

Make curry or garlic butter. For curry butter, melt butter and curry powder in a small skillet until bubbling. For garlic butter, melt butter in a small skillet. Add garlic and cook over low heat for 2 minutes. Add parsley and salt.

Dip the bread cut-outs into the butter, coating each side, and place on a baking sheet. Bake at 375° for 10 minutes, then turn and bake 5 additional minutes or until golden.

Watch carefully, as the timing varies with the oven. Drain on paper towels.

May be stored at room temperature overnight.

❋ May be frozen.

Reheat at 375° for 7 to 10 minutes or until hot. Serve as appetizers or with soup.

Makes 12 to 16 hearts

## Broccoli Bouquets

The broccoli can be parboiled a day before serving and then sautéed just to heat through. This helps retain both color and crispness. Red pimiento ties a bunch of broccoli into a pretty "bouquet" that is a graceful accent to the dinner.

**3 pounds fresh broccoli**
**1 tablespoon salt**
**2 tablespoons butter or margarine**
**2 tablespoons vegetable oil**
**3 cloves garlic, crushed**
**2 tablespoons lemon juice**
  **Pepper to taste**
**1 to 2 whole pimientos, cut into strips for garnish**

Cut the tough end off the broccoli and discard. Peel the stems, leaving the flowerets attached. Cut the bunches into 8 to 10 serving-size portions.

Bring a large pot of water and 1 tablespoon salt to a boil. Add broccoli and boil slowly uncovered for 10 to 12 minutes or until the thickest part of the stem can be pierced with a fork. Remove from heat and immediately plunge the broccoli into a bowl of ice water to stop the cooking process. Remove from water when cool, drain thoroughly on paper towels, and cover with plastic wrap until ready to use.

❋ May be refrigerated overnight.

Before serving, bring broccoli to room temperature. In a large skillet, melt butter or margarine and oil. Add garlic, lemon juice, and broccoli. Sauté broccoli, turning often with tongs, until heated through. Season to taste. Remove to serving plates and garnish each bunch with a strip of pimiento, making a "bouquet."

Serves 8 to 10

## Salmon Wellington

To make this elegant pièce de résistance, individual delicate salmon fillets are topped with Madeira-spiked sautéed artichokes, mushrooms, and onions and then enveloped in a flaky rich pastry dough. The fillets shouldn't be too thin, or they will overcook by the time the pastry is done. Decorate the top with scraps of dough—you can form your lover's initials, hearts, flowers, whatever your romantic self desires.

**Eight 6-ounce salmon fillets, cut about ¾ inch thick**
**1 egg yolk mixed with 1 tablespoon milk for glaze**

FLAKY PASTRY
**½ pound (2 sticks) butter, cold and cut into pieces for food processor, at room temperature for mixer**
**8-ounce package cream cheese, cold and cut into pieces for food processor, at room temperature for mixer**
**2 cups all-purpose flour**

MUSHROOM ARTICHOKE FILLING
**3 tablespoons butter or margarine**
**8-ounce can artichoke bottoms, drained and coarsely chopped**
**1 onion, chopped**
**1 pound mushrooms, coarsely chopped**
**¼ cup Madeira wine**
**Salt and pepper**

LIGHT WHITE WINE SAUCE
**6 tablespoons dry white wine or imported dry vermouth**
**6 tablespoons white wine vinegar**
**2 tablespoons finely chopped shallots or onion**
**1½ cups whipping cream, at room temperature**
**¼ to ½ teaspoon salt**
**White pepper**
**2 tablespoons finely chopped chives or parsley**

Make flaky pastry: In food processor with metal blade or in mixing bowl, mix butter and cream cheese until blended. Add flour and continue mixing until well incorporated. Shape into 2 flat balls and refrigerate for several hours or overnight.

❋ May be refrigerated up to 1 week.

❀ May be frozen.

Make mushroom artichoke filling: Melt butter or margarine in skillet and sauté artichokes and onion until lightly browned. Add mushrooms and Madeira and cook, stirring, until most of the liquid has evaporated. Season to taste. Remove to bowl and chill.

❋ Filling may be refrigerated up to 2 days.

❀ May be frozen.

Roll half the pastry on a floured board into a rectangle approximately 14 inches long and 12 inches wide. Cut into 4 rectangles. Repeat with remaining dough.

Place salmon fillets on a greased baking sheet. Tuck the thinner parts of fillet underneath, making them all the same thickness. Divide mushroom artichoke filling among the fillets and spread evenly on top. Cover each with a rectangle of pastry. Tuck ½ inch of pastry under fillets; trim off excess dough. Do not cover the entire bottom with pastry or it will become soggy. Brush top and sides with egg yolk glaze, being careful not to let glaze drip. Reroll scraps of pastry and cut out small decorations. Place on Wellingtons and glaze the entire pastry again.

❋ May be refrigerated up to 8 hours.

Make light white wine sauce: Place wine,

*Tuck thin strips of salmon underneath thicker parts to make fillets equal size. Spread filling on fillets. Then place rectangles of dough on top of them and tuck edges underneath.*

vinegar, and shallots or onion in medium saucepan. Bring to a boil, lower the heat, and simmer until slightly thickened and reduced to approximately 4 tablespoons. Slowly whisk in the cream. Simmer, stirring occasionally, until sauce thickens to desired consistency. This will take a little time, but as the water evaporates from the cream, it will thicken. Season to taste with salt and pepper. Stir in chives or parsley. Reheat before serving. If sauce becomes too thick, thin down with additional wine or cream. Serve hot.

✱ Sauce may be kept covered at room temperature for 4 hours.

✱ May be refrigerated overnight

Before serving, bring Wellingtons to room temperature for 1 hour. Preheat oven to 425°. Bake Wellingtons for 20 to 25 minutes or until the pastry is golden. At this time, if the fillets are ¾ inch thick, they will be moist and flaky. Spoon a small amount of sauce on each plate, place Wellingtons on sauce, and pass remaining sauce.

Serves 8

*Baked Salmon Wellington is served with a light white wine sauce and Broccoli Bouquets.*

## *Poached Pears in Raspberry Sauce*

Fresh pears poached in raspberry juice blush and absorb a raspberry essence even before they are cloaked in a sauce. These pears retain the shape and texture of fresh pears with the sweet softness of poached. They are bathed in a crimson raspberry sauce perfumed with raspberry brandy.

**4 tablespoons lemon juice**
**8 ripe pears**
**Three 10-ounce packages frozen**
    **raspberries in syrup, thawed**
**6 cups water**
**1 cup sugar**
**¾ cup seedless raspberry preserves**
**2 tablespoons framboise (raspberry**
    **brandy), cognac, or kirsch**
**Mint sprigs for garnish**

*Use melon baller to scoop out seeds. Leave stems attached. As each pear is finished, place it in water with a few tablespoons of lemon juice to prevent from turning dark.*

Fill a medium bowl with water, adding 2 tablespoons lemon juice. Peel pears, leaving stem intact. Working from the base of the pears, use a melon baller to remove the seeds, taking out a ball of seeds at a time, leaving the top intact. Cut a small slice from the bottom so pears will stand straight. As each is peeled, place it in lemon water to keep from discoloring.

Choose a saucepan (about 4 quarts) into which the pears fit comfortably. Drain raspberries, reserving syrup. Pour syrup, water, sugar, and 2 tablespoons lemon juice into pan. Bring to a boil, lower heat, and simmer for 5 minutes or until sugar is dissolved.

❊ Poaching syrup may be stored in refrigerator indefinitely and reused to poach peaches or pears.

❊ May be frozen.

Add pears to syrup, cover, and simmer slowly, turning occasionally until pears are tender when pierced with a knife. The poaching time will depend on the type, size, and ripeness of the pear, anywhere from 10 to 40 minutes. When tender, remove from syrup, place in a bowl, and when syrup is cool, pour it over the pears.

❊ May be refrigerated covered overnight. Turn occasionally.

In a medium saucepan, heat the 3 packages reserved drained raspberries and preserves until boiling. Press through the medium disk of a food mill or through a strainer. For a clear sauce, strain twice to make sure all seeds are out. Add liqueur and refrigerate covered until ready to use.

❋ Sauce may be refrigerated for 1 week.

At serving time, remove pears from syrup and blot with paper towels. Spoon a small amount of sauce onto each dessert plate, dip pears in remaining sauce, and place on plate. Garnish top with a sprig of mint. Serve with fork, spoon, and knife.

Serves 8

*Poached Pears in Raspberry Sauce are garnished with a sprig of mint.*

# St. Patrick's Day Party

## MENU

GREEN GODDESS CUCUMBER CUPS
MARINATED ARTICHOKES
MINIATURE REUBENS

IRISH STEW
BREAD "BOWLS"
CABBAGE CASSEROLE
IRISH BOILED POTATOES
SHAMROCK MINT FREEZE
GREEN BEER

BUTTERSCOTCH BAKED APPLES
IRISH COFFEE

*Whether you are Irish or not (in fact, St. Patrick himself wasn't), St. Patrick's Day is a great excuse to throw a lively party. My menu features a hearty Irish stew, which is always great for a crowd, since it can be prepared ahead, it stretches easily, and leftovers freeze well. I serve the stew in bread bowls, pictured here in a field of lacy green to honor Ireland's national flower, the shamrock.*

*Those of you who can't imagine a traditional St. Patrick's dinner without corned beef will be happy to find it here in the form of miniature Reuben sandwich hors d'oeuvres.*

*Irish whiskey, cinnamon, cloves, and orange and lemon rind, when heated, flambéed, and added to coffee, create a jaunty Irish finale.*

*Although this menu serves 16, I've prepared it for as few as 8 and as many as 48.*

*Pot of Irish Stew and Bread "Bowls" filled with stew.*

## Green Goddess Cucumber Cups

Fresh cucumbers are easily shaped into miniature cups holding a rosette of rich and creamy Green Goddess spread. Each hors d'oeuvre will taste like a refreshing bite of salad.

1 long European or hot-house
   cucumber or 2 regular cucumbers
   Parsley sprigs for garnish

GREEN GODDESS SPREAD
8-ounce package cream cheese, at
   room temperature
¼ cup chopped parsley
1 small clove garlic, crushed
2 teaspoons wine vinegar
1 tablespoon chopped green onion,
   including top
Half a 2-ounce can anchovies,
   mashed
¼ teaspoon dried tarragon

Peel cucumbers and cut into ½-inch rounds. With a melon baller, scoop out the center of the cucumber, leaving a small piece of cucumber on the bottom. If you take out too much and scoop out the bottom, don't be concerned. Drain upside down on paper towels until ready to fill.

Make Green Goddess spread: Mix all spread ingredients in food processor with metal blade or in a small mixing bowl.

Spoon a small dollop of spread into each cucumber cup or fit a pastry bag with a ½-inch open star tip and pipe spread into cups. Refrigerate until firm and then cover loosely with plastic wrap.

✸ May be refrigerated up to 8 hours.

Before serving, garnish with small sprigs of parsley.

Makes about 30 cups

## Marinated Artichokes

These marinated artichokes will taste totally different from those that come store-bought in a jar or a can. My marinade, with its green onion and fresh garlic flavor, will work beautifully as a marinade for any vegetable you want to use.

**9-ounce package frozen artichoke hearts, halves and quarters**
**½ cup pitted ripe or green olives**
**¾ cup Swiss cheese cut into 1-inch cubes (about 3 ounces)**
**½ cup green pepper, cut into 1-inch squares**

GREEN ONION MARINADE
**1 small clove garlic, crushed**
**½ cup vegetable oil**
**3 tablespoons lemon juice**
**2 tablespoons red wine vinegar**
**1 tablespoon green onion dip mix**
**1 tablespoon chopped parsley**
   **Salt and pepper to taste**

Cook artichokes as package directs, 5 to 8 minutes. Rinse under cold water; drain. When cool, mix with olives, cheese, and green pepper.

Make green onion marinade: Mix all marinade ingredients in small bowl or food processor with metal blade. Pour over vegetables and cheese. Cover and refrigerate for several hours or overnight.

✽ May be refrigerated up to 2 days.

Serves 8

## Miniature Reubens

All the delightful taste sensations of a classic Reuben sandwich can be found in these miniature replicas—they are perfect for a large casual party or a cocktail party. If you cut them in half when they're semi-frozen, they will slice easily.

**Two 8-ounce packages cocktail rye bread**
**Mustard**
½ **pound thinly sliced corned beef**
**8-ounce can sauerkraut, drained**
**8-ounce package thinly sliced Swiss cheese**
½ **pound (2 sticks) butter or margarine**

Spread half of the bread slices with mustard. Top with a folded piece of corned beef, covering the bread completely but not extending over the edge. Spread about 1 teaspoon sauerkraut over the meat. Place 2 thin slices of Swiss cheese over sauerkraut; trim edges even with bread. Top with remaining bread.

In large skillet, melt 4 tablespoons butter or margarine. Sauté sandwiches over moderate heat a batch at a time; do not crowd. When underside is golden, turn and brown other side. Add additional butter as needed.

If not serving immediately, place on baking sheet and freeze. When almost frozen, remove from freezer and cut each sandwich in half. Sandwiches are easier to cut when partially frozen.

❋ May be frozen up to 3 months. Reheat frozen.

Before serving, bake at 400° for 10 to 15 minutes until heated through and bubbling.

Makes 36 sandwiches

# Irish Stew

This stew is not at all reminiscent of Irish stews I've had, because this one is much richer in taste. The orange peel adds a wonderful flavor, although I can't really credit the Irish for that—I think I borrowed the idea from the Italians. The flavor of this stew improves with time. This recipe is designed to serve 16, but if your party is smaller it can easily be cut in half. Leftovers will freeze well.

  8 pounds lean lamb leg or rump, or beef, cut into 2-inch cubes
    Flour
  1 tablespoon salt
  ½ teaspoon pepper
  6 to 8 tablespoons vegetable oil
  4 onions, sliced
  2 tablespoons sugar
  6 cups dry red wine (or enough to cover ⅔ of meat)
16-ounce can tomato purée
  2 teaspoons dried basil
  1 teaspoon dried thyme
  4 teaspoons grated orange rind
  4 cloves garlic, crushed
  2 pounds frozen baby carrots, or whole carrots peeled and cut into 2-inch lengths and 1 inch wide
  2 pounds small fresh mushrooms

Dry the meat thoroughly. Dredge in flour which has been mixed with salt and pepper. Heat the oil in a large heavy casserole or Dutch oven. Sauté meat in batches over moderately high heat, one layer at a time, until browned on all sides. Remove meat as it browns.

To same saucepan, add onions and sugar. Sauté, stirring constantly, until glazed and lightly browned. Add a little more oil if pan is too dry. Pour off excess fat. Add the wine to the pan. Over moderate heat, stirring constantly, scrape up all residue which has accumulated in the bottom of the pan. Cook for 2 minutes; stir in tomato purée, basil, thyme, orange rind, and garlic.

Return meat to casserole. Cover and bring to a slow boil. Bake at 325°, stirring occasionally, for 2 to 3 hours, or until fork tender. If sauce bubbles rapidly, reduce temperature to 300°, so the juices will not evaporate. Remove from oven and if not serving immediately place a clean damp dish towel directly on top of the meat. This will prevent it from drying out as it cools.

❋ May be refrigerated for 4 days.

❋ May be frozen.

Before serving, cook carrots in boiling water for 10 to 15 minutes or until almost tender; drain. Remove all fat from stew. Add carrots and mushrooms and simmer on top of the stove or in the oven at 325°, stirring occasionally, until heated through and carrots are tender, about 30 minutes. Season to taste with additional wine, salt, pepper, or orange rind.

Serves 16

## Bread "Bowls"

Hollowed-out rolls make perfect containers to hold individual servings of Irish Stew (preceding recipe). It's like dipping bread into sauce to get every last drop—only better.

**6-inch French or sourdough rolls, 1 per person**
**Garlic Butter (see recipe for Garlic Toast Hearts in Valentine's Day Dinner)**

Cut tops off rolls. Hollow out bread, leaving a shell. Leave rolls uncovered at room temperature for 8 to 12 hours to dry out. Spread inside with garlic butter, using approximately 1 to 2 tablespoons per roll. Replace the tops.

Can be held at room temperature for 4 hours.

Place rolls on a platter. Let guests help themselves in filling their bread "bowls" with stew.

## Cabbage Casserole

Cabbage comes alive with the addition of crunchy bacon, colorful green beans, and spicy onion soup mix.

  3 **heads cabbage (approximately 4 pounds total weight)**
  1 **pound bacon, chopped into 1-inch pieces**
  ¾ **cup chicken broth**
**Three 10-ounce packages frozen French-style green beans**
  2 **envelopes dry onion soup mix**
1½ **teaspoons salt or to taste**
  ½ **teaspoon pepper**

Cut cabbage into thin slices; do not shred. Set aside. In large skillet, fry bacon over moderate heat, stirring occasionally, until crisp. Remove bacon to paper towel and pour drippings into a measuring cup. Reserve ⅓ cup drippings. Pour chicken broth into skillet. Bring to a boil, add green beans, cover, and cook, stirring occasionally, until beans are thawed. Add cabbage, onion soup, and ⅓ cup bacon drippings. Stir well, cover, and simmer for 5 to 6 minutes or until cabbage is cooked but still crisp. Stir in bacon, salt, and pepper. Turn into a 9-by-13-inch casserole.

❀ May be refrigerated overnight.

Before serving, bring to room temperature. Cover casserole and bake at 350° for 25 to 30 minutes or until heated through.

Serves 16

## *Irish Boiled Potatoes*

Traditional Irish boiled potatoes are a classic side dish to Irish Stew. These parsley-garnished potatoes are moist, tender, and buttery.

**6 to 8 pounds small new potatoes (about 3 per person) or large boiling potatoes**
**1 tablespoon salt**
**4 tablespoons (½ stick) butter, at room temperature**
**½ cup chopped parsley**
**Salt and pepper to taste**

Scrub potatoes. If using small potatoes, peel a small band of skin from around the center to keep them from bursting. If using large potatoes, peel, cut into serving-size pieces, and drop them into cold water until ready to use. This will prevent them from discoloring. Put the potatoes into a large saucepan. Cover with cold water and add 1 tablespoon salt. Bring to a boil over high heat, reduce heat, and boil gently for 15 to 20 minutes or until they are tender when pierced with a fork. Drain. Return the potatoes to the pan and put over moderate heat for about 1 minute to evaporate the remaining moisture. Add butter, parsley, salt, and pepper, and toss until butter has melted. Serve immediately.

Serves 12 to 16

## *Green Beer*

Pour beer into a pitcher. Stir in a few drops of green food coloring to tint green.

## Shamrock Mint Freeze

This refreshing, light, mint-green mold cleanses the palate after a hearty dinner and is also a fine complement to any lamb dish.

**Two 20-ounce cans crushed pineapple**
**2 envelopes unflavored gelatin**
**Two 10-ounce jars mint jelly**
**1 pint (2 cups) whipping cream**
**2 teaspoons powdered sugar**
  **Green food coloring**

Drain pineapple, reserving liquid in a medium saucepan. Stir gelatin into syrup and let rest 5 minutes to soften. Place over moderate heat and stir until gelatin is dissolved. Add mint jelly and cook, stirring, until jelly is melted. Remove from heat and stir in pineapple. Pour into a bowl and refrigerate or stir over ice water until mixture thickens slightly.

Whip cream and powdered sugar until soft peaks form. Fold gelatin mixture into cream. Tint green. Pour into an 8-cup mold. Cover with foil and freeze until firm.

❀ May be frozen up to 1 month.

Several hours before serving, go around edges with a sharp knife. Dip mold into warm water and unmold onto serving plate. Return to freezer. Remove from freezer 10 to 15 minutes before serving.

❀ Leftovers may be refrozen.

Serves 12 to 16

# Butterscotch Baked Apples

Imagine juicy baked apples generously stuffed with whiskey-soaked plump raisins and sweet dates. They're coated with a thick, warm butterscotch-caramel glaze.

½ cup raisins
½ cup chopped dates
6 tablespoons whiskey
½ cup coarsely chopped walnuts or pecans
16 baking apples
Two 3¾-ounce packages instant butterscotch pudding
2 cups water
2 cups light corn syrup

A day ahead, or several hours before serving, begin the filling by marinating raisins and dates in 4 tablespoons whiskey. Let soak for 2 to 4 hours or overnight. Stir in nuts.

Peel apples. Cut out core, taking care to remove all seeds and seed pockets. Divide apples between two 9-by-13-inch baking dishes. Divide the filling among the apples and spoon into the cavities. In a medium bowl, mix pudding with 1 cup water; stir well until pudding is dissolved. Stir in 2 tablespoons whiskey, corn syrup, and remaining water. Pour this mixture evenly over the apples, coating them well. Bake at 350° for 40 to 45 minutes or until tender when pierced with a small knife. Baste every 10 to 15 minutes. As the sauce cooks, it will thicken, and frequent basting toward the end of the baking time will give you beautiful caramel-coated apples.

May be held at room temperature for 8 hours or may be refrigerated overnight.

Before serving, bring to room temperature. To serve warm, reheat at 350° for 10 minutes. Spoon sauce over each apple when serving.

Makes 16 baked apples

## Irish Coffee

How else could you end a St. Patrick's Day dinner but with traditional Irish coffee? If you make it in a chafing dish, it's easier to do it in two batches. It will work well, but not as dramatically, in a large pan on the stove.

**Peel of 4 oranges, removed in strips with vegetable peeler**
**Peel of 4 lemons, removed in strips with vegetable peeler**
**Whole cloves**
**4 cinnamon sticks**
**6 tablespoons sugar**
**32 ounces Irish whiskey**
**12 cups strong hot coffee**
**½ pint (1 cup) whipping cream, whipped**

Cut the peel of the oranges and lemons into 1-inch strips. Stud each strip with 2 to 3 cloves. Place peel, cinnamon sticks, and sugar in chafing dish or saucepan. Set over moderate heat, stirring occasionally, until sugar has melted. Pour the Irish whiskey into the pan, stand back, and carefully ignite. Shake the pan back and forth slowly until the flames die out. Add hot coffee all at once and let it simmer for 3 to 4 minutes.

Ladle coffee into Irish coffee glasses or mugs. Top each with a dollop of whipped cream.

Makes 16 servings, about 8 ounces each

# 3
# SPRING
# FEASTS

# Easter Gala Buffet

## MENU

MOLDED EASTER EGG SPREAD
HAM, CHEESE, AND GREEN
PEPPERCORN PÂTÉ

❧

CROWN ROAST OF LAMB OR
ROAST LEG OF LAMB
MINTED PEAR BUNNIES
FRUITED RICE PILAF
SPRING PEAS
CREAMED CARROTS
EASTER NEST BREAD

❧

RASPBERRY VACHERIN
CHOCOLATE EASTER EGG
CHOCOLATE BASKET WITH WHITE
CHOCOLATE STRAWBERRIES

❧

WINE RECOMMENDATION:
A DRY AND FULL-BODIED CABERNET
SAUVIGNON OR A ROBUST, DRY
ZINFANDEL

*Easter is an occasion that celebrates rebirth, both as a joyful religious holiday commemorating the resurrection of Jesus Christ and as a celebration of the reawakening of nature.*

*The perfect entrée for an Easter buffet is succulent spring lamb. Choose between a regal crown roast or a roast leg of lamb; the latter is less formal and less expensive. The flavorful wine-based marinade, which can be used to marinade either of the roasts, is reduced to an essence and then added to the gravy. The lamb is accompanied by fresh peas simmered with lettuce and by carrots cloaked in cream—perfect harbingers of spring.*

*Because an Easter egg motif is irresistible, it is incorporated into the menu in a variety of ways. It appears first in the Molded Easter Egg Spread, then in the Easter Nest Bread, and finally in the delicious chocolate mousselike dessert, the Chocolate Easter Egg. A centerpiece of a wicker basket filled with raw eggs interspersed with spring flowers would complete the pretty picture.*

*This Easter buffet serves 8 to 10.*

*Crown Roast of Lamb stuffed with Fruited Rice Pilaf and garnished with Minted Pear Bunnies.*

43

## *Molded Easter Egg Spread*

Think Easter and you think eggs, so why not mold a chopped-egg spread into a simple egg shape? The ingredients blend beautifully, and it's firm enough even to mold with your hands. The spiced cheese with garlic and herbs perks up the flavor and adds an extra-creamy consistency. Serve as an appetizer with crackers or bread rounds, as shown here, or serve as a light, distinctive luncheon dish.

**8 slices bacon (about ½ pound)**
**Two 4-ounce packages spiced cheese with garlic and herbs (Rondelé or Boursin), at room temperature**
**8 hard-boiled eggs**
**⅓ cup chopped green onion**
**Salt and freshly ground pepper to taste**
**Green onion top, cut into thin strips, for garnish**
**Radish roses for garnish**
**Parsley sprigs for garnish**
**Crackers or bread rounds**

Dice bacon and fry in large skillet until crisp. Remove and drain on paper towels. Place cheese and eggs in food processor with metal blade. Process until mixed but still slightly chunky. Remove to bowl and stir in bacon, chopped green onion, and seasonings. Line a 3-cup mold with plastic wrap. Pack egg spread into mold or mound spread into egg shape with your hands. Cover with plastic wrap and refrigerate until ready to use.

✽ May be refrigerated for 2 days.

Before serving, garnish with green onion strips, small sprigs of parsley, and radish roses if desired. Serve with crackers or bread rounds.

Makes 3 cups spread

## *Ham, Cheese, and Green Peppercorn Pâté*

Green peppercorns are less harsh than black peppercorns, so they lend a subtle spiciness to the blend of smoky ham and pungent Swiss cheese. This pâté is slightly chunky and can double as a sourdough-sandwich spread.

**2 teaspoons green peppercorns**
**8 ounces smoked ham, cut into cubes**
**1 cup shredded Swiss cheese (about 4 ounces)**
**¼ cup parsley leaves**
**½ cup mayonnaise**
**¼ cup sour cream**
**2 teaspoons Dijon mustard**
**Parsley sprigs**
**Crackers or bread rounds**

In food processor with metal blade, process green peppercorns until minced. Add ham, Swiss cheese, and parsley; process until coarsely chopped. Add mayonnaise, sour cream, and mustard. Mix until well blended. Pack into crock. Refrigerate covered with plastic wrap for at least 4 hours for flavors to blend.

✽ May be refrigerated for 3 days.

Garnish with parsley sprigs and serve with crackers or bread rounds.

Makes 2½ cups pâté

## Crown Roast of Lamb

To me, few foods are as festive or elaborate as a crown roast. It should be presented on your loveliest large platter, but you are then faced with the dilemma of having to carve on it. I solved that problem by taking my platter to a lumber yard that cut and finished a piece of wood to fit snugly inside the platter. I hide the rim of the board with a garnishment of parsley.

An unusual aspect of this recipe is that the meat is marinated before roasting for extra flavor and tenderness. The reduced marinade is a rich base for the sauce that is accented by mint jelly and a hint of thyme.

**Marinade for Lamb (see recipe below)**
**16- to 24-rib crown roast of lamb**
**Salt and freshly ground pepper**
**Fruited Rice Pilaf for center of crown (see recipe below)**
**Minted Lamb Gravy (see recipe below)**
**16 to 24 glazed kumquats or paper frills for bone ends**
**Parsley or mint sprigs**
**Minted Pear Bunnies (see recipe below)**

Make marinade for lamb according to recipe. Place roast in a bowl that fits it as snugly as possible and pour marinade over. The marinade will cover only a small portion of the meat. Refrigerate loosely covered with foil for 8 to 12 hours.

Several hours before serving, remove lamb from marinade and bring to room temperature. Reserve marinade for gravy. Dry roast well with paper towels. Sprinkle with salt and pepper. Preheat oven to 450°. Place roast on rack in shallow roasting pan or broiler pan. Cover the bone ends with aluminum foil to keep them from burning. Fill center with a mound of foil to help retain its shape. Put roast in oven and immediately reduce heat to 350°. Roast approximately 1 hour and 30 minutes, about 15 minutes per pound, or until meat thermometer inserted into the meatiest part registers 140° (medium rare) or 150° (medium well done). Remove foil from center of roast after the first 45 minutes of baking, to allow inside to brown.

While roast cooks, make Minted Lamb Gravy according to recipe. Remove roast to platter. Let rest 10 minutes. Fill center with Fruited Rice Pilaf. Remove foil from rib bones and top each with a glazed kumquat or paper frill. Garnish roast with parsley or mint sprigs and Minted Pear Bunnies. Serve with Minted Lamb Gravy.

Serves 8 to 12, allowing 2 to 3 ribs per person

## Roast Leg of Lamb

It's my feeling that most Americans overcook lamb; it's really at its best when served pink. My temperature instructions might seem low to you, but do remember that the roast continues cooking at least 10 minutes after you remove it from the oven. It's easiest to determine temperature with a meat thermometer. If the lamb is cooked to 140°, it will be juicy, pink, and very tender. The marinade not only adds a nice seasoning to the meat, it's a penetrating tenderizer as well.

Marinade for Lamb (see recipe below)

6- to 7-pound leg of lamb, with bone in or boned and rolled

3 tablespoons vegetable oil

1 teaspoon crushed rosemary

1 teaspoon dried thyme

Salt and freshly ground pepper

Minted Lamb Gravy (see recipe below)

Parsley or mint sprigs

Minted Pear Bunnies (see recipe below)

Make marinade for lamb according to recipe. Place lamb in large bowl and pour marinade over. Place in refrigerator, uncovered, and marinate for approximately 24 hours, turning occasionally.

Several hours before serving, remove lamb from marinade; bring to room temperature. Reserve marinade for gravy. Preheat oven to 450°. Dry lamb very well with paper towels. Rub oil on all sides and sprinkle with rosemary, thyme, salt, and pepper. Place lamb on rack in shallow roasting pan or broiler pan. Put in oven and immediately reduce heat to 350°.

While roast cooks, make the gravy according to recipe. Roast lamb for 2 to 2½ hours (approximately 20 minutes per pound) or until a meat thermometer inserted into the meatiest part registers 140° (medium rare) or 150° (medium well done). Baste roast occasionally with pan drippings. Remove roast to carving board and let rest for 15 to 20 minutes before carving. Garnish with parsley or mint sprigs and Minted Pear Bunnies. Serve with Minted Lamb Gravy.

Serves 8 to 10

## Marinade for Crown Roast or Leg of Lamb

2 cups dry white wine (or half dry vermouth and half wine)

¼ cup lemon juice

2 tablespoons olive oil

3 large cloves garlic, crushed

1 large onion, sliced

2 bay leaves

2 tablespoons fresh chopped mint or 1 teaspoon dried mint, crumbled

1 teaspoon dried thyme

Combine all ingredients in bowl. Use as directed in preceding recipes.

Makes marinade for 6- to 7-pound leg of lamb or 24-rib crown roast

## Minted Lamb Gravy

**Reserved Marinade for Lamb (see
preceding recipe)**
**¾-ounce package brown gravy mix**
**1 cup cold water**
**Water or dry white wine**
**1 tablespoon mint jelly or to taste**
**Pinch of thyme**
**Salt and pepper**

Strain marinade into a medium saucepan. Bring
to a boil, reduce heat, and simmer until liquid
is reduced by half to about 1 cup. In a separate
saucepan, stir gravy mix and 1 cup cold water
until blended. Add reduced marinade and bring
to a boil, stirring constantly.

May be made several hours ahead. It will
thicken as it sits.

When lamb has finished cooking, remove excess fat from drippings and stir drippings into
gravy. Stir in additional water or wine to obtain
desired consistency. Season to taste with mint
jelly, thyme, salt, and pepper.

Makes approximately 2½ cups

## Minted Pear Bunnies

When you look at these bunnies, they're so sweet you just have to smile. The pears
are tinted green with food coloring, flavored with peppermint extract, and decorated à la
Peter Cottontail. I really believe that it's foods like these that make a holiday feel special.

**1-pound 13-ounce can pear halves in
syrup**
**¼ to ½ teaspoon peppermint extract**
**Green food coloring**
**Currants or black raisins, snipped**
**Golden raisins, snipped**
**Flaked coconut**
**Sliced almonds**
**Miniature marshmallows**

Drain pears, reserving syrup in medium bowl.
Stir in peppermint extract and enough food coloring to color a deep green. Add pear halves;
marinate at room temperature for approximately 1 hour or until pears have turned a pale
shade of green. If they do not tint, add additional food coloring.

Remove pears from marinade and drain on
paper towels. Place on plate and decorate with
currants for eyes, a snipped white raisin for the
nose, coconut for whiskers, sliced almonds for
ears, and half a miniature marshmallow for the
tail.

❉ May be refrigerated covered with plastic
wrap up to 2 days.

Makes about 9 bunnies (amount varies with
can)

## Fruited Rice Pilaf

I love food textures, and my favorite rice recipe really represents them. The crunch of golden toasted almonds, the juicy softness of fruit, tender fluffy rice grains, and sweet and spicy cinnamon and cardamom explore many taste sensations.

½ cup blanched almonds
4 tablespoons (½ stick) butter or margarine
1 large onion, chopped
2 cups long-grain white rice, uncooked
4½ cups boiling chicken broth
1 cup golden raisins
1 large green apple, peeled, cored, and chopped into ½-inch pieces (about 1½ cups)
⅓ cup chopped green onion
Salt and pepper

BOUQUET GARNI
12 whole peppercorns
12 whole cloves
1 large cinnamon stick, broken into pieces
2 cloves garlic, sliced
6 whole cardamom pods or ¼ teaspoon powdered cardamom

Dice almonds and toast at 350° for 15 to 20 minutes, stirring occasionally, until golden. Set aside.

Melt butter or margarine in heavy saucepan. Sauté onion until soft. Add rice and sauté, stirring often, until lightly browned.

Make bouquet garni: Cut cheesecloth into approximately a 4-inch square. Place peppercorns, cloves, pieces of cinnamon stick, slices of garlic, and cardamom onto cloth. If using cardamom pods, hit lightly with a meat mallet or other heavy object, breaking the pod and exposing the seeds. Bring edges of cloth together at the top, making a small pouch. Tie string around top and cut off excess cheesecloth. Alternatively, all ingredients may be placed in a tea or spice strainer.

Slowly stir chicken broth into rice. Add bouquet garni, cover, and simmer 15 to 20 minutes or until almost all liquid is absorbed. Add raisins and apple. Mix lightly. Cover and simmer 5 additional minutes or until all liquid has been absorbed.

Stir almonds and green onion into rice. Remove bouquet garni. Add salt and pepper to taste.

Serves 10 to 12

## Spring Peas

The French method of cooking peas is the best. You don't need cooking liquid, for the lettuce supplies moisture and gently steams the peas to perfection. A teaspoon of fines herbes or chervil is a sophisticated touch.

1 head iceberg lettuce (about 1 pound 6 ounces)
3 tablespoons butter or margarine
4 pounds fresh peas (4 cups unshelled) or two 10-ounce packages frozen petit peas
1 tablespoon sugar
1 teaspoon chervil or fines herbes
2 chicken bouillon cubes, crumbled
½ teaspoon salt
1 bunch green onions, sliced (about ½ cup)

Cut lettuce into thin slices, approximately 1 inch long; do not shred. Melt butter or margarine in a medium saucepan. Cover with a layer of lettuce. If using frozen peas, separate frozen peas with hands and sprinkle 1 package over lettuce. In a small bowl, mix sugar, herbs, chicken bouillon cubes, and salt. Sprinkle half the seasoning mixture over peas and top with a layer of green onions. Continue with another layer of lettuce, peas, seasonings, and green onions.

May be assembled and held at room temperature for 4 hours.

Before serving, cook over moderately high heat for 7 to 10 minutes, stirring occasionally to distribute heat. Drain excess liquid, if necessary, and serve immediately.

Serves 8

## *Creamed Carrots*

The easy way of cooking carrots is with the peel on. Run them under cold water and the peel slips off but the flavor stays where it belongs, inside the carrot. Be sure to add the whipping cream slowly so that the carrots can absorb each drop.

2 **pounds carrots**
4 **tablespoons (½ stick) butter or margarine**
**Salt and freshly ground white pepper**
¾ **cup whipping cream, at room temperature**
2 **tablespoons chopped parsley (optional)**

Cut a small slice off both ends of carrots. Do not scrape or peel them. Place the carrots in a large bowl of cold water and soak them for about 15 minutes.

Bring a large pot of salted water to a boil. Add carrots and cook uncovered until tender, but still firm. The cooking time will vary with the size and age of the carrots, from 15 to 25 minutes. Remove from heat, drain, and plunge carrots into a bowl of cold water to stop the cooking. When cool, peel the carrots under running water by gently pushing off the skin with your hands. Cut the carrots into ¼-inch slices.

❋ May be covered and refrigerated overnight.

Before serving, bring carrots to room temperature. Melt the butter or margarine in a medium saucepan. Add the carrots and sauté for about 5 minutes. Season to taste with salt and pepper. Add 1 tablespoon of the cream and stir until it is absorbed. Continue with remaining cream in the same manner. As each tablespoon of cream is absorbed, add another until carrots are nicely coated. Remove to serving bowl and garnish with chopped parsley, if desired.

Serves 8

## *Chocolate Easter Egg*

This fantastic concoction is somewhere between a rich fudge and a velvety chocolate mousse, so you may prefer spooning it; it's too rich to cut into perfect slices. As the chocolate mixture needs two days to set, be sure to start this ahead.

12 **ounces semisweet chocolate**
3 **tablespoons instant coffee granules**
¾ **cup water**
1½ **cups sugar**
¾ **pound (3 sticks) unsalted butter, at room temperature**
6 **eggs**
1 **pint (2 cups) whipping cream Candied lilacs or violets for garnish (optional)**

In a medium saucepan, combine chocolate, coffee, and water over low heat, stirring constantly until chocolate is melted and mixture is smooth. Add sugar and stir until dissolved. Cut butter into small pieces and stir into hot mixture. Immediately remove from heat and stir until butter is melted. Whisk in eggs one at a time. Line a 10-cup metal bowl with several layers of freezer foil. Pour in chocolate mixture. Bake at 350° for 1 hour or until the top has formed a thick crust. Remove from oven and cool. Mixture will sink and crack as it cools. Cover top with foil and refrigerate for a minimum of 2 days.

❉ May be refrigerated for 1 week.

❁ May be frozen.

Before serving, remove chocolate from pan with the foil. Tear or pull off foil. Place on serving platter crust side down. Whip cream until stiff. Spread whipped cream over chocolate to cover completely, or fill a pastry bag fitted with ½-inch star tip and pipe rosettes over chocolate. Garnish with candied lilacs or violets, if desired.

❉ May be refrigerated several hours.

Serves 10 to 12

*Baked Easter Nest Bread with tinted coconut "nest."*

## Easter Nest Bread

Food should not only look good when it's decorated, but should be 100 percent edible. Easter Nest Bread uses most of its dough for the nest, and the rest becomes the eggs. A real conversation piece that's almost too pretty to eat.

1 package active dry yeast
¼ cup warm water (100° to 115°)
1 cup milk
¼ pound (1 stick) butter
5 to 5½ cups all-purpose flour
½ cup sugar
1 teaspoon salt
2 eggs, at room temperature
¼ cup orange juice
2 tablespoons grated orange rind

Sprinkle yeast over warm water, stirring until dissolved. Set aside. In small saucepan, heat milk and butter until lukewarm. In mixing bowl, place 2 cups flour; add warm milk with butter, sugar, salt, and yeast mixture. Mix until blended. Beat in eggs, one at a time. Add orange juice and rind. Beat 2 minutes, scraping down sides occasionally. Mix in 3 cups additional flour. Dough should be fairly stiff. If it is too soft, add a little more flour. Knead on floured board or with dough hook, adding more flour if needed, until smooth and elastic, about 8 to 10 minutes. Shape dough in a ball, place in a greased bowl, and turn to grease all surfaces.

**TINTED COCONUT**
**Green food coloring**
**Water**
**1 cup flaked coconut**

**SUGAR GLAZE**
**¾ cup powdered sugar**
**Hot water**
**Red and yellow food coloring**

*Cut remaining dough into strips and braid them.*

*Stand braid up on its edge around the sides of a springform pan. Shape approximately one third of the dough into small eggs and place on a baking sheet.*

Cover with buttered plastic wrap and a damp towel and let rise in a warm place until double in bulk, about 2 hours.

Punch dough down and let dough rest 10 minutes. Use a third of the dough to make eggs: Break off small balls of dough and shape into approximately ½-inch elongated eggs. You should have at least 20. Place on greased baking sheet. Use remaining two-thirds dough to make nest. Divide dough in half. Spread half into bottom of a greased 10-inch springform pan or cake pan. Roll remaining dough into a rectangle ½ inch thick and about 12 inches long. Cut into six ½-inch strips. Braid 3 of the strips. Stand braid up along side of pan; it should go halfway around the pan. Press braid into dough on bottom. Repeat with remaining 3 strips, making another braid. Attach to braid in pan, pressing ends together securely. Press braid against sides of pan and flatten bottom dough, forming a nest. Cover nest and eggs and let rise 45 minutes to 1 hour or until nearly double.

Preheat oven to 350°. Bake eggs 15 to 20 minutes and nest 30 to 40 minutes or until golden brown. Remove from oven and cool.

❋ Nest and eggs may be frozen.

Make tinted coconut: Mix a few drops green food coloring and a teaspoon of water together. Place coconut in a small bowl, add green food coloring and water, and toss until desired color is attained. Place in bottom of nest.

Make sugar glaze: Place sugar in small bowl. Add 1 teaspoon hot water. Stir. Continue to add hot water a few drops at a time until sugar is a thin spreading consistency. Divide sugar in thirds. Tint a third pink, a third yellow, and leave a third white. Brush or spread glaze on eggs. Let dry. Place as many eggs as desired on coconut in nest. Serve remaining eggs separately as rolls.

Serves about 10

## Raspberry Vacherin

Three sweet crunchy layers of airy meringue are sandwiched between alternating layers of raspberry sherbet and cassis-flavored whipping cream. Ruby-red berry sauce is spooned over the top. This pastel-colored dessert reminds me of an Easter bonnet and all the goodness of spring.

MERINGUE LAYERS
**4 egg whites**
   **Dash of salt**
**¼ teaspoon cream of tartar**
**1 cup sugar**
**½ teaspoon vanilla extract**

**2 pints raspberry sherbet, softened**

RASPBERRY CASSIS FILLING
**½ pint (1 cup) whipping cream**
**2 tablespoons crème de cassis**
**2 tablespoons seedless raspberry preserves**

Make meringue layers: Line 2 baking sheets with parchment or waxed paper. Draw three 8-inch rounds on paper. If using waxed paper, grease and flour circles. Beat egg whites until frothy. Add salt and cream of tartar and beat until stiff. Add sugar, 1 tablespoon at a time, beating well after each addition until meringue stands in firm, shiny peaks. Beat in vanilla. Divide meringue among rounds and spread evenly, making a smooth surface. Bake at 250° in center rack of oven for 1 hour. If baking both sheets in one oven, rotate them halfway through the baking time. Turn off oven and allow meringues to cool in oven and dry out for 4 hours or overnight.

If meringues are thoroughly dried, they will keep well in airtight containers for at least 1 week.

Line an 8-inch cake pan with foil or plastic wrap. Fill with sherbet; spread top evenly. Freeze solid.

Make raspberry cassis filling: Whip cream until soft peaks form. Add crème de cassis and preserves and beat until stiff.

Assemble torte by placing 1 meringue layer on a small baking sheet. Remove sherbet from cake pan and tear off paper. Place sherbet on meringue; top with second meringue. Spread raspberry cassis filling over; top with third meringue. Wrap in foil and freeze until firm.

❀ May be frozen covered with foil for 1 week.

FROSTING
**1 pint (2 cups) whipping cream**
**1 tablespoon crème de cassis**

RASPBERRY CASSIS SAUCE
 **2 cups fresh strawberries**
**10-ounce package frozen raspberries**
   **in syrup, thawed**
 **3 tablespoons crème de cassis**
**12 whole strawberries for garnish**

   **Green garden leaves for garnish**
   **(optional)**

Place torte on serving platter. Make frosting: Whip cream until soft peaks form. Add crème de cassis and beat until stiff. Spread on top and sides of torte. Pipe rosettes on top, if desired.

❉ May be frozen overnight.

Make raspberry cassis sauce: Hull and halve strawberries; place in small bowl. In small saucepan, heat raspberries to boiling. Strain to remove seeds. Add strained raspberries and crème de cassis to strawberries. Refrigerate for at least 1 hour before serving.

❉ Sauce may be refrigerated 8 hours.

Before serving, dip 12 strawberries in sauce. Drain on paper towels to remove excess sauce and place on top of torte. Garnish platter with leaves, if desired. Pass remaining sauce.

Serves 12 to 14

*Place soufflé dish upside down on small board or platter. Press foil around dish. Pipe lacy pattern of chocolate on bottom of dish. Overlap circles of chocolate from the sides to bottom and continue piping on the sides of the dish. Freeze until firm.*

*Begin second layer and proceed as for first.*

*Pipe third layer in same manner.*

*When chocolate is firm and cold, remove soufflé dish by pulling it out from underneath the foil. Turn basket right side up and carefully pull off foil; it is easiest to do this in pieces.*

*Pull paper off handle.*

*Pipe a border around top of basket using star tip.*

*Pipe other side of handle.*

*Draw handle on waxed paper. Pipe handle using star tip.*

*Dab a small amount of chocolate on each side of basket and hold handle in place using palm of hand until chocolate hardens and glues handle in place.*

# Chocolate Basket

This recipe takes some time, but it's not difficult to make. After my students saw how easy it was, most of them went home and successfully duplicated beautiful lacy chocolate baskets. The basket refrigerates or freezes almost indefinitely. If you store it without the handle, it will take less space and you can attach the handle right before serving. If not eaten immediately, this delectable edible container can be used over and over again—vary the filling according to your whim.

**1 pound semisweet chocolate, chopped**
**White Chocolate Strawberries (see next recipe)**

EQUIPMENT
**2- to 4-cup soufflé dish or 6 custard cups**
**Heavy-duty aluminum foil**
**1 small pastry bag**
**1 small plastic coupler to hold tips or a second small pastry bag**
**1 writing tip (#2 or #3)**
**1 small star tip (#18 or #20)**

Place a soufflé dish or custard cups upside down on a small board or baking sheet. Press aluminum foil over top and sides, letting it extend about 2 inches on bottom. Press foil tightly around bottom edge, making a sharp, definitive edge. Place in refrigerator or freezer.

In top of double boiler over very low heat, slowly melt chocolate. Stir until smooth. Let sit 15 minutes or until thick enough to pipe. If it becomes too firm while working, remelt slightly. Fit a small pastry bag with a writing tip. Fill with some of the chocolate. Pipe a continuous drizzle of chocolate in a lacy design over bottom and sides of mold, as pictured. Do not be concerned if chocolate drips slightly. If it drips too much, the chocolate is too warm. Refrigerate or freeze for 5 to 10 minutes or until chocolate is firm. Repeat with a second layer in the same manner. Refrigerate or freeze until firm. Repeat with a third layer; refrigerate or freeze until chocolate is firm, at least 20 minutes.

Remove soufflé dish by carefully pulling it out from underneath the foil. Turn basket right side up and remove foil by slowly and carefully pulling it away from sides and bottom of basket. Remove writing tip from coupler (or use another pastry bag) and replace it with a star tip. Pipe a decorative chocolate border around top edge of basket. Refrigerate while making handle.

Line a baking sheet that will fit into your refrigerator or freezer with waxed paper or parchment. To make handle, measure the diameter of the basket; mark that width on the paper. Draw the curved shape of a handle. Using room-temperature chocolate (it cannot be too warm or the design won't show) and star tip, pipe zigzag lines around arc, following your handle pattern. Refrigerate or freeze until firm.

Turn over and pipe similar pattern on other side. Refrigerate or freeze until firm.

Attach handle to basket by using melted chocolate as "glue" and dabbing it on each side of the basket. Using the palm of your hand, hold handle in place until it sticks.

✳ May be refrigerated for several months.

❅ May be frozen.

Fill with White Chocolate Strawberries.

Makes 1 large basket or 6 small custard-cup-size baskets

## White Chocolate Strawberries

These berries are an eye-catching color contrast to the semisweet chocolate basket (preceding recipe). Use Toblerone or a white dipping chocolate from a candymaking supply store, as white chocolate does not always melt.

**16 to 20 large strawberries, with stems attached**

**6 ounces white chocolate, chopped**

Line a baking sheet that will fit into the refrigerator with waxed paper. Pat strawberries clean with paper towels; do not wash. Melt the chocolate in the top of a double boiler over hot water. Holding each strawberry by the leaves, dip it into the melted chocolate. Place strawberries on the prepared baking sheet. Refrigerate until firm.

✳ May be refrigerated uncovered overnight.

Makes 15 to 20 strawberries

*Dip strawberries in white chocolate and place on waxed paper. Refrigerate until firm.*

*Chocolate Basket filled with strawberries dipped in white chocolate.*

# Passover Seder

MENU

HAROSET
GEFILTE FISH LOAF
VEGETABLE SOUP WITH
MATZOH BALLS

STUFFED BRISKET OF BEEF WITH
BROCCOLI FARFEL STUFFING
ASPARAGUS WITH
LEMON MATZOH SAUCE
MATZOH FRUIT KUGEL

CHOCOLATE POPPY
SEED TORTE
FROZEN STRAWBERRY
MERINGUE TORTE

*The Passover Seder is the beautiful ritualistic dinner which commences the week-long celebration of the freedom of Jewish slaves from Egyptian bondage. The table is set with the traditional Seder Plate, which holds a roasted bone (usually a lamb shank), a roasted hard-boiled egg, parsley, bitter herbs (usually fresh horseradish), and haroset, a mixture of chopped apples and nuts.*

*In this menu the traditional Passover foods, such as gefilte fish and brisket, grace the Seder table in somewhat untraditional ways. A carrot-flecked gefilte fish loaf, delicious served warm or cold, is simple to prepare and easy to serve. The tasty broccoli stuffing for the brisket is made with matzoh farfel for this holiday, but an herbed bread stuffing can be substituted other times of the year. The Frozen Strawberry Meringue Torte, a light, luscious, and low-calorie dessert, is a perfect conclusion to a rich and hearty meal.*

*The menu for this Passover Seder serves 10 to 12.*

*Vegetable Soup with Matzoh Balls.*

## Haroset

Haroset is a traditional offering at the Passover Seder. It's slightly sweet and slightly tart, and the consistency can be altered to your own preference.

¼  cup raisins
¼  cup chopped dates
4  tablespoons red wine
2  green apples, peeled and chopped
   (about 3 cups)
½  cup chopped walnuts (about 4
   ounces)
1  teaspoon ground cinnamon
1  to 2 tablespoons sugar

In a small bowl, soak raisins and dates in red wine for several hours or overnight. In food processor with metal blade or in mixing bowl, combine all ingredients together. The consistency may be as coarse or fine as you prefer.

Makes about 3 cups

## Gefilte Fish Loaf

It's easier, more practical, and more economical to serve gefilte fish in loaf form. Cut into slices and place on individual plates lined with lettuce leaves. Garnish with fresh dill and red horseradish for an eye-pleasing presentation.

**3 pounds firm, white-fleshed fish fillets such as whitefish, carp, pike, scrod, or halibut**
**2 medium onions, coarsely chopped**
**3 carrots, peeled**
**1 teaspoon salt**
**2 large eggs**
**⅓ cup ice water**
**1 tablespoon kosher salt**
**1 teaspoon sugar**
**½ teaspoon white pepper**
**2 rounded tablespoons matzoh meal**
**2 tablespoons freshly grated horseradish or 1 tablespoon prepared horseradish**
**2 to 3 tablespoons fresh chopped dill or 2 to 3 teaspoons dried dill**
**Lettuce leaves**
**Sprigs of fresh dill or parsley**
**Red horseradish**

Have fish dealer remove all skin and bones from fish. Cut fish into small pieces and place in mixing bowl with onion. Refrigerate while preparing carrots.

In food processor with metal blade, chop carrots into very small dice. Place in a small pot, cover with water, add 1 teaspoon salt, and bring to a boil. Boil for 2 minutes. Drain and run under cold water to stop the cooking. Set aside.

Divide the fish and onions in half. Place half at a time in food processor with metal blade. Purée until smooth. To each batch add 1 egg, half the ice water, and the kosher salt, sugar, and white pepper. When finely puréed, remove to bowl. Stir in matzoh meal, horseradish, carrots, and dill. Taste, and correct seasonings.

Grease a 9-by-5-by-3-inch loaf pan. Cut a piece of parchment or waxed paper to fit the bottom of the pan and grease the paper. Spoon fish into pan, spreading top evenly. Set loaf pan in a baking pan and fill with about 2 inches of boiling water. Bake at 325° for 50 to 60 minutes or until center feels firm to the touch. Remove from oven and cool for 5 minutes. Run a sharp knife around sides and reverse the pan onto a piece of aluminum foil. Remove the pan and the paper.

❋ If not serving immediately, cool and wrap in foil. May be refrigerated up to 3 days.

May be served warm or cold. Slice and serve on lettuce leaves garnished with fresh dill or parsley and horseradish.

Serves 10 to 12

## Vegetable Soup with Matzoh Balls

A savory, satisfying, earthy vegetable soup that can begin with homemade stock or kosher chicken broth. It's lighter than most vegetable soups and is a refreshing change of pace from the traditional chicken soup.

3 tablespoons pareve margarine or rendered chicken fat

2 large onions, chopped

2 carrots, peeled and chopped into ½-inch pieces

3 large leeks, cleaned and chopped, white part only

½ cup celery root, peeled and chopped into ½-inch pieces

1 small turnip, peeled and chopped into ½-inch pieces

1 small rutabaga, peeled and chopped into ½-inch pieces

1 small head green cabbage, cored and shredded

11 cups chicken broth

3 peppercorns

1 teaspoon dried thyme

1 teaspoon dried basil

Salt and pepper to taste

2 tomatoes, seeded and chopped

Matzoh Balls (see next recipe)

Melt margarine or chicken fat in a large soup pot. Add vegetables and sauté, stirring, for about 15 minutes or until soft. Add chicken broth, peppercorns, thyme, and basil. Cover, bring to a boil, reduce heat, and simmer for about 2 hours, stirring occasionally.

Strain, reserving vegetables. Add as many reserved vegetables to broth as desired.

❋ May be refrigerated up to 5 days.

❈ May be frozen.

Before serving, reheat and season to taste. Add chopped tomatoes and matzoh balls and cook until heated through.

Serves 8 to 10

## Matzoh Balls

These matzoh balls have a slight almond crunch and are a family recipe that has been handed down through the generations.

4 large eggs
3 tablespoons rendered chicken fat
1 cup matzoh meal
⅓ cup chicken broth
¼ cup finely ground almonds
1½ teaspoons salt or to taste
2 tablespoons finely chopped parsley
½ teaspoon powdered ginger (optional)

In medium bowl, beat the eggs and chicken fat together. Stir in the matzoh meal. Add the chicken broth, almonds, salt, parsley, and ginger, if using. Stir well. Refrigerate for 1 hour or more. With wet hands, form into 1½-inch balls.

In a soup pot, bring 4 quarts of salted water to a boil. Reduce to a simmer and drop in the balls. Cover the pot and cook at a low simmer for 20 minutes. Do not lift the lid while cooking or the matzoh balls will boil instead of steam and will become tough. Drain and add to soup.

❋ May be refrigerated for several days.

❋ May be frozen.

Makes about 28 matzoh balls

## Stuffed Brisket of Beef with Broccoli Farfel Stuffing

A pocket is easily cut into a brisket to hold a hearty broccoli farfel stuffing. When the brisket is sliced, it frames the colorful stuffing as pretty as a picture.

BROCCOLI FARFEL STUFFING
- 3 tablespoons rendered chicken fat
- 1 large onion, chopped
- ½ pound mushrooms, coarsely chopped
- 2 cloves garlic, crushed
- 10-ounce package frozen chopped broccoli, thawed
- 1½ cups matzoh farfel
- 1 whole egg
- 1 egg yolk
- 1 teaspoon salt
- 1 teaspoon dried basil or 2 tablespoons fresh basil
- ⅛ teaspoon freshly ground pepper

BRISKET
- 3- to 5-pound first-cut brisket
  Salt and pepper
  Paprika
- 2 onions, quartered
- 3 carrots, peeled and cut into 2-inch pieces
- 1 cup beef broth
- 1½ cups dry red wine
- 2 tablespoons Dijon mustard
- 1 to 2 tablespoons potato starch mixed with an equal amount of cold water (optional)

Make broccoli farfel stuffing: Melt chicken fat in skillet. Sauté chopped onions until soft. Add mushrooms and garlic and sauté until most of the liquid has evaporated. Place in medium bowl and cool slightly. Stir in broccoli and farfel. Mix egg and egg yolk and add to broccoli farfel mixture. Stir in seasonings. Set aside.

Make a pocket in brisket by cutting horizontally through the center of the meat, leaving a ¾-inch border uncut on three sides. Loosely push stuffing into pocket. Do not overstuff. Skewer closed with turkey lacers or trussing needle. Press on top of meat with hands to distribute stuffing evenly. Sprinkle both sides of meat with salt, pepper, and paprika.

Place onions and carrots in bottom of roaster or Dutch oven. Place brisket on vegetables. Broil until top is brown. Turn meat over and brown other side. Reduce oven to 300°. In a small bowl, whisk beef broth, wine, and mustard together. Pour over brisket. Cover and bake 3 to 4 hours or until tender when pierced with a fork. Baste occasionally. If sauce boils too rapidly, reduce heat to 275°.

When meat is tender, remove from oven. If not serving immediately, place meat in a bowl and cover with a damp towel. This will prevent the top from drying out. Strain pan juices for sauce, discarding vegetables.

❉ Meat and sauce may be refrigerated up to 2 days. Wrap meat securely in foil. Store sauce in a covered bowl.

❊ Meat, well wrapped in foil, may be frozen. Freeze sauce separately. Defrost in refrigerator overnight.

Before serving, remove fat from sauce. Bring meat and sauce to room temperature. Place meat in casserole or roasting pan; pour sauce over meat. Cover and reheat at 350° for 45 minutes or until meat is heated through. Remove meat to serving platter and let rest for 10 minutes before slicing. Heat sauce in saucepan.

*Cut slit in brisket. Keep knife horizontal to bottom and leave a three-quarter-inch border uncut on three sides.*

*Stuff the brisket.*

*Sew the brisket closed.*

*Stuffed Brisket of Beef garnished with cooked carrots.*

Season sauce to taste with salt, pepper, wine, or mustard. If a thicker sauce is desired, remove pan from heat and stir in starch and water mixture. Return to heat and stir constantly until sauce comes to a boil and thickens. Slice meat into ¼-inch-thick slices. Spoon a small amount of sauce over meat. Pass remaining sauce.

Serves 8 to 12

*Variation:* Here is my year-round version: Substitute 4 tablespoons butter or margarine for the chicken fat. Substitute 1¾ cups herb-seasoned bread stuffing for the matzoh farfel, and 1 to 2 tablespoons cornstarch for the potato starch.

## Asparagus with Lemon Matzoh Sauce

Bread crumbs can be substituted for matzoh meal at other times of the year, but after you taste it this way, I doubt you'll want to make any substitutions.

**4 pounds asparagus**
**½ pound (2 sticks) pareve margarine**
   **or butter**
**2 tablespoons plus 2 teaspoons**
   **lemon juice**
**2 cloves garlic, crushed**
**4 tablespoons matzoh meal**
   **Salt and pepper to taste**

Wash the asparagus. Cut or snap off tough ends. Peel the stalks with a vegetable peeler, pulling from stem end toward tip. Gather into bunches of 6 to 8 and tie into bundles.

❋ May be refrigerated overnight. Stand in a pitcher filled with about 2 inches of water and cover with a plastic bag over the top.

Fill a large sauté pan or skillet with water. Bring to a boil, add asparagus, and simmer, uncovered, until tender but firm. Timing will vary with size and age of asparagus, about 8 to 10 minutes after water returns to a boil.

In a small saucepan, melt margarine or butter. Stir in lemon juice, garlic, and matzoh meal. Do not boil or sauce will separate. Season to taste.

Drain asparagus, place on platter, and cut off strings. Pour sauce over top.

Serves 10 to 12

# Matzoh Fruit Kugel

Golden matzoh kugel is a real hit with my family. It's fruity with a dash of sweetness, and it's pretty to look at when dotted with currant jelly.

5 matzohs
6 large eggs
2 unpeeled red apples, shredded
1 small unpeeled pear, shredded
8-ounce can crushed pineapple, drained
¾ cup golden raisins
3 tablespoons sugar
Grated rind of 1 lemon
1 tablespoon lemon juice
1 teaspoon ground cinnamon
2 teaspoons vanilla extract
3 tablespoons rendered chicken fat or margarine
2 tablespoons sugar mixed with ½ teaspoon ground cinnamon
2 tablespoons currant jelly

Break matzohs into a bowl and cover with water. Soak 2 minutes and drain.

In a large bowl, mix eggs until fluffy. Stir in apple, pear, pineapple, raisins, sugar, lemon rind and juice, cinnamon, and vanilla. When well mixed, stir in matzohs.

Preheat oven to 325°. Place chicken fat or margarine in a 9-by-13-inch casserole and heat in oven until melted. Swirl pan, coating it well with the fat. Pour excess fat into matzoh fruit mixture. Pour mixture into casserole, spreading evenly. In a small bowl mix sugar and cinnamon for topping. Sprinkle over top and dot with currant jelly.

❋ May be refrigerated overnight.

Before serving, bring to room temperature. Bake at 325° for 45 minutes or until top is golden and kugel is solid. Cut into squares to serve.

Serves 10 to 12

## Chocolate Poppy Seed Torte

The reason I've included this cake in the Passover menu is because it has no flour. Substitute Grand Marnier for the orange juice in the glaze and this torte will make any day a holiday. The poppy seeds are simple to grind; just put them in a blender if you don't have a coffee grinder and let them whirl for about a minute. They add a marvelous nutty flavor. Be sure not to let the cake overbake; it becomes firmer as it cools and is rich, fudgy, and velvety.

6 ounces semisweet chocolate
¾ cup poppy seeds (about 3½ ounces)
¼ pound (1 stick) unsalted margarine or butter, at room temperature
¾ cup sugar
6 large eggs, separated
Dash of cream of tartar
⅓ cup orange marmalade
Grated rind of 1 orange for garnish (optional)

CHOCOLATE GLAZE
3 ounces semisweet chocolate
1½ tablespoons orange juice
3 tablespoons unsalted margarine or butter, at room temperature

Grease and line the bottom of an 8-by-2-inch or 9-by-2-inch cake pan or springform pan with parchment or waxed paper. Set aside. Melt 6 ounces chocolate in top of double boiler over simmering water. Grind poppy seeds in a coffee grinder or blender for about 40 seconds or until they begin to pulverize and are partially ground.

In mixing bowl, with electric mixer cream together margarine or butter and sugar. Add egg yolks one at a time, beating after each addition. Stir in poppy seeds and chocolate. In separate bowl, beat egg whites until frothy. Add cream of tartar and beat until stiff peaks form. Stir a small amount of whites into chocolate mixture to lighten it, then gently fold in the rest. Pour into prepared pan.

Bake at 350° for 40 to 50 minutes or until cake tester or toothpick inserted near center comes out almost clean and top is cracked and crusty. A small amount of chocolate on cake tester means cake will be moist and fudgy. Do not overbake. Remove to cooling rack and cool 10 minutes. Invert pan on rack and pull off paper. Cool completely.

✻ May be refrigerated 2 days.

❀ May be frozen.

Cut cake in half horizontally. Place top layer, cut side up, on serving plate lined with waxed paper. Spread with marmalade. Set bottom layer smoothest side up on top.

Make chocolate glaze: In double boiler over simmering water, melt chocolate. Stir in orange juice. Remove from heat and stir in margarine or butter. Refrigerate or stir over ice water until thick enough to spread. Spread over top and sides of cake. Sprinkle orange rind lightly around top of cake, if desired. Remove waxed paper from platter. Refrigerate torte several hours before serving.

❊ May be refrigerated overnight.

❊ May be frozen, but glaze will lose its shine.

Serves 10

## Frozen Strawberry Meringue Torte

Everyone wants to serve a dessert that's light yet still elegant. We're taught to believe egg whites must be isolated in order to whip well, but I added fruit, sugar, lemon juice, and vanilla and discovered that it will whip up to a light, frothy, and creamy filling. This torte is low in calories and goes directly from freezer to table.

MACAROON NUT CRUST
 5 **ounces almond macaroons (about 1½ cups)**
 2 **tablespoons unsalted margarine or butter, melted**
 ½ **cup chopped pecans or walnuts**

FILLING
 2 **egg whites, at room temperature**
 1 **cup sugar**
 2 **cups sliced strawberries**
 1 **tablespoon lemon juice**
 1 **teaspoon vanilla extract**

STRAWBERRY SAUCE
10-**ounce package frozen sliced strawberries**
 3 **tablespoons frozen undiluted orange juice concentrate or 2 tablespoons orange marmalade**
 1 **tablespoon currant jelly**
 1 **cup fresh strawberries, sliced**

Make macaroon nut crust: In food processor with metal blade, process macaroons and butter until coarsely ground. Add nuts and process until mixture begins to hold together. Press into the bottom of a 10-by-3-inch springform pan. Bake at 350° for 7 to 10 minutes or until golden. Cool.

In a large bowl of an electric mixer place egg whites, sugar, 2 cups sliced strawberries, lemon juice, and vanilla. Beat on low speed to blend. Increase to high speed and beat until firm peaks form when beaters are withdrawn, about 10 to 15 minutes. Pour into cooled crust. Cover and freeze until very firm, a minimum of 6 hours.

❊ May be frozen for 3 weeks.

Serve torte directly from freezer, as it will not become totally solid.

Make strawberry sauce: Slightly defrost strawberries and orange juice concentrate. Purée strawberries and concentrate or marmalade in food processor fitted with metal blade. Mix in currant jelly. Remove to a bowl and stir in sliced strawberries. Serve cold.

❊ Sauce may be refrigerated overnight.

Cut torte in wedges and serve with strawberry sauce.

Serves 12

## 4
# A FAMILY
# AFFAIR

# Mother's Day
# Breakfast in Bed

## MENU

GRAPEFRUIT BASKETS WITH
FRESH FRUIT SALAD

MAPLE ALMOND OMELET SOUFFLÉ, OR
MEXICAN OMELET, OR
ITALIAN OMELET GRATINÉ, OR
BANANA PANCAKES, OR
OVERNIGHT CINAMMON FRENCH
TOAST WITH CINNAMON SYRUP

PEANUT BUTTER AND
JELLY MUFFINS, OR
HONEY-GLAZED PINEAPPLE
BRAN MUFFINS, OR
APPLE CHEESE MUFFINS

MOTHER'S EYE-OPENER

In 1914, President Woodrow Wilson proclaimed the second Sunday of May a national holiday to commemorate mothers. Mothers truly deserve some pampering, and what better way is there than to serve them breakfast in bed?

This breakfast menu is truly wonderful in or out of bed, any day of the week, but is especially nice for those Sundays when friends drop by for a late breakfast or brunch. Many of these recipes are easy enough for the children to make—such as the cinnamony French toast, kirsch-laced fruit salad, rich peanut butter and jelly muffins, or banana pancakes. Others, such as the Maple Almond Omelet Soufflé, may need Dad's participation.

You'll find three spectacular omelets here, each with an original twist. One is sweetened with maple syrup, another has the crunch of tortillas, and the third is topped with cream and Parmesan cheese, and broiled until glazed and crusty.

All of the entrées serve 2 to 4.

*On the tray, Grapefruit Basket with Fresh Fruit Salad and Mother's Eye-Opener. On the plate, Maple Almond Omelet Soufflé and Peanut Butter and Jelly Muffin garnished with a fresh strawberry fan.*

## Grapefruit Baskets

A lovely introduction to any meal. I have made these for large crowds, as they can be made a day ahead and are perfect for showers or brunches. One grapefruit will give you two baskets.

**2 medium to large grapefruit**
  **Ribbon to tie handles**
  **Fresh Fruit Salad (see following recipe)**

Cut grapefruit in half. Take 2 toothpicks and insert into the grapefruit rind ¼ inch apart and about ¼ inch from the cut edge, as pictured. Repeat on the opposite side with two more toothpicks. Place the grapefruit on its side and cut a thin slice halfway down, stopping at the toothpicks. Repeat on opposite side. The slice remains attached between the toothpicks. Using a grapefruit knife, cut around inside edge and remove all grapefruit pulp, leaving a shell.

✻ Baskets may be refrigerated overnight, covered with a damp towel.

Before serving, fill baskets with Fresh Fruit Salad. Pull strips up from each side of grapefruit, making handles. Tie handles together with colored ribbon.

Makes 4 baskets

*Cut grapefruit in half. Slice until you reach toothpicks.*

*Remove grapefruit pulp.*

*Fill with fruits and tie handles together with ribbon.*

## Fresh Fruit Salad

Imported kirsch—I use it rather than domestic here—adds flavor to this refreshing fruit salad. To cut down on preparation time, have handy a zester, corer, vegetable peeler, serrated cutter, and melon baller.

1 teaspoon orange rind or zest
2 tablespoons orange juice
2 tablespoons sugar
2 tablespoons kirsch or orange-flavored liqueur (optional)
¼ pound seedless grapes (about ¾ cup)
¾ cup fresh pineapple, cut into 1-inch pieces
½ cup orange segments, cut into 1-inch pieces
½ cup grapefruit segments, cut into 1-inch pieces
1 apple, peeled and chopped
½ cup small whole or sliced strawberries

Make orange marinade by mixing orange rind and juice, sugar, and kirsch or orange liqueur together in a small bowl.

Place all fruit but strawberries in a bowl. Pour marinade over. Refrigerate for 1 hour or longer.

✳ May be refrigerated overnight.

Before serving, stir in strawberries.

Serves 4

*Variation:* Vary fruits with season, such as melon balls, berries, and peaches. Do not marinate soft fruit; stir them into the marinade before serving.

## Mexican Omelet

Tortillas usually hold a filling; in this recipe they are bite-size and cooked along with the eggs to form the slightly crunchy omelet itself. The omelet encases a zesty and creamy avocado filling.

½ cup chopped avocado
¼ cup sour cream
1 tablespoon chopped canned green chilies
1 tablespoon chopped green onion
1 teaspoon lemon juice
   Dash of Tabasco sauce
6 eggs
   Dash of salt
3 tablespoons butter or margarine
1 corn tortilla, cut into bite-size pieces
¾ cup shredded Monterey Jack cheese (about 3 ounces)

In a small bowl, mix avocado, sour cream, chilies, green onion, lemon juice, and Tabasco. Set aside.

Preheat oven to 325°. Mix eggs with salt until blended. Melt butter or margarine in a 7- to 8-inch omelet pan. Add half the tortilla pieces and cook until soft. Pour in half the eggs and cook 2 to 3 minutes, lifting eggs to allow uncooked mixture to flow underneath. Do not cook firm; eggs must be very soft, for they will continue to cook in the oven. Sprinkle top with cheese. Spread half the avocado filling over half the omelet. Place pan in oven and bake 5 to 7 minutes or until cheese is melted. Fold in half. Repeat for second omelet.

Makes two 7- to 8-inch omelets

## Italian Omelet Gratiné

Robust, chunky, and herb-scented describe this easy-to-make tomato sauce filling. I like to double it and freeze it in individual portions so it will be ready when I need it. The omelet is delicious with the filling alone, but the addition of cream and Parmesan cheese over the top, browned until bubbly, makes it extra moist and very rich.

ITALIAN TOMATO FILLING
- ¼ **cup chopped onion**
- 1 **clove garlic, crushed**
- 1 **tablespoon vegetable oil**
- ¼ **cup thinly sliced green pepper**
- 2 **mushrooms, sliced**
- **8-ounce can tomato sauce**
- ¼ **teaspoon dried oregano**
- ¼ **teaspoon dried basil**
  **Dash of sugar**
  **Salt and pepper to taste**

OMELET
- 6 **eggs**
  **Dash of salt**
- 3 **tablespoons butter or margarine**
- 6 **tablespoons whipping cream, at room temperature**
- 6 **tablespoons grated Parmesan cheese**

Make Italian tomato filling: In small saucepan, sauté onion and garlic in oil until soft. Add green pepper and mushrooms and cook until slightly wilted, but not limp. Add tomato sauce, oregano, basil, and sugar and simmer for 10 to 15 minutes or until thickened slightly. Season to taste.

Set aside.

❄ Filling may be frozen.

Mix eggs with salt until blended. Melt half the butter or margarine in a 7- to 8-inch omelet pan. Add eggs and cook, lifting eggs to allow uncooked mixture to flow underneath. Do not cook firm; eggs should be very soft, as they will continue to cook under the broiler. Preheat broiler to highest setting. Spread half the tomato filling over half the omelet. Fold over and remove to an ovenproof platter. Spoon 3 tablespoons cream over top and sprinkle with 3 tablespoons Parmesan cheese. Broil until top is golden brown. Repeat with second omelet in same manner.

Makes two 7- to 8-inch omelets

## Maple Almond Omelet Soufflé

If you like pancakes and omelets you'll love this delectable combination of both flavors. It's light as air and the almonds on the bottom form a crunchy crust.

- 3 **egg yolks**
- 3 **tablespoons maple syrup**
- 2 **tablespoons whipping cream or half-and-half**
- ½ **teaspoon vanilla extract**

Beat egg yolks until light and creamy. Mix in the maple syrup, cream or half-and-half, and vanilla.

In a separate mixing bowl, beat egg whites until frothy. Add cream of tartar and beat until

3 egg whites, at room temperature
  Dash of cream of tartar
2 tablespoons butter or margarine
¼ cup sliced almonds
  Maple syrup for serving (optional)

soft peaks form. Fold whites into the yolk mixture.

Preheat oven to 350°. Melt butter or margarine in a 8- to 9-inch omelet pan. Sprinkle almonds on the bottom and spoon over the egg mixture. Over low heat, cook the omelet for about 5 minutes or until sides begin to brown and the underside is golden when lifted with a spatula. Be careful not to cook over too high a heat or the almonds will burn. Place pan in oven and bake for 5 to 8 minutes or until top is puffed and browned. If your omelet pan does not have an ovenproof handle, cover it with a double thickness of aluminum foil. Slide omelet onto serving plate, flipping top half over bottom one to fold omelet in half. Pass additional syrup, if desired.

Serves 2

## Banana Pancakes

I made these one morning for my children. After the first bite, there was complete silence. Then my oldest, Cheryl, said, "But Mom, how will your readers know that these are not *just* pancakes?!"

¾ cup whole wheat flour
¼ cup all-purpose flour
⅓ cup all-bran cereal
2 teaspoons baking power
  Dash of salt
1¼ cups milk
2 tablespoons vegetable oil
1 medium banana, finely chopped
  (about ¾ cup)
  Syrup for serving

In medium bowl, stir together flours, bran, baking powder, and salt. Add milk and oil. Stir to combine; batter will be slightly lumpy. Stir in banana. Using a scant ¼ cup for each, cook pancakes on hot, lightly greased griddle, turning once. Serve with syrup.

Makes 12 pancakes

## Overnight Cinnamon French Toast

These may be kept covered on the baking sheet overnight, and if you don't get to them the next day, put them in Baggies and they can be refrigerated for two more days. The end result will be light, moist, spongy on the inside, crispy on the outside French toast.

3 eggs
½ cup milk
2 tablespoons sugar
⅛ teaspoon baking powder
¼ teaspoon ground cinnamon
1 teaspoon vanilla extract
6 slices bread — egg, French, or sourdough — sliced about ¾ inch thick
4 tablespoons butter or margarine Cinnamon Syrup (see following recipe)

In a medium bowl, whisk together the eggs, milk, sugar, baking powder, cinnamon, and vanilla until blended. Place bread on a rimmed baking sheet and slowly pour the batter over. Turn the bread until it is all coated with the batter. Press a piece of waxed paper directly on the bread to cover it. Refrigerate overnight.

Before serving, melt butter or margarine in skillet. Fry bread over moderate heat until golden on both sides. Do not crowd. Serve with Cinnamon Syrup.

Makes 6 slices toast

## Cinnamon Syrup

The perfect topping for Cinnamon French Toast (preceding recipe), pancakes, and waffles is this creamy, cinnamon-fragrant syrup.

1 cup sugar
½ cup light corn syrup
¼ cup water
½ teaspoon ground cinnamon
½ cup whipping cream or evaporated milk

In small saucepan, stir together sugar, corn syrup, water, and cinnamon. Stirring constantly, bring to a boil over moderate heat; boil for 2 minutes. Remove from heat. Stir in cream or evaporated milk. Cool at least 30 minutes. Syrup will thicken as it cools.

❋ May be refrigerated for several months.

Serve warm or at room temperature.

Makes 1⅓ cups

## Peanut Butter and Jelly Muffins

Peanut butter and jelly lovers, these muffins are for you. They still taste like fluffy buttermilk muffins, but with the added flavor of peanut butter. The jelly is spooned over the top, but as the muffins bake, it ends up in the middle. The added wheat germ makes them extra healthful, too.

2 large eggs
1 cup water
6 tablespoons peanut butter
1 teaspoon vanilla extract
1⅓ cups buttermilk biscuit mix
⅔ cup wheat germ
½ cup sugar
½ teaspoon strawberry or raspberry jelly per muffin

In mixing bowl or food processor with metal blade, combine egg, water, peanut butter, and vanilla. Mix until smooth. Add biscuit mix, wheat germ, and sugar; mix until dry ingredients are incorporated. Do not overmix. Spoon batter into greased or paper-lined 2½-inch muffin pans, filling them three-fourths full. Top each with ½ teaspoon jelly. Bake at 375° for 20 to 25 minutes or until puffed and golden brown.

❋ May be frozen.

Serve warm or at room temperature. Top with a dollop of jam or jelly, if desired.

Makes 12 muffins

## Honey-Glazed Pineapple Bran Muffins

These muffins have an earthy aroma and a whisper of sweetness from crushed pineapple and golden honey.

1 large egg
2 tablespoons vegetable oil
2 tablespoons honey
¾ cup buttermilk
¼ cup whole wheat flour
⅓ cup all-purpose flour
¼ cup sugar
1½ cups all-bran cereal
¼ teaspoon salt
¼ teaspoon baking soda
Heaping ¼ teaspoon cinnamon
¼ cup raisins
¼ cup canned crushed pineapple, well drained
¼ cup honey for glaze
Butter, for serving

In mixing bowl or food processor with metal blade, mix egg, oil, honey, and buttermilk until blended. Add flours, sugar, bran, salt, baking soda, and cinnamon. Mix until blended; do not overmix. Lightly mix in raisins and pineapple. Spoon into greased 2½-inch muffin pans, filling them three-fourths full. Bake at 400° for 18 to 20 minutes or until skewer inserted into center comes out clean. Let cool 10 minutes and remove from pan.

Melt honey in small saucepan. Let sit about 4 minutes or until slightly thickened. Brush on tops of warm muffins.

❋ May be frozen.

Serve with butter.

Makes 10 to 12 muffins

## Apple Cheese Muffins

These are moist, fine-textured apple muffins with a generous amount of shredded Cheddar cheese in the batter as well as on top. It's rather like having your own hot apple pie with a melted cheese topping, all neatly contained in a muffin cup.

¼ pound (1 stick) butter, at room temperature
⅔ cup sugar
2 large eggs
¼ cup apple juice
1¾ cups all-purpose flour
1 teaspoon baking soda
1 teaspoon baking powder
½ teaspoon salt
1 teaspoon cinnamon
¼ teaspoon almond extract
1 large green apple, peeled, cored, and coarsely chopped (about 1½ cups)
¾ cup golden raisins
2½ cups shredded sharp Cheddar cheese (about 10 ounces)
Butter, for serving

In mixing bowl or food processor with metal blade, cream butter and sugar until light and fluffy. Add eggs one at a time, beating well. Mix in apple juice. Add flour, baking soda, baking powder, salt, cinnamon, and almond extract. Mix until incorporated. Do not overmix. Stir in apples, raisins, and 1 cup cheese. Batter will be very thick. Spoon batter into greased or paper-lined 2½-inch muffin pans, filling them two-thirds full. Sprinkle top of each muffin with remaining cheese. Bake at 375° for 20 to 25 minutes or until knife inserted in center comes out clean.

❀ May be frozen.

Serve warm with butter.

Makes about 20 muffins

## Mother's Eye-Opener

What a way to start the day! Ice-cold, thick, and creamy with fresh fruit; if you're the Mom you deserve the rum!

1½ cups milk
6-ounce can frozen orange or tangerine juice concentrate, defrosted slightly
1½ cups cubed fresh pineapple (about ½ pineapple)
1 ripe banana
6 to 7 ice cubes
¾ cup dark rum
Orange slices for garnish (optional)

Place all ingredients except orange slices in blender. Mix until thick and smooth. Pour into glasses and garnish each with a fresh orange slice, if desired.

Makes four 8-ounce servings

*Variation:* Mix all ingredients except rum and orange slices in blender. Fill glasses half full. Fill rest with champagne.

# Father's Day
# Seafood Supper

MENU

CRUNCHY APPETIZER PIE
❧

SPINACH AMARETTO SALAD
❧

SEAFOOD BROCHETTES, OR
FILET OF SOLE IN PARCHMENT, OR
BAKED FISH IN
LEMON YOGURT SAUCE
❧

CREAMY POTATO PUFF
ASPARAGUS AU GRATIN, OR
STUFFED SQUASH
❧

CHOCOLATE CHIP ALMOND TORTE
WITH HAZELNUT FUDGE SAUCE
❧

WINE RECOMMENDATION:
A CRISP AND DRY SAUVIGNON
(FUMÉ) BLANC, OR A SPICY WHITE
WINE SUCH AS A GEWÜRZTRAMINER

*It was a grateful daughter who thought up the idea of Father's Day back in 1910. In deference to all those dads who love to fish, I offer three great ways of preparing the bounty of their catch. The first is en brochette—fish steaks are cut into cubes and interspersed with shrimp and thin lemon slices. The second is baking fillets in parchment. These perfect parchment packages contain not only the fish but the vegetables as well. Both are basted with a creamy tarragon sauce, leaving them moist and flavorful. The parchment packages bake on cookie sheets, which means there's a minimum of clean-up. Last, I offer a recipe for fish baked whole—either a single large fish or individual ones—coated and served with a lemony yogurt sauce enhanced by the exotic aromas of cardamom and coriander.*

*The no-fail rule for cooking fish is this: ten minutes for every inch measured at the thickest part of the fish. This holds true for any method of preparation.*

*My Father's Day dessert, which can be prepared and frozen weeks in advance, is for all you chocolate-nut lovers. Rich, crunchy, and topped with a heavenly hot chocolate sauce, it gives hot fudge sundaes some tough competition.*

*This menu serves 8.*

## Crunchy Appetizer Pie

Crushed cheese crackers form a fine-textured top and bottom crust to hold a tangy filling of finely chopped fresh raw vegetables bound together with sour cream.

8-ounce box cheese crackers, finely crushed (about 2 cups)
3 tablespoons melted butter or margarine
1 pint (2 cups) sour cream
½ cup pimiento-stuffed green olives
½ cup finely chopped celery
½ cup finely chopped green pepper
½ cup finely chopped onion
2 tablespoons lemon juice
1 teaspoon salt
1 teaspoon Worcestershire sauce
¼ teaspoon paprika
  Several dashes of Tabasco sauce
  Anchovy fillets (optional)
  Pimiento strips
  Green pepper strips
  Sliced ripe and green olives
  Curly lettuce

Mix cheese crumbs with melted butter or margarine and press half into the bottom of a 9-inch springform pan. Set remaining crumbs aside.

In a medium bowl, stir together sour cream, olives, celery, green pepper, onion, lemon juice, salt, Worcestershire sauce, paprika, and Tabasco sauce until blended. Spread sour cream mixture over crumb base; smooth top. Sprinkle remaining half of cracker crumbs evenly over the top. Press in gently. Cover with plastic wrap and refrigerate for at least 4 hours for flavors to blend.

❋ May be refrigerated for 2 days.

Before serving, remove sides of springform. Place pie on serving platter and decorate top with alternating strips of anchovy, pimiento, and green pepper. Place slices of green and black olives around top edge. Surround pie with curly lettuce. Cut into pie-shaped wedges to serve.

Serves 10 to 12

*Variation:* To serve 6, mix 1½ tablespoons butter with a 5-ounce box of cheese crackers, halve the remaining ingredients, and make in an 8-inch springform.

## Spinach Amaretto Salad

The fragrant mellow flavor of Amaretto adds a subtle sweetness to this rendition of a classic favorite, the spinach salad. If you like a wilted salad, pour the dressing over very hot; if not, let cool a bit before adding.

2 **pounds spinach (about 4 bunches)**
1 **pound bacon, diced**
½ **cup salad oil**
2 **large cloves garlic, crushed**
6 **anchovy fillets, chopped fine (optional)**
½ **cup red wine vinegar**
½ **cup lemon juice**
4 **teaspoons Worcestershire sauce**
1 **teaspoon dry mustard**
¼ **cup Amaretto liqueur**
  **Salt and pepper to taste**
¼ **pound mushrooms, thinly sliced**
1 **small red onion, thinly sliced**

Wash spinach. Remove large stems and tear into bite-size pieces. Store in plastic bags in refrigerator until ready to use.

To make dressing, place bacon in a large skillet. Cook over moderate heat, stirring occasionally, until bacon is crisp and all fat is rendered. With a slotted spoon, remove bacon from skillet and drain on paper towels. Reserve ⅓ cup bacon fat and discard the rest. Return bacon fat to skillet and add oil, garlic, anchovies, vinegar, lemon juice, Worcestershire, mustard, Amaretto, salt, and pepper. Simmer until blended.

❋ Dressing may be refrigerated overnight and reheated before serving.

When ready to serve, place spinach, mushrooms, onion, and reserved bacon in large salad bowl. Pour hot dressing over and toss well.

Serves 8

## Seafood Brochettes

A hearty lemon beer marinade is good with any fish, and my brochettes using shrimp, scallops, and swordfish only scratch the surface of suggestions. Any one fish works beautifully alone as well. Be sure to cut all the fish the same size so that when they cook they will be done at the same time.

½ pound (2 sticks) butter
⅔ cup room-temperature beer, measured after foam subsides
6 tablespoons catsup
6 tablespoons lemon juice
¼ cup Worcestershire sauce
6 cloves garlic, crushed
½ teaspoon salt
¼ teaspoon freshly ground pepper
24 small or 12 large sea scallops (about 1¼ pounds)
12 ounces swordfish or halibut steak
24 medium shrimp (about 1 pound), peeled and deveined
1 lemon, thinly sliced

To make marinade, melt the butter over low heat in a medium saucepan. Stir in beer, catsup, lemon juice, Worcestershire, garlic, salt, and pepper. Cool before using.

If the scallops are large, cut them in half. Cut the swordfish or halibut into 24 cubes, about 1 inch across. Place the seafood in a shallow glass dish, keeping each type separate. Pour the marinade over and toss the fish gently to thoroughly coat it. Marinate in the refrigerator 4 to 6 hours, turning occasionally. Thread the shrimp, scallops, swordfish or halibut, and lemon slices on eight 15- to 18-inch skewers, putting 3 pieces of each on a skewer. Broil or barbecue 4 to 5 inches from the heat for 3 to 4 minutes in a broiler, or about 6 minutes on the barbecue. Turn the skewers, brush seafood with the marinade, and broil 3 to 4 minutes or barbecue 6 minutes longer.

Serves 8

## *Baked Fish in Lemon Yogurt Sauce*

Coriander and cardamom are universally popular spices that are beginning to be enjoyed in this country for their piquant flavor. They masterfully season a tangy lemon yogurt sauce that tenderizes and highlights fresh fish.

**Two 4-pound whitefish or red snapper, or eight 10- to 12-ounce trout**
**Salt and pepper**
½ **pound (2 sticks) butter or margarine**
2 **teaspoons salt**
2 **teaspoons ground coriander**
½ **teaspoon ground cardamom**
   **Freshly ground pepper**
4 **tablespoons lemon juice**
2 **teaspoons cornstarch**
1 **pint (2 cups) plain yogurt**
3 **to 4 tablespoons chopped fresh dill or 2 teaspoons dried dill**
   **Lemon wedges for garnish**
   **Sprigs of dill or parsley for garnish**

Have fish dealer butterfly-fillet the fish, leaving the head and tail intact, but removing the entire center bone. Open fish out, run hands along meat of fish, and remove any small bones with tweezers. Sprinkle fish with salt and pepper.

To make the sauce, melt butter in a medium saucepan over low heat. With a whisk, mix in salt, coriander, cardamom, pepper, and lemon juice. Stir cornstarch into yogurt and whisk into pan. Do not boil.

❁ Sauce may be held at room temperature for 4 hours or refrigerated overnight and reheated.

Brush inside of fish with sauce. Fold fish in half and brush top with sauce. Sprinkle with dill. Place foil over tail of large fish to prevent it from burning. Using heavy foil, line a shallow baking dish large enough to hold the fish; butter the foil. Preheat oven to 425°. Measure the thickest part of the fish from top to bottom. Bake for 10 minutes per measured inch, approximately 20 to 30 minutes. Baste with sauce every 10 minutes. The fish is done when it has lost its opaqueness when flaked with a fork.

While the fish bakes, reheat lemon yogurt sauce over low heat until hot. Do not boil. Remove fish to serving platter. Drizzle with sauce. Garnish with lemon wedges and fresh dill sprigs or parsley.

Pass remaining sauce.

Serves 8

## Fillet of Sole in Parchment

Cooking fish in a package, whether it be foil or parchment, ensures a very moist, flavorful, and slimming entrée. Other vegetables, such as spinach seasoned with a little cream and Pernod, work equally as well as the tomatoes and cucumbers in the recipe. If you use parchment, it will puff up and brown; cut an X in the top, letting the guests open their own packets. This keeps the fragrant juices in until the last possible moment.

**Eight 6-ounce fillets of sole**
**Salt and pepper**
 3 **medium shallots or 3 tablespoons**
     **finely chopped onion**
 3 **medium cloves garlic**
 ¾ **cup vegetable oil**
 ¼ **cup Dijon mustard**
 1 **tablespoon lemon juice**
 1 **teaspoon dried tarragon**
 1 **teaspoon Pernod (optional)**
 8 **to 10 ripe plum-shaped tomatoes**
     **or small, ripe tomatoes (about 1¼**
     **pounds) sliced ⅛ inch thick**
 ⅔ **cup julienned or shredded peeled**
     **cucumber (about one 8-inch piece)**
 2 **tablespoons melted margarine or**
     **vegetable oil**

Cut 8 pieces of parchment paper into heart shapes approximately 12 inches long and 14 inches wide. Fold parchment in half. Dry fish well. Place 1 fillet on one half of parchment, next to center fold. Season with salt and pepper.

In food processor fitted with metal blade, or in blender, process shallots or onion and garlic until minced. Add oil, mustard, lemon juice, tarragon, and Pernod (if you wish), and process until the mixture has formed a thick sauce.

Divide sauce among fillets, spreading evenly over each. Top with 3 to 4 tomato slices, overlapping slightly, and 1 tablespoon cucumber. Salt again lightly. Fold paper in half. Seal packages by starting at rounded end, rolling and crimping edges together tightly. Twist tip of heart to seal. Place packages on baking sheet.

❄ May be refrigerated up to 8 hours.

*Cut heart shape out of parchment. Fold parchment in half and place fillet next to center fold. Spread fillet with tarragon-mustard sauce. Top with tomato slices and shredded cucumber.*

*Crimp edges of parchment to seal.*

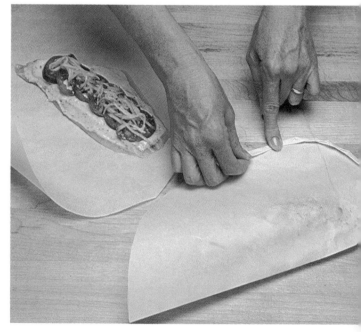

*Cut an X in the top of each parchment package and fold back edges to serve.*

Preheat oven to 500°. Place oven rack in lowest position in oven. Brush top of packages with melted margarine or oil. Bake 8 to 10 minutes or until puffed and browned. Place on serving plates and cut an X in the top of each package. Fold back corners and serve.

Serves 8

## *Creamy Potato Puff*

Potatoes are lighter and more fluffy when baked first and then mashed. Cream cheese and eggs make these potatoes velvety and rich, and the French-fried onions add a touch of crunch.

4 baking potatoes (about 10 ounces each)

8-ounce package cream cheese, at room temperature, cut into cubes

1 medium onion, finely chopped

3 eggs

3 tablespoons flour

1 teaspoon salt

¼ teaspoon white pepper

3-ounce can French-fried onions

4 tablespoons dry sherry (optional)

Bake potatoes. Scoop out insides and put into a large mixing bowl. Mash potatoes or put through ricer. Add cream cheese and beat until smooth. Add onion, eggs, flour, salt, and pepper and beat until light and fluffy. Spoon into an ungreased round 1½- to 2-quart casserole or soufflé dish. Sprinkle onion rings over the top. Cover with foil.

❋ May be refrigerated up to 2 days.

❋ May be frozen.

Before serving, bring to room temperature. Drizzle top with sherry, if desired. Bake, covered, at 325° for 30 minutes. Remove foil and bake 20 more minutes or until potatoes are bubbling and top is golden and crusty.

Serves 8

## Asparagus au Gratin

The sauce that binds this gratin is gentle enough not to overpower the delicate taste of asparagus but flavorful enough to enhance it. If increasing the recipe, I like to spoon some of the sauce on the bottom of the casserole as well as on the top. This sauce is lovely with cauliflower and broccoli, too.

3 **pounds fresh asparagus**
6 **tablespoons butter or margarine**
1 **small onion, thickly sliced**
6 **tablespoons flour**
2 **cups chicken broth**
1 **cup half-and-half**
½ **to 1 teaspoon salt**
  **White pepper to taste**
  **Dash of ground nutmeg**
1½ **cups shredded sharp Cheddar cheese (about 6 ounces)**

Wash asparagus. Cut or snap off tough ends. Peel the stalks with a vegetable peeler, pulling from stem end toward tip. Gather into bunches of 6 to 8 and tie into bundles. Fill a large sauté pan or skillet with water. Bring to a boil, add asparagus, and simmer, uncovered, until tender but firm. Timing will vary with size and age of asparagus, about 8 to 10 minutes after water returns to a boil. Remove from saucepan and immediately plunge into cold water to stop the cooking. Cut off strings and drain asparagus on paper towels. Arrange in shallow 7-by-11-inch casserole.

To make the sauce, melt butter or margarine in medium saucepan. Sauté onion over low heat until very soft, about 15 minutes; do not brown. Discard onion. Stir flour into butter and cook, over low heat, for 1 to 2 minutes. Remove pan from heat and stir in chicken broth and half-and-half. Return to moderate heat; whisk constantly until sauce comes to a boil and is smooth and thick. Season with salt, pepper, and nutmeg. If not using immediately, place a buttered piece of waxed paper directly on top of the sauce to keep skin from forming. Pour sauce over center of asparagus, leaving tips and ends exposed. Sprinkle sauce with cheese.

❋ May be refrigerated covered overnight.

Before serving, bring to room temperature. Bake at 400° for 15 minutes or until cheese is melted and asparagus is heated through.

Serves 8

## Stuffed Squash

A creative way of cooking squash is to scoop out the pulp and combine it with mushrooms, fragrant basil, and Swiss cheese. Bind it together with a small amount of sour cream and place the mixture back in the squash shell to bake.

4 medium zucchini (about 2 pounds), or 8 medium pattypan or scaloppini squash
  Salt
3 tablespoons butter or margarine
½ pound mushrooms, coarsely chopped
½ teaspoon salt
1 tablespoon chopped fresh basil or 1 teaspoon dried basil
¼ teaspoon pepper
1 cup shredded Swiss cheese (about 4 ounces)
3 tablespoons sour cream

Scrub squash and cook in boiling salted water to cover until tender but still firm when pierced with a fork. Timing will depend on type and size of squash, approximately 5 to 10 minutes. Drain. If using zucchini, cut off stem. Cut in half lengthwise; scoop out pulp, leaving ¼-inch shells. If using pattypan or scaloppini squash, scoop out enough of the center to make a cavity for filling. Chop pulp and reserve for stuffing. Drain shells upside down on paper towels while preparing mushroom stuffing.

In medium skillet melt butter or margarine and sauté mushrooms until moisture has evaporated, about 3 minutes. Stir in salt, basil, pepper, and reserved squash pulp. Cook 2 minutes. Remove from heat and stir in cheese and sour cream.

✽ Stuffing may be refrigerated overnight.

Divide stuffing equally among squash. Place in shallow baking dish.

✽ May be refrigerated overnight.

Before serving, bring to room temperature. Bake uncovered at 350° for 10 to 15 minutes or until hot and bubbling.

Serves 8

# Chocolate Chip Almond Torte with Hazelnut Fudge Sauce

First you make a simple buttery chocolate crust. Then egg whites and whipping cream are beaten stiff and placed in the freezer until very cold but not frozen solid. Warm melted dark chocolate and golden toasted almonds are quickly folded in. When hot hits cold, chunks of chocolate are formed. The filling will remain pure white with deep chocolate chunks. It's poured into the crust, kept frozen, and then served in wedges with a rich hazelnut fudge sauce.

### CHOCOLATE WAFER CRUST
- **16 chocolate wafer cookies, crushed (about 1 cup)**
- **3 tablespoons melted butter**

### FILLING
- **4 egg whites, at room temperature**
- **Dash of salt**
- **Dash of cream of tartar**
- **¼ cup sugar**
- **1 pint (2 cups) whipping cream**
- **1 tablespoon vanilla extract**
- **Eight 1-ounce squares semisweet chocolate**
- **½ cup diced almonds, roasted at 350° for 10 to 15 minutes or until golden, stirred occasionally**

### HAZELNUT FUDGE SAUCE
- **6-ounce imported milk chocolate bar with hazelnuts or 6-ounce milk or semisweet chocolate bar, chopped**
- **½ cup half-and-half**

Make chocolate wafer crust: In small bowl or food processor with metal blade blend cookie crumbs and butter. Press into bottom of an 8-by-3-inch springform pan.

In large mixing bowl, beat egg whites until frothy. Add salt and cream of tartar and beat until soft peaks form. Add the sugar 1 tablespoon at a time, beating well after each addition. Transfer mixture to a large bowl that can be put in the freezer. In same mixing bowl, beat the cream and vanilla until stiff. Fold cream into whites and place bowl uncovered in freezer until top is almost solid and icy, and underneath the mixture is very cold but not frozen, 1 to 1½ hours.

Meanwhile, in top of double boiler over simmering water, melt chocolate. Add almonds. While the mixture is *hot,* quickly fold it into the very cold cream mixture. Small chunks of chocolate slivers will form when the hot mixture hits the cold. Pour into crust, cover tightly with foil, and freeze until solid.

❋ May be frozen up to 3 months.

Remove from freezer and let sit at room temperature about 45 minutes or until soft enough to cut.

Make hazelnut fudge sauce: In double boiler, melt chocolate bar and ¼ cup half-and-half over simmering water. When melted, stir in as much half-and-half as needed to obtain desired consistency.

❋ Sauce may be refrigerated for several weeks.

Remove sides of springform, cut torte into wedges, and serve with warm fudge sauce, thinned with cream if necessary.

Serves 8 to 10

# Anniversary Dinner

MENU

SMOKED SALMON SPREAD

BRIE EN CROÛTE OR
BAKED BRIE WITH PITA PETALS

BUTTER OR BOSTON LETTUCE
AND WALNUT SALAD
FILLETS OF BEEF CHASSEUR
CAULIFLOWER WITH PURÉE
OF PEAS AND WATERCRESS
WILD RICE CASSEROLE
SPICED PEACHES WITH
CURRANT JELLY

CHOCOLATE-FILLED
CREAM PUFF HEART

WINE RECOMMENDATION:
A DRY, FULL-BODIED CABERNET
SAUVIGNON

*Anniversaries are a special time for toasting, and whether you're giving an intimate dinner for 8 or a golden wedding celebration for 40, you'll want to go all out and create an unforgettable meal. My menu is designed for 16, but can easily be divided in half or doubled.*

*Romance runs throughout the meal, with a creamy heart-shaped Smoked Salmon Spread, a delectable Brie en Croûte decorated to fit the occasion, and a wonderful dark chocolate Cream Puff Heart for a love-filled finale.*

*Here's a list of traditional themes for anniversary gifts and also of modern themes that are gaining popularity.*

|  | Traditional | Modern |
|---|---|---|
| 1st | paper | clocks |
| 5th | wood | silverware |
| 10th | tin/aluminum | diamond jewelry |
| 15th | crystal | watches |
| 20th | china | platinum |
| 25th | silver | silver |
| 40th | ruby | ruby |
| 50th | gold | gold |

*Happy anniversary! and many more to come.*

*The Cream Puff Heart is glazed with dark chocolate and filled with chocolate cream.*

## Smoked Salmon Spread

It's all the goodness of cream cheese and lox without the bagel. It's smooth, oniony, creamy, and a fragile pale pink in hue. This spread can be molded and shaped into a heart and decorated creatively. It becomes the perfect hors d'oeuvre to serve with an anniversary toast.

1 pound smoked salmon, shredded very fine for mixer, cut into large pieces for food processor
Four 8-ounce packages cream cheese, at room temperature
½ cup chopped green onions
Four 0.6-ounce packages green onion dip mix
1 pint (2 cups) sour cream
½ teaspoon dried dill
2 tablespoons capers, rinsed
1 green onion top, cut into thin strips for garnish
1 slice smoked salmon for garnish
Cucumbers, cut into thin rounds
Crackers or bread rounds

If using a food processor, divide ingredients into two batches. In food processor with metal blade or in mixing bowl with electric mixer, mix salmon, cream cheese, green onions, dip mix, sour cream, and dill until well blended. Stir in capers. Spread mixture into a 6-cup mold lined with plastic wrap or shape spread into heart or other shape with your hands. Refrigerate, covered with plastic wrap, until firm.

❋ May be refrigerated up to 2 days.

Before serving, if made in a mold, invert onto a platter and pull off the paper. Garnish with strips of salmon around the top edge to form a border and green onion strips to make an arrow. Serve with cucumber rounds and crackers or bread rounds.

Makes 6 cups or 16 to 20 servings

## Brie en Croûte

Spread creamy spiced cheese on Brie. Wrap it all in flaky puff pastry, bake until golden, and you've got an impressive appetizer. Be sure to let it sit for several hours before serving or the cheese will be too soft. The special beauty of it is that it can be prepared in advance, frozen, and baked when needed.

Two 4½-ounce packages spiced cheese with garlic and herbs (Rondelé or Boursin)
2 tablespoons whipping cream
2-pound Brie cheese (8 inches in diameter)
1-pound package frozen puff pastry, defrosted
1 egg beaten with 1 tablespoon water for wash

In mixing bowl, beat spiced cheese and cream until smooth. Spread on top of Brie, covering the top evenly.

Remove 1 sheet of puff pastry. Place on lightly floured board and roll into approximately a 14-inch square. Brush with egg wash. Place Brie in center. Trim pastry into a circle 2 inches larger than the cheese. Brush edges of pastry with egg wash again. Press a portion of dough against the side of the cheese. Cut along crease and place cut edge of pastry against bottom edge of cheese. Repeat with remaining dough, covering entire sides of cheese. Roll second piece of pastry into a 14-inch square. Brush

*Cut pastry into circle two inches larger in diameter than the Brie. Brush edges with egg wash.*

*Diagonally cut edge of pastry and fold it against cheese.*

*Fold and crimp dough around edge.*

*Wrap other side with another circle of dough in same manner so cheese is completely enclosed. If pastry gets dry, brush again with egg wash to seal.*

with egg wash. Turn Brie over and place rind down in center of pastry. Cut into a circle 2 inches larger than the cheese. Brush edges of pastry with egg wash. Repeat folding and cutting the dough, covering the sides with a double thickness of pastry. Brush top and sides with egg wash. Reroll pastry scraps and cut out decorations. If making a border, place it ½ inch in from outer edge. Place decorations on top and brush them with egg wash.

❋ May be refrigerated covered overnight.

❊ May be frozen for 2 weeks.

Before serving, bring to room temperature. Preheat oven to 400°. Place on ungreased baking sheet and bake for 35 to 45 minutes or until pastry is golden. Let rest at room temperature for at least 2 hours before serving or the cheese will be too soft to cut. Serve cut in wedges.

Serves 16 to 20

*Baked Brie en Croûte decorated with pastry heart and braid.*

## Baked Brie with Pita Petals

Both Brie recipes here are delicious, but they are different. This one is served just out of the oven, warm and melted. It's perfect for a buffet, for it can stay on a hot tray for hours. The toasted pita becomes very crispy, great for dipping in the Brie.

**2-pound Brie cheese**
**1½ cups sliced almonds (about 6 ounces)**
**3 tablespoons butter or margarine**
**3 to 4 rounds large pita bread Butter**

Place the Brie in an 11-inch to 12-inch oven-proof dish with at least 1-inch-high sides, such as a quiche dish. Sauté almonds in 3 tablespoons butter or margarine until lightly browned; set aside.

Make pita petals: Slip a knife into edge of pita bread, dividing it in half horizontally. Butter each half. Cut each half into 8 triangles. Repeat with remaining bread. Place triangles on baking sheets. Bake at 325° for 10 to 15 minutes or until golden. Watch carefully as they burn easily.

Pita may be stored airtight for several weeks. ❊ May be frozen. Reheat at 350° until hot, about 5 minutes.

Bake Brie at 350° for 20 to 30 minutes or until heated through and cheese feels soft to the touch. It is all right if the rind breaks slightly. Remove from oven and top with toasted almonds. Surround cheese with pita petals for dipping. Serve immediately. May be kept warm on a hot plate, if desired.

Serves 16 to 20

## Fillets of Beef Chasseur

This dish is marvelous to make for a crowd, for it is one of the only fillet dishes I know that benefits by being prepared a day ahead. The drippings that stick to the bottom of the pan when you brown the meat will become the essence of a delicious sauce, so be sure *not* to use a nonstick pan. Give the meat room while sautéing as well as in the casserole, so it will brown and not steam. I have written the recipe for 16; you will have enough sauce to increase the number of steaks to 20, if desired.

16 filet mignon steaks (6 to 8 ounces each) cut 1 inch thick
2 large cloves garlic, crushed
1 tablespoon seasoned salt
½ teaspoon seasoned pepper
¼ pound (1 stick) plus 2 tablespoons butter
4 tablespoons brandy
6 tablespoons all-purpose flour
4 teaspoons tomato paste
1 teaspoon crushed garlic
1½ cups dry red wine
2 cups chicken broth
1 cup beef broth
½ teaspoon Worcestershire sauce
4 tablespoons currant jelly
1 pound mushrooms, sliced

Place steaks on a work surface in a single layer. In a small bowl, make a paste of the 2 cloves garlic, seasoned salt, and pepper. With hands, rub seasonings on both sides of steaks. Heat 2 tablespoons butter in a large, heavy skillet (not nonstick) until very hot. Sauté 6 steaks at a time over moderately high heat until brown on each side but still raw in the middle. Do not crowd. If butter begins to burn, reduce heat slightly. Divide steaks between two 9-by-13-inch casseroles; leave at least 1-inch space between steaks.

Add brandy to skillet. Cook over moderate heat, stirring constantly, scraping up all brown bits which stick to the bottom of the pan. Add ¼ pound butter; when melted and foamy, stir in the flour. Reduce heat to low and cook, stirring constantly, until mixture is golden. Stir in tomato paste and 1 teaspoon garlic; the mixture will be thick and grainy. Remove pan from heat and whisk in wine, chicken broth, and beef broth. Return to moderate heat and bring to a boil, stirring constantly. Reduce heat and simmer, stirring occasionally for 10 minutes or until reduced by approximately a third. Stir in Worcestershire sauce and currant jelly. When jelly has melted, stir in mushrooms. Adjust seasonings. Sauce should be coating consistency. If too thick, thin down with water, broth, or wine. Cool completely. Pour over steaks in casseroles; sauce should not come more than halfway up the steaks.

❋ May be refrigerated covered with foil overnight.

Before serving, bring to room temperature, about 2 hours. Preheat oven to 400°. Bake uncovered for 15 to 20 minutes for medium rare, 20 to 25 minutes for medium to medium well done. If baking two casseroles in one oven, rotate them halfway through the baking time. When serving, spoon sauce from pans over steaks. Serves 16

## Butter or Boston Lettuce and Walnut Salad

Toasted walnuts and walnut oil make this a special salad. Butter lettuce allows the absorption of every drop of the walnut essence.

4 heads butter or Boston lettuce (about 1½ pounds)
1 cup walnut oil
9 tablespoons red wine vinegar
1 tablespoon plus 2 teaspoons Dijon mustard
1 tablespoon sugar
Salt and freshly ground pepper
Two 14-ounce cans hearts of palm, drained and sliced
1 cup chopped walnuts (about 4 ounces), toasted at 350° for 10 to 15 minutes and stirred occasionally
¾ cup sliced green onions (1 large bunch)

Wash lettuce. Dry, tear into bite-size pieces, and store in plastic bags in refrigerator until ready to use.

❋ May be refrigerated overnight.

To make dressing, mix walnut oil, vinegar, mustard, and sugar in glass jar or bowl. Season well with salt and lots of pepper. Taste before serving, and add more vinegar and seasonings, if needed.

❋ Dressing may be refrigerated for 3 days.

Before serving, place lettuce in large salad bowl. Add hearts of palm, walnuts, and green onions. Toss with as much dressing as needed.

Serves 14 to 16

## Spiced Peaches with Currant Jelly

There is certainly nothing on your grocer's shelf to compare to these peaches. They seem to be the perfect garnish for beef, ham, or poultry. The number of peach halves varies with each can, so if you are making this for 16 people, buy three cans, use all the peaches, but use the juice from only two cans. The rest of the recipe's proportions remain the same.

**Two 1-pound 13-ounce cans peach halves**
**1¼ cups light, or golden, brown sugar, firmly packed**
**1 cup white vinegar**
**2 cinnamon sticks**
**2 teaspoons whole allspice**
**4 teaspoons whole cloves**
**12 to 16 teaspoons currant jelly**

Drain peaches, reserving syrup. Combine syrup with brown sugar, vinegar, cinnamon sticks, allspice, and cloves. Bring to a boil and simmer for 10 minutes. Add peaches and simmer for 5 minutes. Cool peaches in syrup at room temperature for 4 to 8 hours. With a slotted spoon, lift peaches from syrup and place in shallow ovenproof casserole.

❋ May be refrigerated, covered, up to 2 days.

Before serving, bring peaches to room temperature. Fill center of each with 1 teaspoonful currant jelly. Place under medium broiler until jelly has melted and peaches are warm.

Makes 12 to 16 peach halves (amount varies with the can)

## Chocolate-Filled Cream Puff Heart

This beautiful heart-shaped cream puff is made up of sixteen smaller puffs filled with a light, rich, smooth chocolate filling and drizzled with a dark, satiny chocolate glaze. You can make this as one large heart, as I do here, or divide the dough in half and make two smaller hearts.

CREAM PUFF PASTRY
- 1½ cups water
- 12 tablespoons (1½ sticks) butter, cut into small pieces
- ¾ teaspoon salt
- 1½ cups all-purpose flour
- 1½ teaspoon sugar
- 6 large eggs

Make cream puff pastry: In a heavy saucepan over moderate heat, bring water, butter, and salt to a boil. When mixture boils and butter melts, remove from heat. Immediately stir in flour and sugar. Using a wooden spoon, stir vigorously until mixture leaves sides of saucepan. Return to heat and continue stirring for 1 to 2 minutes to dry out the dough. Remove from heat and place dough in mixing bowl. Break in one egg and mix well. Continue adding the additional eggs, one at a time, beating after each addition until well incorporated. The finished dough will be smooth and shiny.

Lightly grease and flour a baking sheet or line it with parchment. Draw a heart approximately 10 inches high and 10 inches wide on the parchment or trace it with the tip of a knife onto the flour-lined pan. Drop dough by spoonfuls following lines of the heart; each dollop of dough should touch the next and be approximately 3 inches wide. Bake at 400° for 25 to 35 minutes or until pastry is puffed and golden. Remove from oven, but leave temperature at 400°. Cut heart in half horizontally (don't be concerned if it breaks; the filling and frosting will cover all cracks). Place top half cut side up on another baking sheet, keeping pieces in the same order. Bake both halves for an additional 10 to 15 minutes or until dry. Remove from oven and cool.

❀ Puff may be frozen in a box or wrapped in foil. Defrost at room temperature.

*Spoon cream puff dough onto parchment.*

CHOCOLATE CREAM FILLING
- 3 cups whipping cream
- ¾ cup plus 2 tablespoons powdered sugar
- ½ cup unsweetened cocoa
- 2 teaspoons vanilla extract or 4 tablespoons Kahlúa or crème de cacao

CHOCOLATE GLAZE
- 4 ounces unsweetened chocolate
- 3 tablespoons butter or margarine
- 1⅓ cups sifted powdered sugar
- 4 tablespoons water

Make chocolate cream filling: Beat cream until soft peaks form. Add sugar, cocoa, and vanilla or liqueur, and beat stiff. Spoon or pipe filling through large star tip onto bottom of heart. Place top on, letting filling show in between.

Make chocolate glaze: In a small heavy saucepan, melt chocolate and butter or margarine. Stir in sugar and water. Cool slightly before using. If mixture becomes too stiff, thin with additional water. Drizzle glaze over top of heart. Refrigerate for several hours.

❉ May be refrigerated overnight.

Serves 14 to 16

*The Chocolate-Filled Cream Puff Heart baked, filled, and glazed.*

# 5

# SPECIAL CELEBRATIONS

# Saluting the Graduate

MENU

GOLDEN CELEBRATION PUNCH
❧

CLASSIC PIZZA
QUICK DEEP-DISH PIZZA
❧

CHEESY SPAGHETTI
HOMEMADE PASTA
PASTA WITH BROCCOLI SAUCE
BOLOGNESE SAUCE WITH PASTA
LINGUINI ALFREDO CON PESTO
❧

ANTIPASTO SALAD
❧

ICE CREAM SUNDAE BAR

ASSORTED ICE CREAM BALLS
FUDGY FUDGE SAUCE
HOT PEANUT BUTTER TOPPING
CHOCOLATE BUTTERSCOTCH SAUCE
BLUEBERRY SAUCE

*Graduates come in all ages, from nursery school toddlers to grown-up MDs, but pasta and pizza never fail to please everyone. Here is a variety of entrées—you can create your own menu to accommodate the age and sophistication of the crowd. Cheesy Spaghetti is perfect for the younger set, while adult palates will appreciate the blend of vegetables, garlic, and prosciutto in the Bolognese sauce or the unusual combination of classic Alfredo sauce and pesto in the Linguini Alfredo con Pesto.*

*If you've eaten homemade pasta you know how far superior it is to packaged pasta. If you don't have the equipment to make your own, you might want to buy freshly made pasta from a specialty gourmet shop.*

*A crowd of any age will delight in a make-your-own sundae bar with a wide selection of extraordinary sauces.*

*These recipes are designed to serve 8.*

## Golden Celebration Punch

This punch is sweet, golden, and fruity. I've found it to be very popular with the younger set, but grown-ups enjoy it too.

2 cups water
2 cups sugar
1 cup pineapple juice
2 cups apricot nectar
1 cup orange juice
½ cup lemon juice
3 pints (6 cups) ginger ale, chilled
1 pint pineapple sherbet

In a medium saucepan, bring water and sugar to a boil. Simmer for 5 minutes or until sugar is dissolved. Cool.

In a large bowl or pitcher, mix pineapple juice, apricot nectar, orange juice, lemon juice, and sugar syrup. Stir well and refrigerate until chilled.

❋ May be refrigerated for 2 days.

Before serving, pour fruit mixture into a punch bowl. Add ginger ale and top with scoops of sherbet.

Makes 24 four-ounce servings

## Cheesy Spaghetti

When my children were younger, they used to beg me to make the spaghetti with the cheese—"you know, the one that's not gourmet." I could never find words to describe it better, and I've got to admit that I like it too. It's perfect for all kids' parties.

3 pounds lean ground beef
2 teaspoons salt
3 cloves garlic, crushed
2 teaspoons dried oregano
2 teaspoons dried basil
Four 10½-ounce cans tomato soup
15-ounce can tomato sauce
1 pound mozzarella cheese, shredded
Two 1-pound packages spaghetti

In large saucepan, sauté meat, breaking it up with a fork, until it loses its pink color. Pour off fat. Stir in salt, garlic, oregano, basil, tomato soup, and tomato sauce. Cook, stirring occasionally, 15 minutes or until heated through and mixed well.

❋ May be refrigerated for 2 days.

❋ May be frozen.

Before serving, reheat sauce. Stir in cheese and cook over low heat, stirring constantly, until melted. Cook spaghetti according to package directions and toss with sauce.

Serves 12 to 14

## Homemade Pasta

The Italians have all kinds of rules for which sauces go over homemade pasta and which go over store-bought. As for me, I'll take homemade pasta, under or over any kind of sauce. The tenderness of "the real thing" is a true delicacy. Once you've made your own, it's hard to go back.

1¾ cups all-purpose flour
1 teaspoon salt
1 large egg
6 egg yolks

Place 1½ cups flour, salt, whole egg, and yolks in food processor with metal blade or in mixer. Process or mix until blended and dough forms a ball. The dough should not be too wet. Add remaining flour, if necessary, 1 tablespoon at a time, mixing until smooth.

Divide the dough into four balls. Wrap three balls in a towel, so they do not dry out while you work. Lightly flour one ball of dough. Set pasta machine at widest setting; press down on dough lightly and put through machine. Flour dough very lightly, fold it into thirds, and put it through the rollers a second time. Repeat the folding and rolling, lightly flouring the dough only if it is sticky, until dough is soft and smooth, about 4 to 6 times.

When dough is smooth, it is ready to be stretched. Reset roller on pasta machine for a thinner setting. Do not fold or flour dough unless necessary, and put through the machine. Reset roller a notch at a time, and work pasta through machine without folding it, until it reaches desired thickness, usually about 1/16 inch. Place over pasta rack or counter to dry while repeating process with remaining dough. Dough is ready to be cut when it is dry to the touch, but not brittle.

Cut the pasta, using the narrow or wide roller of pasta machine. If not using immediately, place noodles on large trays, toss lightly with flour, and cover with towel.

May be held several hours at room temperature.

❋ May be frozen. Before freezing, dry at room temperature for 1 to 2 hours or until dry, but not brittle. Dust lightly with flour and place in plastic bags. Do not defrost before cooking.

Bring 6 quarts of water and 1½ tablespoons salt to a boil. Add noodles. Bring water back to a boil and cook uncovered until noodles are tender, but firm to the bite. Timing depends on the freshness and size of the noodles, from 3 minutes for fresh to 10 minutes for frozen. Drain and toss with desired sauce.

Makes approximately 12 ounces; serves 4 as a main dish and 6 to 8 as a side dish or first course

## Pasta with Broccoli Sauce

I was once in a restaurant where I was served a marvelous pasta dish with broccoli in the sauce. I have no idea how their sauce was made, but here's my rendition. They served it over the heavier type of mostaccioli noodle, but my classes prefer it over homemade. I know you'll love this sauce with whichever pasta you choose.

1 large bunch broccoli (about 1¾ pounds)
⅓ cup olive oil
1½ tablespoons crushed garlic
½ cup chicken broth
¼ pound (1 stick) butter or margarine
¼ cup chopped fresh basil or 1 teaspoon dried basil
½ teaspoon dried oregano
Salt and pepper to taste
1 recipe Homemade Pasta (above), cut for fettucine, or 8 to 12 ounces store-bought fettucine or mostaccioli
¾ cup freshly grated Parmesan cheese

Cut stalk and stems off broccoli and discard. Steam flowerets on a rack or steamer over boiling water until crisp-tender, about 5 minutes; do not overcook. Drain and place in a bowl of ice water to stop the cooking. When cool, cut flowerets into ½-inch pieces.
❋ May be refrigerated overnight.

Heat olive oil in a medium saucepan. Sauté garlic until pale golden. Add chicken broth and butter or margarine. Stir in basil, oregano, salt, and pepper.
❋ May be refrigerated overnight.

Before serving, cook pasta as directed; drain. Reheat sauce, stir in broccoli, and cook until heated through. Place cooked pasta in large bowl. Add sauce and Parmesan cheese and toss well.

Serves 6 as a side dish or first course

## Bolognese Sauce with Pasta

Vegetables, garlic, and prosciutto puréed in the food processor combine to make a rich coarse-textured base for the sauce. Ground pork and veal, fragrant with herbs and spices, add to the robust flavor, and whipping cream binds the two together.

½ pound prosciutto ham
2 onions
2 small carrots, peeled
4 cloves garlic
3 stalks celery
6 sprigs parsley
3 tablespoons olive oil
½ pound ground pork
½ pound ground veal
1½ cups chicken broth
1½ cups dry red wine
1-pound 12-ounce can whole tomatoes, undrained and finely chopped
8-ounce can tomato paste
¼ teaspoon ground nutmeg
½ teaspoon dried oregano
½ teaspoon dried thyme
½ teaspoon dried basil
½ pound chicken livers, chopped
¾ cup whipping cream, at room temperature
2 recipes Homemade Pasta (above), cut for fettucine, or 1½ pounds spaghetti
Freshly grated Parmesan cheese

In food processor with metal blade, process ham, onions, carrots, garlic, celery, and parsley until finely ground. In a large saucepan, heat olive oil. Sauté ham and vegetables over moderately high heat until golden, about 10 minutes. Stir in the ground pork and veal and cook, stirring and breaking up meat, until it is browned. Pour off excess fat. Add the broth and wine and simmer 5 minutes. Stir in tomatoes with their juice, tomato paste, and seasonings. Reduce heat and simmer uncovered, stirring occasionally, until mixture is reduced and thickened, about 1 hour. Flavor will improve if mixture is refrigerated overnight.

✳ May be refrigerated for 2 days.

❋ May be frozen for 3 months.

Before serving, bring sauce to a slow boil, stirring occasionally. Add chicken livers and simmer for 15 minutes. Adjust seasonings. Add cream. Cook pasta as directed; drain. Ladle a small amount of sauce into a large bowl. Top with pasta and more sauce. Toss well. Spoon onto plates, topping each serving with additional sauce. Serve with Parmesan cheese.

Serves 8 as a main dish

## Linguini Alfredo con Pesto

When I really want to toss calories to the wind, I combine two of my favorite pasta sauces—a pesto and a sauce Alfredo for a spectacular linguini extravaganza.

½ cup olive oil

½ cup chopped fresh parsley

½ cup chopped pine nuts or walnuts

3 tablespoons dried basil or ½ cup chopped fresh basil

2 cloves garlic, crushed

1½ teaspoons salt

¼ teaspoon pepper

¼ pound (1 stick) butter, at room temperature

1½ recipes Homemade Pasta (above), cut as linguini, or 1-pound package linguini

1⅔ cups freshly grated Parmesan cheese

½ cup whipping cream, at room temperature

¼ pound (½ stick) butter, at room temperature

1 large egg, at room temperature

Make pesto sauce by combining olive oil, parsley, nuts, basil, garlic, ½ teaspoon salt, and pepper.

❋ May be refrigerated for 2 weeks.

❋ May be frozen.

Before serving, melt 6 tablespoons butter in a small saucepan. Add pesto and heat until bubbling.

Cook pasta as directed. Drain and immediately transfer to a large bowl. Add Parmesan cheese, cream, 2 tablespoons butter, egg, and 1 teaspoon salt. Toss well. Reheat pesto sauce if necessary. Pour hot pesto over and toss again. Serve immediately.

Serves 8 as a side dish or first course

## Quick Deep-Dish Pizza

This pizza is so easy to make because it begins with a store-bought hot roll mix. Just pat the dough into shape, and it bakes into a thick, light, and crunchy crust. The topping is full of the hearty good flavor of sausage, the thick essence of tomatoes, and a generous sprinkling of herbs.

13¾-ounce package hot roll mix
¾ cup warm water (110° to 115°)
1 egg, at room temperature
½ pound bulk sausage or lean ground beef
¼ cup chopped onion
1 clove garlic, crushed
15-ounce can tomatoes, undrained and chopped
4 tablespoons tomato paste
1 teaspoon dried basil
1 teaspoon dried oregano
1 teaspoon salt
Dash of pepper
½ teaspoon sugar
2 cups shredded mozzarella cheese (about 8 ounces)

In a large bowl, dissolve yeast from roll mix in water; stir to dissolve. Add egg and whisk until incorporated. Stir in flour mixture from mix and blend well. With greased hands, pat dough out onto bottom and halfway up sides of a greased rimmed baking pan 15½ by 10½ by 1 inch. Cover and let rest in warm place for 15 minutes. Press dough up sides again, making a border. Bake at 375° for 20 minutes or until golden.

❋ Crust may be frozen. Bring to room temperature before filling.

Make tomato meat filling: In medium skillet, cook sausage or ground beef, onion, and garlic until meat is brown. Drain off excess fat. Add remaining ingredients (except cheese). Cook, stirring occasionally, over moderate heat until thickened, about 20 minutes.

❋ Filling may be refrigerated for 2 days.

❋ May be frozen.

Spread filling over the crust. Sprinkle with the cheese. Bake at 375° until bubbly and cheese has melted, about 20 to 25 minutes. Let stand 5 minutes before cutting.

Serves 8

# Classic Pizza

This is everything a pizza should be. The crust can be shaped as thin or thick as you like; the larger the pan, the thinner the crust. There's lots of cheesy, chewy topping, and the zesty sauce is simmered until it's very thick and rich.

PIZZA CRUST
¼ cup warm water (100° to 115°)
1 teaspoon sugar
1 package active dry yeast
2 cups all-purpose flour
1 teaspoon salt
2 tablespoons olive oil
¼ to ½ cup warm water

TOMATO SAUCE
3 cloves garlic, crushed
1 onion, chopped
2 tablespoons olive oil
1-pound 12-ounce can whole
    tomatoes, drained and chopped
4 tablespoons tomato paste
1 teaspoon dried basil
½ teaspoon dried oregano
1 teaspoon salt
    Freshly ground pepper to taste
    Tabasco sauce to taste

TOPPINGS
7½-ounce can caponata eggplant
    appetizer (optional)
1 pound mozzarella cheese,
    shredded
¼ cup thinly sliced green pepper
4 ounces peperoni, thinly sliced
⅓ cup sliced ripe olives, drained
Half a 2-ounce jar diced pimiento,
    drained

Make pizza crust: Place ¼ cup warm water in a measuring cup. Add sugar and yeast and stir until dissolved. Set aside for 10 minutes or until bubbly. Place flour, salt, and olive oil in food processor with metal blade or in mixing bowl. Add yeast mixture and mix until blended. Slowly add warm water, mixing continuously, until dough is thoroughly moistened and begins to form a ball. Continue processing or mixing until ball is formed. Remove to an oiled bowl, turn dough on all sides to coat with oil, cover with buttered plastic wrap and a towel, and set in a warm place until doubled in bulk, about 1 hour. Pat dough into a 12- to 15-inch pizza pan. Crimp the edges well to form a rim.

Make tomato sauce: In a medium saucepan, sauté garlic and onion in olive oil until soft. Add chopped tomatoes, tomato paste, basil, and oregano and cook over moderate heat, stirring occasionally, until reduced to a thick purée, about 30 minutes. Season to taste with salt, pepper, and Tabasco.

Makes sauce for two 15-inch pizzas
❋ Sauce may be refrigerated for 1 week.
❊ May be frozen.

Spread sauce over crust. Spoon caponata over sauce. Sprinkle lightly with cheese. Layer green pepper, peperoni, olives, and pimiento alternately with cheese, ending with some of the olives, peppers, and pimiento.

Bake at 425° on bottom rack of oven until crust is golden brown and filling is bubbling, about 20 to 25 minutes.

❊ May be frozen. Underbake slightly. Reheat frozen pizza at 425° for 20 to 25 minutes.

Serves 8

# *Antipasto Salad*

An antipasto salad doesn't need a recipe. It's a great way of using up all the leftovers in your refrigerator, so don't be afraid to experiment with yours. The dressing is one of my favorites. I often serve it over plain romaine and call it an Italian Caesar Salad, but it's versatile enough to use over anything. Please try it with the anchovies, even if you use half the amount called for in the recipe. Make this dressing in your food processor and the anchovies will be puréed, adding a marvelous flavor.

**1 head iceberg lettuce (about 1½ pounds)**
**2 bunches romaine lettuce (about 2 pounds)**
**2 medium zucchini (about ¾ pound), thinly sliced**
**1 cup cubed provolone or fontina cheese**
**1 cup sliced celery**
**4-ounce can sliced ripe olives, drained**
**½ cup chopped green onions**
**8¾-ounce can garbanzo beans, drained**
**2 cloves garlic, crushed**
**6 anchovy fillets, finely chopped (optional)**
**6 tablespoons extra-virgin or good-quality olive oil**
**6 tablespoons salad oil**
**6 tablespoons red wine vinegar**
**4 tablespoons lemon juice**
**1 teaspoon salt or to taste**
**Freshly ground pepper**

Tear greens into bite-size pieces. Add zucchini, cheese, celery, olives, green onions, and garbanzos and toss well.

To make Italian dressing, process all remaining ingredients in food processor with metal blade or in blender. Adjust seasonings.

❄ Dressing may be refrigerated for one week.

Before serving, mix dressing well and toss salad with as much dressing as needed.

Serves 12 to 14

*Variation:* 2 ounces Gorgonzola cheese may be crumbled over the top.

## *Ice Cream Sundae Bar*

A sundae bar buffet is easy on the host or hostess and a treat for all ages. Make sauces ahead and store them in the refrigerator until ready to use. When making hot sauces, it is important to store them in a wide-mouth container so they will be easy to remove when cold. It is best to reheat sauces in a double boiler. They can remain on a buffet table for about one hour before becoming too hard to spoon. Recipes for four fabulous sauces follow, and another three—Butterscotch-Rum Sauce, Raspberry Cassis Sauce, and Strawberry Sauce—appear in previous recipes. Check the index.

Here are some tips to help set up your buffet:

- Serve 2 to 3 different types of ice cream. Allow 1 to 2 scoops per person.
- One quart of ice cream yields approximately 8 medium balls.
- To make ice cream balls in advance, line baking sheets with waxed paper. Scoop ice cream into balls and place on paper. Freeze until solid. Transfer to covered containers, separating layers with waxed paper. Cover well. They will keep for 1 week.
- Serve a variety of at least 3 types of sauces.
- Allow approximately 2 ounces of sauce per serving. If a recipe makes 2 cups sauce, it will yield enough for 8 scoops of ice cream.
- Allow approximately 2 tablespoons whipped cream per person; ½ pint whipping cream, whipped, will serve 12.
- Serve a variety of condiments. Some suggestions are:
  Chopped walnuts or pecans
  Sliced almonds
  Coarsely crushed chocolate chip or Oreo cookies
  Toasted coconut
  M and M candies
  Crushed English toffee

## Fudgy Fudge Sauce

Homemade hot fudge is far superior to bottled varieties—and so simple to make and so easy to keep it's a shame not to always have it on hand. With vanilla ice cream in your freezer, you always have a delicious impromptu dessert.

**Four 1-ounce squares unsweetened**
  **chocolate**
**1 cup sugar**
**1 cup whipping cream**
  **Dash of salt**
**1 teaspoon vanilla extract**

Combine chocolate, sugar, whipping cream and salt in a small, heavy saucepan. Stir over low heat until chocolate is melted. Increase heat to moderate and bring to a boil. Boil, stirring constantly, until sauce becomes smooth and thick, about 4 minutes. Remove from heat and stir in vanilla.

❉ May be refrigerated for several months. Store in a wide-mouth container or bowl, as it hardens when cold. It will thin down when reheated.

Reheat in heavy saucepan or in double boiler over simmering water, stirring constantly. If too thick, thin with a little hot water or cream.

Makes 1¾ cups; serves 6

## Hot Peanut Butter Topping

My son, Kenny, a peanut butter lover, asked me once if he could put a spoonful of peanut butter on his ice cream. I thought the idea sensational, but the method all wrong. We melted a package of peanut butter chips and voilà! My son and I still can't understand why this sauce is not a part of every ice cream parlor's repertoire.

**Half a 12-ounce package peanut**
  **butter chips**
**¾ to 1 cup whipping cream**
**¼ cup chopped peanuts**

In medium saucepan, mix peanut butter chips and ¾ cup cream. Melt over low heat, stirring constantly, until chips are melted. Add remaining cream if needed to obtain desired consistency.

❉ May be refrigerated for several weeks in a wide-mouth container.

Reheat in heavy saucepan or in double boiler. Serve warm over vanilla ice cream. Sprinkle chopped peanuts over top.

Makes about 2 cups; serves 8

## Chocolate Butterscotch Sauce

Butterscotch, chocolate, and marshmallow cream make an outrageously rich and creamy sauce.

14-ounce can sweetened condensed
   milk
6-ounce package butterscotch chips
Four 1-ounce squares unsweetened
   chocolate
7-ounce jar marshmallow cream
½ cup milk
1 teaspoon vanilla extract

Combine all ingredients in top of a double boiler. Place over simmering water and stir until melted and smooth.

❋ May be refrigerated for several months in wide-mouth container.

Reheat in double boiler. If too thick, thin with additional milk.

Makes 2½ cups; serves 12

## Blueberry Sauce

This is a little like eating blueberry pie à la mode, upside down.

12-ounce package frozen blueberries
   or 1½ cups fresh blueberries
¼ cup sugar
¾ teaspoon cinnamon
¼ teaspoon nutmeg
½ teaspoon grated lemon rind

Mix all ingredients in medium saucepan and bring to a boil. Boil over moderately high heat, stirring occasionally, for 10 minutes or until sauce thickens slightly. Sauce will continue to thicken as it cools.

❋ May be refrigerated for 2 weeks.

Serve at room temperature.

Makes 1½ cups; serves 6

# Baby Shower Brunch

MENU

PINK STORK COCKTAIL
FILO ARTICHOKE PIE
❧

CHUNKY CHICKEN SALAD OR
ORIENTAL TUNA SALAD
LEMON PECAN POPOVERS WITH
LEMON HONEY BUTTER
BUCKET OF FROZEN FRUIT
SWEET-AND-SOUR CUCUMBER CHIPS
❧

ICE CREAM BOMBE
BABY CARRIAGE APRICOT CAKE
❧

RECOMMENDED BEVERAGES:
CITRUS ICED TEA (SEE LABOR DAY
PICNIC) OR HOT TEA AND COFFEE

*Baby showers are exciting, happy times, with the opening of presents, the exchange of experiences, and the sharing of dreams and hopes for the future.*

*The theme for this fun-filled celebration can be carried out in the decorations as well as in the food. Baby bottles filled with fresh flowers and baby cups full of candy or mints add a playful touch to the table. A sand bucket used as a mold for a frozen fruit salad and a moist Amaretto-apricot cake, cut and decorated as a baby carriage, help to carry out the theme.*

*Baby showers are most often luncheons, and here you have a choice of two splendid main-dish salads, one with chicken and one with tuna. The popovers, with their hint of lemon and crunch of pecan, are easy to prepare and heavenly when served piping hot, spread lavishly with Lemon Honey Butter.*

*This lively menu, which serves 12 to 16, is fun for the hostess as well as the guests.*

*The Bucket of Frozen Fruit serves as the centerpiece for a playfully decorated luncheon table.*

121

## Pink Stork Cocktail

This wonderful mélange of flavors is perfect for a women's get-together. Be sure to use coconut syrup, available at most supermarkets, not coconut cream. For a change of pace, try substituting one cup of cubed bananas for the pineapple.

24 large strawberries, fresh or frozen
   (about 12 ounces frozen)
 1 cup chopped fresh pineapple
 ½ cup coconut syrup
 ½ pint (1 cup) whipping cream
 ½ to ¾ cup brandy
 2 cups ice cubes
   Strawberries for garnish

Place half the ingredients (except garnish) in blender container. Cover and blend until thick and smooth. Repeat with remaining ingredients. Pour into glasses and garnish each with a strawberry.

Makes eight 4-ounce servings

## Filo Artichoke Pie

Many people are afraid of working with filo. Once you've tried it and see how easy it is, it could become an important part of your culinary repertoire. The only trick is learning that until you brush it with butter it must be kept covered. The filling of this pie is creamy and cheesy, and the artichokes add a slight resiliency as well as a delicate flavor; the crust is flaky and buttery.

**Five 6-ounce jars marinated artichoke hearts**
**1 pound ricotta cheese**
**½ cup sour cream**
**4 eggs**
**¾ cup chopped green onions (about 1 bunch)**
**¾ cup grated Parmesan cheese (about 3 ounces)**
**1 cup shredded Swiss cheese (about 4 ounces)**
**¼ cup chopped fresh basil or 2 teaspoons dried basil**
**½ teaspoon salt**
**Freshly ground pepper**
**¼ pound (1 stick) melted butter**
**8 to 10 sheets filo dough (about ½ pound)**

Drain artichoke hearts and chop them into small pieces. In mixing bowl, mix ricotta cheese, sour cream, and eggs until well blended. Stir in green onions, Parmesan and Swiss cheeses, basil, salt, pepper, and artichoke hearts.

Lightly butter the bottom and sides of a 9-by-13-inch baking dish. Place four sheets of filo on a lightly dampened towel. Keep the remaining filo covered with a damp towel to prevent it from drying out. Lightly brush each sheet with butter. Place them, one at a time, in the baking dish, letting ends extend over the sides of the dish. Pour in artichoke filling; spread evenly.

Remove one sheet of filo, brush with butter, and fold in half. Lay lengthwise on top of the artichoke cheese filling. Fold the extended edges of filo over the top. Butter the remaining 3 sheets, fold them in half, and lay them one on top of the other. Tuck edges into pan with the tip of a sharp knife. Brush top with butter. Cover with plastic wrap.

❋ May be refrigerated for 2 days.

❅ May be frozen for 3 months.

Before serving, bring to room temperature. Bake at 400° for 25 to 35 minutes or until filo is golden. Let rest 10 minutes and cut into squares. Serve on plates with fork.

Makes 16 appetizer servings or 8 main-dish servings

## *Oriental Tuna Salad*

Tuna is given a new look in this crunchy but creamy salad. It's gloriously presented in a pineapple shell.

2 **cups mayonnaise**
4 **teaspoons curry powder**
¼ **teaspoon garlic powder**
4 **tablespoons sour cream**
Two 12½-**ounce cans tuna (oil or water packed), drained**
Two 10½-**ounce packages frozen peas, thawed**
2 **cups chopped celery**
Two 8-**ounce cans water chestnuts, drained and chopped**
2 **cups chopped fresh pineapple**
2 **large whole pineapples with fronds, for serving**
5-**ounce can chow mein noodles**

Mix mayonnaise, curry powder, garlic powder, and sour cream together in medium bowl.

Coarsely flake tuna in a large bowl. Add peas, celery, water chestnuts, and pineapple. Toss lightly with dressing.

❋ May be refrigerated overnight.

Cut pineapple in half lengthwise right through the fronds. Remove the fruit, leaving a shell. This is easiest to do with a grapefruit knife.

Right before serving, toss chow mein noodles into salad. Mound into pineapple halves.

Serves 14 to 16

# Chunky Chicken Salad

Chicken salad is made both unusual and easy in this recipe. Fresh green beans are cooked just until they are no longer raw and still crispy to the bite. They're added to a crunchy and tangy salad studded with almonds. The simplest way of poaching chicken is to oven-poach it. This ensures even cooking with a minimum of attention on your part. The key to a juicy chicken salad is to slightly undercook the chicken so all its flavors stay sealed in.

8 **whole chicken breasts, skinned, boned, and split (about 8 to 12 ounces each, net weight)**
  **Salt and pepper**
1 **pound fresh green beans, cut into 1-inch slices on the diagonal**
2 **cups whole or slivered blanched almonds**
2 **tablespoons butter**
1 **cup mayonnaise**
1 **cup sour cream**
2 **tablespoons lemon juice**
2 **teaspoons Worcestershire sauce**
2 **tablespoons Dijon mustard**
1 **teaspoon soy sauce**
1 **teaspoon salt**
¼ **teaspoon white pepper**
4 **cups thinly sliced celery**
2 **cups sliced green onions (about 3 bunches)**
12 **hard-boiled eggs, coarsely chopped**
  **Tomatoes for garnish**
  **Hard-boiled eggs for garnish**

Poach chicken by placing breasts in two 9-by-13-inch casseroles or 1 large shallow casserole. Pour in water to depth of ½ inch and sprinkle chicken with salt and pepper. Tear a sheet of waxed paper long enough to cover the casserole. Butter one side. Place buttered side directly on chicken. Tuck edges into dish. Bake at 350° for 18 to 25 minutes, depending on the size. Chicken breasts are done when they are still slightly pink when cut into. They will look slightly underdone, but will continue cooking when they are removed from the oven. Immediately remove from casserole to a plate to cool.

❋ Breasts may be refrigerated overnight.

❋ May be frozen for 2 months.

Bring a small pot of water to a boil. Add beans, bring back to a boil, and cook for 3 minutes. Drain.

❋ Beans may be refrigerated for 2 days.

Sauté almonds in a small skillet in 2 tablespoons butter until golden.

❋ Almonds may be stored in airtight container or refrigerated for 1 week.

To make dressing, mix mayonnaise, sour cream, lemon juice, Worcestershire, mustard, soy sauce, 1 teaspoon salt, and pepper together in medium bowl. Refrigerate several hours for flavors to blend.

❋ Dressing may be refrigerated overnight.

Several hours before serving, cut chicken into ¾-inch pieces. Add green beans, celery, onions, and eggs. Toss with dressing.

❋ Salad may be refrigerated for 6 hours.

Before serving, toss with almonds. Mound salad on large lettuce-lined platter and garnish with tomato and egg wedges.

Serves 16 to 18

## Lemon Pecan Popovers with Lemon Honey Butter

This wonderful recipe comes from my good friend and colleague, Richard Nelson. The popovers have a fine, even texture with a nutty crunch of pecans and a slight tang of lemon. Generously spread the lemon honey butter over their crusty brown tops.

2 cups all-purpose flour
¼ cup very finely chopped pecans
2 cups milk
4 large eggs
¼ teaspoon salt
2 teaspoons finely grated lemon rind

LEMON HONEY BUTTER
¼ pound (1 stick) butter, at room temperature
2 tablespoons honey
2 teaspoons lemon juice
2 tablespoons finely grated lemon rind

In a mixing bowl, mix flour, pecans, milk, eggs, salt, and 2 teaspoons lemon rind until well blended. Batter may be slightly lumpy.

❋ May be refrigerated up to 2 days.

Make lemon honey butter: Beat butter until smooth. Add honey, lemon juice, and 2 tablespoons lemon rind and mix until well blended. Serve at room temperature.

❋ Butter may be refrigerated for 4 days.

❄ May be frozen.

Before serving, heavily butter twelve 6-ounce custard cups, popover pans, or heavy 2½-inch muffin tins. Fill two-thirds full of batter.

May sit at room temperature for 2 hours.

Preheat oven to 425°. Bake popovers for 30 to 35 minutes or until puffed and browned. Serve immediately with lemon honey butter.

Makes 12 popovers

## *Sweet-and-Sour Cucumber Chips*

These easy-to-make crunchy cucumber chips have all the flavors of pickles but are so light that people think they're eating zucchini.

**2 large cucumbers (about 1¾ pounds)**
**¾ teaspoon salt**
**½ cup green pepper, cut into ¼-inch dice**
**½ cup thinly sliced onion**
**½ cup white vinegar**
**½ cup plus 2 tablespoons sugar**
**1½ teaspoons celery seed**

Peel cucumbers. Slice into ¼-inch slices. Place in colander in sink and sprinkle with salt. Let stand 2 hours. Drain well and place in medium bowl with green pepper and onion. In another bowl combine vinegar, sugar, and celery seed. Stir until sugar is dissolved. Pour over vegetables and refrigerate for a minimum of 24 hours.

✳ May be refrigerated for several months.

Serve with a slotted spoon.

Makes about 3½ cups or 8 servings

## Bucket of Frozen Fruit

We all like to be kids once in a while, and a baby shower is definitely the place to relive childhood. This frozen fruit mixture could be molded in a loaf pan, but think of all the fun you'd be missing! If you invite more guests than the recipe calls for, you might want to make 1½ times the recipe and pour some into smaller molds which could be placed around the bucket.

**4-ounce package whipped cream
cheese, at room temperature
4½-ounce carton frozen whipped
dessert topping, thawed
21-ounce can cherry pie filling
Two 11-ounce cans mandarin orange
segments or mandarin orange
segments with pineapple tidbits,
drained
2 gumdrops**

Stir together cream cheese and whipped dessert topping. Add pie filling and orange or orange and pineapple tidbits; stir well to distribute the fruit. Pour mixture into two 2½-cup or one 4½- to 5-cup plastic bucket or mold. Cover; freeze overnight or until firm.

❀ May be frozen for 1 month.

Remove from freezer and go around edge of mold with tip of a knife. Dip mold briefly into warm water and unmold onto platter. Turn right side up. Return to freezer if not ready to serve.

Insert a toothpick at an upward angle into each side where the handles will be attached. Place plastic handle from the bucket over toothpicks and secure them in place with a gumdrop.

Before serving, bring to room temperature until soft enough to cut. A 4½- to 5-cup bucket will take about 1 hour, smaller molds 30 to 45 minutes.

To serve, slice into wedges, or cut bucket in half crosswise and cut halves into wedges.

Makes 4½ cups or 10 servings

*Bucket of Frozen Fruit in the foreground and Chunky Chicken Salad garnished with green beans in the background.*

## Ice Cream Bombe

Whipping cream, Grand Marnier, and chocolate-coated almonds folded into softened vanilla ice cream help make this the best bombe I've ever tasted. If serving it as the only dessert, frost it with dainty rosettes of whipped cream flavored with Grand Marnier.

  1 **quart raspberry sherbet**
1½ **pints vanilla ice cream**
   **Three one-ounce squares**
   **semisweet chocolate**
 ½ **cup slivered almonds, toasted on**
   **a baking sheet at 350° for 10 to 15**
   **minutes, stirred occasionally**
 ½ **pint (1 cup) whipping cream**
  3 **tablespoons Grand Marnier**
   **Strawberries for garnish**
   **(optional)**
   **Mint or lemon leaves for garnish**
   **(optional)**

Lightly oil a 2-quart (8-cup) ring mold or stainless steel bowl. Reserve 2 cups sherbet and return to freezer. Using the back of a spoon, spread remaining sherbet around the sides of the mold, coating it evenly. Freeze firm.

Remove ice cream from freezer and soften slightly. Melt chocolate in double boiler over simmering water; add almonds. Whip cream and Grand Marnier until soft peaks form. Fold the hot chocolate mixture into the softened but still very cold ice cream. Fold in the whipped cream.

Fill the sherbet-lined mold with the ice cream mixture and freeze until firm. Spread reserved sherbet over the top. Cover with foil.

❀ May be frozen for 1 month.

To unmold, go around edge of mold with the tip of a knife. Dip mold briefly in warm water several times and invert onto serving plate. Return to freezer. Before serving, garnish with strawberries and mint or lemon leaves, if desired.

Serves 12 to 14

*Baby Carriage Apricot Cake decorated with jelly beans and licorice whips.*

## Baby Carriage Apricot Cake

This is a simple sheet cake shaped into a baby carriage, decorated and trimmed with whipped cream and candies. It's very whimsical and adds a touch of fun to a happy occasion.

18½-ounce package yellow cake mix
3¾-ounce package vanilla instant
   pudding
3¾ large eggs
1 cup sour cream
¾ cup Amaretto liqueur
7 canned apricot halves, drained
   and chopped
2 to 3 cups whipping cream,
   whipped

In mixing bowl, with electric mixer beat cake mix, pudding, eggs, sour cream, and Amaretto until blended. Increase speed and beat on high 2 minutes. Add chopped apricots and mix until well incorporated. Pour batter into greased and floured 9-by-13-inch baking pan. Bake at 350° for 40 to 45 minutes or until cake tester inserted in center comes out clean. Let cool in pan for 10 to 20 minutes; turn out onto rack to cool.

❋ May be frozen.

**Red and blue food coloring**
**Pink and blue jelly beans**
**Red licorice whips**
**Gumdrops**
**Assorted candies if desired**

Draw paper diagram of baby carriage as pictured. Use a 2½-inch to 3-inch round cookie cutter to outline arc for wheels in diagram and to cut out wheels. Cut cake into baby carriage using diagram as a guide. Whip cream until soft peaks form. Tint pink or blue and beat stiff. Frost cake and wheels. Outline carriage and wheels with pink and blue jelly beans. Place licorice whips radiating out from center of wheels as spokes. Place a gumdrop in the center of the spokes. Decorate with additional candies if desired.

❋ May be refrigerated several hours before serving.

Serves 16 to 20

*Variation:* Cake may be baked in a greased and floured 10-inch fluted tube pan at 350° for 45 to 55 minutes. While still warm, brush top and sides with ¾ cup hot apricot preserves which have been heated and strained.

*Make baby carriage stencil out of paper and cut shapes out of cake.*

# Sweet Sixteen Luncheon

MENU

PINEAPPLE-COCONUT FRAPPES
AVOCADO-ONION DIP
🐝

MUSHROOM HAM QUICHE
CUPS
SPINACH QUICHE CUPS
SODA FOUNTAIN JELL-O MOLDS
ZUCCHINI BREAD
MIXED-UP SALAD
🐝

CHOCOLATE CAKE
BANANA SPLIT PIE
🐝

RECOMMENDED BEVERAGES:
ASSORTED SOFT DRINKS OR PUNCH

*Having raised four teenagers, I really believe I can claim a tad of experience in this area, besides a badge of courage!*

*I've concocted a menu that is perfect for teenagers and has proved successful many times over. Teens are health-oriented, and they'll love this light and easy menu. So will their vegetarian friends, as most of the menu is meat-free except for the Mushroom Ham Quiche Cups. (The ham can be eliminated, however, if desired.)*

*The Pineapple-Coconut Frappe and the Avocado-Onion Dip are terrific "ice-breakers" when served as soon as the guests arrive. For dessert you can choose between the super-fudgy chocolate birthday cake or the decadent Banana Split Pie, but for this important occasion you may want to go all out and serve them both.*

*This Sweet Sixteen luncheon serves 12.*

*Mushroom and Spinach Quiche Cups are served along with Soda Fountain Jell-O Molds.*

133

## Pineapple-Coconut Frappes

This frothy, fruity, and creamy drink is a favorite of my own teenagers. They made it for their Sweet Sixteens, and it's become a traditional teenage party drink ever since.

1½ cups pineapple juice
  8-ounce can cream of coconut
  1 cup fresh pineapple cubes
    Ice cubes or crushed ice

Place juice, cream of coconut, and pineapple in blender container. Add enough ice to fill to 1 inch from top. Blend until smooth.

Makes 5 cups; about 8 servings

## Avocado-Onion Dip

I was convinced that the old standby, onion soup dip, had had its day until I added avocado to it. What a face-lift!

  3 large avocados, peeled and mashed
½ cup sour cream
  2 tablespoons onion soup mix
  2 dashes of Tabasco sauce
  1 medium tomato, chopped
    Chips or raw vegetables

Mix all ingredients except chips and vegetables in food processor with metal blade or in mixing bowl. Place in bowl with avocado pit in center and a piece of plastic wrap directly on top of spread to prevent it from turning brown. Refrigerate until chilled.

❋ May be refrigerated for 2 days.

Serve with chips or vegetables.

Makes 2¾ cups; about 12 servings

## *Crêpes for Quiche Cups*

Crêpes and quiches are everyone's favorites, and the following recipes combine the best of both. Crêpes are molded into standard 2½-inch muffin tins to form miniature quiche cups. Make sure the crêpes are no larger than 5 inches in diameter so that they'll fit into the cups properly. This is my standard never-failed crêpe batter. The addition of brandy is a trick I learned from a caterer. You can barely taste it, but it has a magical tenderizing effect. Freeze the filled cups unbaked. When ready to serve, just pop them from freezer to oven.

**3 large eggs**
**1 cup milk**
**¼ to ½ cup water**
**1 cup all-purpose or superfine flour**
**Dash of salt**
**2 tablespoons brandy**
**3 tablespoons melted butter**

Blend eggs, milk, ¼ cup water, flour, salt, brandy, and butter in blender or food processor with metal blade. Scrape down sides and blend again. Batter may be used immediately or may be covered and refrigerated.

❉ May be refrigerated overnight.

If batter is too thick, thin with additional water. To make 5-inch crêpes for quiche cups, you will need a 7-inch crêpe pan that measures 5 inches across the bottom. If pan is not nonstick, brush it with butter or oil. Heat pan over moderately high heat, lift pan from heat, and pour in 1 to 2 tablespoons of batter, tilting the pan in all directions, swirling the batter to cover the entire bottom in a very thin layer. Return to heat and cook over moderately high heat until underside is browned. Then carefully turn over with a spatula. Cook for 1 to 2 minutes or until browned slightly. Slide onto plate and continue with remaining batter.

❉ Crêpes may be refrigerated for 5 days stacked with waxed paper between them to keep them separate. Seal in plastic bag.

❉ May be frozen. Package same as for refrigerating.

Bring to room temperature before filling. Crêpes defrost well in a microwave oven.

Makes 20 to 24 five-inch crêpes

## Mushroom Ham Quiche Cups

This recipe is cheesy with Jack and Parmesan and chunky with ham and mushrooms. The basic quiche batter is puréed in the food processor or blender and then you can stir in any meat or vegetable that you like. The filling is divided among the quiche cups and baked to a bubbly golden brown.

¼ pound mushrooms, coarsely
   chopped
½ cup chopped onion
1 clove garlic, crushed
2 tablespoons butter or margarine
2 large eggs
2 tablespoons all-purpose flour
½ cup sour cream
½ pint (1 cup) small-curd cottage
   cheese
½ cup grated Parmesan cheese
1 cup shredded Monterey Jack
   cheese (about 4 ounces)
½ cup finely chopped cooked ham
   Tabasco sauce to taste
   Salt and pepper to taste
   Twelve 5-inch Crêpes for Quiche
   Cups (see preceding recipe)
   Parmesan cheese for topping

In medium skillet, sauté mushrooms, onion, and garlic in butter or margarine until soft. Set aside to cool. In food processor with metal blade or in blender, mix eggs, flour, sour cream, and cottage cheese until well blended. Remove to a bowl and stir in mushroom mixture, Parmesan cheese, Jack cheese, and ham. Season with Tabasco sauce, salt, and pepper.

Grease twelve 2½-inch muffin cups. Lay crêpes brown side up over cups. Spoon 2 heaping tablespoons onto center. Gently bring sides together as pictured and push into cups. Cups should be three-fourths full. Sprinkle tops with Parmesan cheese.

❋ May be refrigerated covered with foil overnight.

❋ May be frozen for 2 weeks. Do not defrost before baking.

Before serving, preheat oven to 350°. Bake filled cups until golden brown for 25 to 30 minutes, if not frozen, or for 40 to 45 minutes, if frozen. Do not overbake or quiche will be dry. Remove cups from muffin tins by inserting a small spatula or knife underneath and lifting them out.

Makes 12 cups

*Variation*: 6 slices of cooked diced bacon may be substituted for the ham.

*Place crêpes over muffin cups. Spoon on filling and press into cups.*

*Mushroom Ham and Spinach Quiche Cups served on a platter. The Soda Fountain Jell-O Molds are topped with whipped cream and maraschino cherries.*

## Spinach Quiche Cups

This quiche filling explores that splendid relationship of spinach and cheese.

**2 large eggs**
**2 tablespoons all-purpose flour**
**½ cup sour cream**
**½ pint (1 cup) small-curd cottage cheese**
**Dash of nutmeg**
**¼ cup grated Parmesan cheese**
**½ cup shredded Swiss cheese (about 2 ounces)**
**½ cup shredded sharp Cheddar cheese (about 2 ounces)**
**10-ounce package frozen chopped spinach, thawed, drained, and squeezed dry**
**Salt and pepper to taste**
**Tabasco sauce to taste**
**Twelve 5-inch Crêpes for Quiche Cups (see recipe above)**
**Parmesan cheese for topping**

In food processor with metal blade or in blender, mix eggs, flour, sour cream, cottage cheese, and nutmeg until well blended. Remove to a bowl and stir in cheeses and spinach. Season to taste with salt, pepper, and Tabasco sauce.

Grease twelve 2½-inch muffin cups. Lay crêpes brown side up over cups. Spoon 2 heaping tablespoons onto center. Gently bring sides together as pictured and push into cups. Cups should be three-fourths full. Sprinkle tops with Parmesan cheese.

❋ May be refrigerated overnight.

❋ May be frozen for 2 weeks. Do not defrost before baking.

Preheat oven to 350°. Bake filled cups until golden brown, 25 to 30 minutes if not frozen or 40 to 45 minutes if frozen. Do not overbake or quiche will be dry. Remove cups from muffin tins by inserting a small spatula or knife underneath and lifting them out.

Makes 12 cups

## Soda Fountain Jell-O Molds

This idea suits kids of all ages. For large informal buffets, make one giant soda in a brandy snifter. Vary fruits, nuts, and flavors to your liking.

3-ounce package lime gelatin
3-ounce package strawberry gelatin
8-ounce container frozen dessert
   topping
2 bananas, coarsely chopped
   Whipped cream or frozen dessert
   topping
12 to 14 maraschino cherries with
   stems

In separate bowls, make lime and strawberry gelatin according to package directions. Chill each until almost jelled, or thick enough to "plop" when dropped from a spoon. Add 4 ounces of dessert topping to each flavor and mix with rotary or electric mixer until frothy. Fill 8 to 10 six-ounce glasses half full with lime gelatin. Place a few pieces of banana over top and cover with strawberry gelatin. Cover with plastic wrap and refrigerate.

❋ May be refrigerated overnight.

Before serving, pipe or dollop a rosette of whipped cream or topping in the center of each glass. Top with a maraschino cherry. Cut drinking straws in half and place two at an angle next to the cream in each glass.

Makes 8 to 10 servings

## Mixed-Up Salad

My teenage daughter Caryn is a vegetarian and says she could live on this salad for the rest of her life. The dressing is similar to French, but subtly sweetened with the goodness of honey.

2 bunches romaine lettuce
1 head iceberg lettuce
½ cup lemon juice
½ cup catsup
½ cup chopped onion
1 teaspoon salt
3 tablespoons honey
1 cup salad oil
1 large cucumber, peeled and
   coarsely chopped
1 pint cherry tomatoes, stemmed
   and cut in half
2 small avocados, peeled and diced
¾ cup coarsely chopped black olives
2 cups croutons

Tear lettuce into bite-size pieces. Wash, dry, and store in plastic bags until ready to use.

Make dressing by combining lemon juice, catsup, onion, salt, honey, and oil in food processor with metal blade or in blender.

❋ Dressing may be refrigerated for several weeks.

Before serving, place lettuce in large salad bowl. Add remaining ingredients and toss with dressing.

Serves 12 to 14

# Zucchini Bread

Zucchini bread is unlike any other. You can see the zucchini, but you can't really taste it. It just makes the bread incredibly moist. This is a fine-textured loaf with a slight crunch of chopped nuts. It's crusty on the outside, soft on the inside, and much more cinnamon-scented than most.

2 large eggs
1 cup sugar
½ cup vegetable oil
2 teaspoons vanilla extract
1 cup shredded zucchini (about 8 ounces)
1½ cups all-purpose flour
½ teaspoon salt
½ teaspoon baking soda
¼ teaspoon baking powder
2 teaspoons ground cinnamon
½ cup chopped walnuts or pecans
Butter for serving

In mixing bowl or food processor with metal blade, beat eggs until frothy. Add sugar, oil, and vanilla. Beat until well blended. Add zucchini, flour, salt, baking soda, baking powder, and cinnamon. Mix just until blended. Stir in nuts. Grease and flour a 9-by-5-by-3-inch loaf pan; spoon batter into pan. Bake the bread at 350° for 50 to 60 minutes or until cake tester inserted in center comes out clean. Remove from oven and cool 10 minutes. Invert onto cooling rack and turn right side up to cool.

✳ May be refrigerated for 3 days. Wrap in foil.

❋ May be frozen.

Before serving, reheat at 350° until hot, about 10 minutes. Slice and serve with butter.

Makes 1 loaf; serves about 8

## Chocolate Cake

This has been my family's "celebration cake" for just about as long as I can remember. It's a wonderfully moist, rich chocolate cake with a shiny, dark chocolate frosting.

CAKE
**Three 1-ounce squares unsweetened chocolate**
**¼ pound (1 stick) unsalted butter or margarine**
**2 cups sugar**
**2 large eggs**
**1 teaspoon vanilla extract**
**½ cup buttermilk**
**2 cups all-purpose flour**
**2 teaspoons baking soda**
**1 teaspoon salt**
**1 cup boiling water**

CHOCOLATE FROSTING
**Four 1-ounce squares unsweetened chocolate**
**9 tablespoons half-and-half**
**1 tablespoon vanilla extract**
**3 tablespoons unsalted butter or margarine**
**Pinch of salt**
**3 cups sifted powdered sugar**

Make the cake: Grease and flour two 9-inch layer cake pans; set aside. Preheat oven to 350°. Melt chocolate in double boiler. In a large mixing bowl, cream butter or margarine and sugar until light and fluffy. Add eggs, one at a time, beating after each addition. Mix in vanilla and melted chocolate, beating until smooth. Add buttermilk, flour, soda, and salt; mix until incorporated. Add boiling water and beat smooth. Batter will be thin. Divide batter evenly between the two cake pans. Shake the pans slightly to even out the tops. Bake in the middle of the oven for 25 to 30 minutes. To ensure even baking, rotate pans halfway through the baking time. Bake until cakes begin to come away from the sides of the pans or the tops barely leave an impression when lightly pressed with fingertip. Do not overbake or cake will be dry. Remove to cake racks and cool 10 minutes. Place racks over top and invert cakes onto them. Cool completely.

May be wrapped in foil and stored at room temperature overnight.

❈ May be frozen.

Make the chocolate frosting: In a small, heavy saucepan, place chocolate, half-and-half, vanilla, butter or margarine, and salt. Stir over low heat until chocolate is melted. Mix well with a wooden spoon. Remove from heat and stir in 1 cup powdered sugar at a time until frosting is smooth. Use immediately, as it hardens quickly. If frosting becomes too stiff, add hot water a teaspoon at a time.

Place one cake layer bottom side down on a serving platter lined with 4 strips of waxed paper extending from underneath the cake on all sides to protect the platter while frosting. Spread approximately a quarter of the frosting over the layer. Top with second layer, bottom side up. Frost the sides and then the top. If you have extra frosting and wish to decorate the cake, put frosting into a small pastry bag fitted with a small star tip and pipe a border of small rosettes around the top and bottom edge. Carefully remove the waxed paper strips.

✳ Cake will improve in flavor if allowed to stand at room temperature overnight. May be refrigerated several days.

Serves 12

## Banana Split Pie

My daughter Margi helped me create this when she was about eight, and although it sounds like it's for kids, I've never seen adults devour anything so fast. Remember its easy good taste for summer or outdoor barbecues.

1 cup vanilla wafer or shortbread cookie crumbs
2 to 3 tablespoons butter or margarine
1 pint vanilla ice cream
1 pint strawberry ice cream
1 pint chocolate ice cream
10-ounce jar chocolate fudge sauce
10-ounce jar strawberry ice cream topping
2 small bananas, sliced
1 cup fresh strawberries, sliced
6 ounces English toffee (optional)

Mix cookie crumbs and butter or margarine in food processor with metal blade or in small bowl. Press into bottom of a 9-by-3-inch springform pan. Slightly thaw ice cream. Alternate scoops, covering the bottom with different flavors. Drizzle heavily with fudge and strawberry sauce. Scatter banana and strawberry slices over and in between sauce and ice cream. Repeat with remaining ice cream, sauce, and fruit. Crush toffee coarsely with rolling pin and sprinkle on top of pie, if desired. If not, reserve some fudge sauce and drizzle over top. Cover with foil and freeze.

✳ May be frozen 1 month.

Bring to room temperature 30 to 40 minutes before serving. Remove sides of springform and cut into wedges.

Serves 12 to 16

# Wedding Reception

MENU

GOLDEN SAUSAGE RINGS
FETA SHRIMP TRIANGLES
FLAKY MUSHROOM TARTLETS
CURRANT-STUDDED PÂTÉ
CHUTNEY-FROSTED CHEESE SPREAD
❧

CHICKEN BREASTS IN FILO
VEAL AU VIN WITH QUENELLES
MARINATED GARDEN FEAST
CHAMPAGNE RICE PILAF
❧

CHOCOLATE MOUSSE FRANGELICO
STRAWBERRIES ROMANOFF
LEMON BAVARIAN
RASPBERRY ALMOND TRUFFLES
ORANGE PECAN TRUFFLES
❧

CHAMPAGNE RECEPTION PUNCH
PINK PASTEL PUNCH

*Weddings are truly one of the loveliest and most memorable celebrations of our whole lives. Though planning and preparing the wedding meal will take some work, it is a labor of love that will guarantee memories to last a lifetime.*

*This menu serves 24, but it has been chosen specifically because of its elegance and its flexibility to accommodate any number of guests. Both the Chicken Breasts in Filo and the Veal au Vin can easily be divided or multiplied simply by doubling or tripling the ingredients. A rule of thumb for the chicken in filo is to allow one-third cup stuffing per breast and ½ pound filo for each eight breasts. This and the veal are favorites of mine, and I often serve them also at smaller dinner parties.*

*For a large celebration, you'll want a selection of hot hors d'oeuvre to pass on trays, as well as spreads that can be grouped on a table or set in different spots throughout the room.*

*Three grand dessert recipes are included. You've absolutely got to have one wonderfully rich chocolate dessert, but the other two here are dreamy and light, and also irresistible. They may be served with great pride along with a wedding cake, or even in place of one.*

*A champagne punch is very festive and much more appropriate for a wedding than an open bar, while a refreshing nonalcoholic punch is just right for a large group that includes children.*

*Clockwise from left: Lemon Bavarian, traditional wedding cake, Raspberry Almond Truffles and Orange Pecan Truffles, Strawberries Romanoff, Chocolate Mousse Frangelico with chocolate hearts.*

## Golden Sausage Rings

Bulk sausage is formed into a roll and then rolled inside mustard-coated puff pastry. It's cut into slices which become rings of flaky pastry on the outside and spicy sausage on the inside.

1 **pound frozen puff pastry, defrosted in refrigerator or at room temperature until pliable but still cold**

2 **pounds hot bulk sausage meat or 1 pound hot and 1 pound regular bulk sausage meat**

4 **tablespoons stone-ground or Dijon mustard**

1 **egg mixed with 1 tablespoon water for wash**

On a lightly floured board, roll one sheet of pastry to a 12-by-12-inch square. Cut in half. Mix sausage together if using hot and regular and divide sausage into four equal parts. On a lightly floured board, shape one part into a sausage shape approximately 12 inches by 1 inch. Spread 1 tablespoon mustard in a 1-inch band along center of pastry. Place sausage roll on mustard. Brush one long edge with egg wash. Roll. Brush pastry with egg wash. Cut into twelve 1-inch pieces. Repeat with remaining pastry and sausage. Place rings seam side down on greased rimmed baking sheets. Bake at 375° for 20 minutes or until golden, if serving immediately. Underbake slightly if refrigerating or freezing. Remove to paper towels.

❁ May be refrigerated overnight.

❀ May be frozen. Before reheating bring to room temperature.

Reheat at 375° for about 10 minutes or until heated through.

Makes 48 rings

## Feta Shrimp Triangles

Crisp pita bread triangles are the base for an exotic Middle Eastern–style topping that's creamy, slightly salty, and fragrant with cumin and mint. They freeze beautifully and are just the right choice for the cocktail hour.

4 **pita breads (about 5 to 6 inches round)**
**Butter**
8 **ounces feta cheese**
8 **ounces baby shrimp or medium shrimp, chopped**
2 **large cloves garlic, crushed**
½ **cup mayonnaise**
½ **teaspoon chili powder**
½ **teaspoon ground cumin**
2 **tablespoons chopped fresh mint or 1 to 2 teaspoons dry mint, crushed**
**Sesame seeds**
**Paprika**

Slip knife into edge of pita breads, dividing them in half horizontally. Spread each half with butter. Cut each half into 5 to 6 triangles. (If bread is large, cut into 8 to 10 triangles.) Place on baking sheet and bake at 300° for 15 to 20 minutes, or until lightly browned.

To make topping, crumble feta cheese into a medium bowl. Add shrimp, garlic, mayonnaise, chili powder, cumin, and mint, mixing with a fork until blended. Spread topping generously on toasted triangles. Sprinkle tops with sesame seeds and dust with paprika. Place on broiler pan and broil until tops are brown and bubbly.

❋ May be frozen. Reheat on baking sheet at 450° for 5 to 10 minutes or until heated through.

Makes about 40 triangles

*Baked Flaky Mushroom Tartlets in muffin tins in background; tartlets on serving platter in foreground.*

## Flaky Mushroom Tartlets

Chopped creamy morsels of mushrooms peek through layers upon layers of flaky, buttery puff pastry. This simple way to make puff pastry comes from my friend, pastry teacher Flo Braker. The rich filling is flavored deliciously with blue cheese, and the end result is luscious melt-in-your-mouth hors d'oeuvre. These tartlets are made in miniature muffin tins, with 1½-inch hollows.

EASY PUFF PASTRY
 **2 cups all-purpose flour**
 **½ pound (2 sticks) unsalted butter, cold and cut into pieces for food processor; at room temperature for mixer**
 **½ cup sour cream**
 **1 egg yolk**

Make easy puff pastry: In food processor with metal blade or in mixing bowl, place flour and butter, and process until blended. In a small bowl, mix sour cream and egg yolk. Add to flour/butter mixture and process until incorporated. Remove to work surface and shape into a ball. Divide dough in half. Flatten each half into a disc. Wrap in plastic wrap and chill until cold enough to roll.

❋ Pastry dough may be refrigerated for five days.

❋ May be frozen.

MUSHROOM FILLING

**4 tablespoons (½ stick) butter or margarine**
**1 small onion, chopped**
**¾ pound mushrooms, chopped**
**2 tablespoons all-purpose flour**
**½ cup whipping cream**
**½-ounce package blue cheese dip mix or 1½-ounce package blue cheese**
**½ teaspoon lemon juice**
**Salt and pepper to taste**

Make mushroom filling: In large skillet, melt butter or margarine. Sauté onion until soft. Add chopped mushrooms and cook, stirring occasionally, until all liquid has evaporated. Stir in flour; cook over low heat until well incorporated. Stir in cream, blue cheese dip mix or blue cheese, and lemon juice. Bring to a boil, stirring occasionally until thickened. Taste and season with salt and pepper.

On a lightly floured board, roll half the pastry into a rectangle about ⅛ inch thick. Cut into 2½-inch squares. Reroll scraps to make more squares for a total of 16 to 18 squares. Place one square over the top of each muffin hollow in an ungreased muffin tin. Repeat with remaining dough. Place a teaspoon of mushroom filling in the center of each square. Bring corners of pastry up to center. Lightly press centers together. Push tartlets gently into muffin tins.

Bake at 400° for 25 to 30 minutes or until golden. Serve immediately or remove to racks to cool.

❈ Baked tartlets may be frozen. Reheat on baking sheets at 350° for 10 to 15 minutes or until heated through.

Makes 34 to 36 tartlets

*Cut pastry into squares and place them over tops of miniature muffin tins. Place a spoonful of filling onto center of square.*

*Bring corners into center and gently push into muffin tin.*

## Currant-Studded Pâté

This liver and mushroom pâté is very smooth, like a mousse, and is studded with currants plumped in white wine.

¼ cup currants
½ cup dry white wine
12 tablespoons (1½ sticks) butter
½ pound fresh mushrooms, coarsely chopped
⅓ cup chopped green onions
1 teaspoon salt
1 clove garlic, crushed
1 pound chicken livers
¼ teaspoon Tabasco sauce
¼ pound (1 stick) butter, at room temperature
Bread rounds or crackers

Marinate currants in white wine for 4 hours or overnight. Drain, reserving the juices. Melt 4 tablespoons butter in a large skillet. Sauté mushrooms, green onions, salt, and garlic until soft, about 3 minutes. Add livers and sauté over moderately high heat, turning until livers are browned outside but pink within. Stir in the reserved wine and Tabasco sauce. Cover and simmer slowly for 5 minutes. Cool.

Transfer mixture to a food processor fitted with the metal blade or to a blender. Process until smooth. Add remaining stick of butter and blend until smooth. Remove to a bowl and stir in currants. Spoon into a 3-cup crock or pâté mold. Cover and refrigerate for at least 4 hours.

❊ May be refrigerated for 2 days.

❊ May be frozen for 1 month.

Before serving, bring to room temperature. Serve with bread rounds or crackers.

Makes 3 cups; serves about 12

## Chutney-Frosted Cheese Spread

This spread has the velvety softness of a blend of cheeses, enhanced by the flavors of curry and chutney. Use a fluted quiche pan to mold the cheese with a pretty ruffled edge.

4 cups shredded Cheddar cheese
(about 1 pound)
2 cloves garlic, crushed
Two 3-ounce packages cream cheese,
at room temperature
2 to 3 teaspoons curry powder
¾ cup chopped green onions (about 1
large bunch)
4 tablespoons mayonnaise
Salt
9-ounce jar Major Grey's Chutney
¼ cup chopped green onions, with
tops for color
Crackers or bread rounds

If using food processor, you may have to divide this in two batches, processing half at a time. In food processor with metal blade or in mixing bowl, mix Cheddar cheese, garlic, cream cheese, curry powder, ¾ cup green onions, and mayonnaise until blended. Season to taste.

Spread cheese into a 7-inch quiche pan with a removable bottom or a 5-cup bowl or mold lined with plastic wrap. Refrigerate overnight.

❋ May be refrigerated for 1 week.

❋ May be frozen. Defrost in refrigerator overnight.

Before serving, place chutney on a cutting board and chop into small pieces. If cheese is made in quiche pan, spread the chutney over the top. Sprinkle ring of green onions around outer edge. Remove sides. If cheese is made in bowl or mold, remove plastic wrap. Frost top and sides with chutney. Sprinkle with green onions, if desired.

❋ May be refrigerated for 8 hours.

Serve with crackers or bread rounds.

Makes about 5 cups; serves 16

## Chicken Breasts in Filo

*I used to make this dish by sautéing the chicken breasts and precooking the stuffing before wrapping the chicken in the filo dough. One day I was in a rush and decided to cut out both those steps, which turned out to be a real timesaver. In fact, it made the chicken more tender. The green peppercorns used in the stuffing are unripened black peppercorns. They are milder in flavor and softer in texture.*

12 whole boned chicken breasts (8 to 10 ounces each, net weight), skinned and split (if breasts are smaller, use 24 whole breasts)
Green Peppercorn and Spinach Stuffing (see below)
2 pounds filo dough
¾ pound (3 sticks) unsalted butter, melted
12 tablespoons (1½ sticks) cold butter
Pink Madeira Sauce (see below)

GREEN PEPPERCORN AND
SPINACH STUFFING
6 cups chopped fresh spinach leaves (about 1 pound, 8 ounces)
3 cups shredded Swiss cheese (about ¾ pound)
1½ cups ricotta cheese
1 large onion, finely chopped (about 1 cup)
6 hard boiled eggs, coarsely chopped
2 large cloves garlic, crushed
2 heaping tablespoons green peppercorns, finely crushed in blender, coffee grinder, or food processor
2 teaspoons salt

Pound or have meatman pound chicken breasts very thin. Sprinkle with salt and pepper.

Make Green Peppercorn and Spinach Stuffing: In very large bowl, mix all ingredients together until thoroughly mixed and crushed peppercorns are well distributed.

❋ May be refrigerated overnight.

Makes 8 cups, ⅓ cup per chicken breast

Spread ⅓ cup stuffing over each breast. Beginning at one end, roll up once, fold in sides and roll as for jelly roll. Place 1 sheet of filo on a damp towel. Keep remaining filo covered while not using, so it will not dry out. Brush filo with butter. Fold in half widthwise. Turn filo so narrow end faces you. Place one rolled chicken breast about 2 inches from end of filo. Top chicken with ½ tablespoon cold butter. Roll filo over chicken once and then fold in sides. Continue rolling to end of filo. Place on rimmed baking sheet seam side down. Brush top with butter. Repeat with remaining chicken and filo.

❋ May be refrigerated overnight, covered with foil.

❋ May be frozen for 2 weeks. Freeze in single layer until solid and then wrap securely. Defrost on baking sheets.

## PINK MADEIRA SAUCE

- **6 tablespoons butter or margarine**
- **6 tablespoons all-purpose flour**
- **6 tablespoons dry Madeira wine**
- **3 cups chicken broth**
- **2 tablespoons tomato paste**
- **1 cup sour cream**
- **1 cup chopped chives or green onion tops**
- **1 teaspoon salt or to taste**
  **White pepper to taste**

*Spread stuffing on pounded chicken breasts. Roll up folding sides in toward center. Place seam side down.*

*Roll chicken breasts in buttered and folded sheet of filo. Filo bows in foreground.*

Make filo bows by placing one sheet of filo on damp towel, narrow side toward you. Brush with butter. Cut into 3-inch strips. With fingers, crimp the center of each strip together down length of dough to form a bow. Place on baking sheet. Make one bow per chicken breast. Bake bows at 400° for 5 to 8 minutes or until golden brown. Watch carefully.

May be stored airtight overnight.

❈ May be frozen.

Make Pink Madeira Sauce: In medium saucepan, melt butter. Add flour and cook, stirring until mixture is golden. Remove from heat and whisk in Madeira and chicken broth. Return to heat and cook, stirring until mixture boils and thickens. In a small bowl mix tomato paste and sour cream. Add a little of the hot sauce to the bowl, mix thoroughly, and return to saucepan. Stir in chopped chives or green onions, salt, and pepper. If not serving immediately, place a piece of waxed paper directly on top to keep a skin from forming.

May be held at room temperature for several hours. Sauce will thicken as it sits.

❈ May be refrigerated overnight.

Reheat slowly; do not boil. If sauce is too thick, thin down with additional Madeira or cream.

Before serving, bring chicken to room temperature. Place on baking sheets at least 1 inch apart. Bake at 400° for 25 to 30 minutes or until golden. If baking 2 baking sheets in one oven, rotate them halfway through the baking time. Reheat filo bows at 400° 2 to 3 minutes. Place chicken breasts on serving platter, top each with a filo bow, and drizzle with Pink Madeira Sauce. Pass remaining sauce.

Makes 24

## Chicken Breasts in Filo for Eight

4 whole large chicken breasts or 8
  small ones
½ pound filo
¼ pound (1 stick) butter, melted
4 tablespoons (½ stick) cold butter

GREEN PEPPERCORN AND
SPINACH STUFFING
2 cups chopped spinach leaves
  (about 8 ounces)
1 cup shredded Swiss cheese
½ cup ricotta cheese
½ medium onion, chopped
2 hard-boiled eggs, chopped
1 clove garlic, crushed
2 heaping teaspoons green
  peppercorns, crushed
½ teaspoon salt

PINK MADEIRA SAUCE
2 tablespoons butter or margarine
2 tablespoons all-purpose flour
2 tablespoons Madeira
1 cup chicken broth
2 teaspoons tomato paste
⅓ cup sour cream
⅓ cup chopped chives or green onion
  tops
½ teaspoon salt or to taste
  White pepper to taste

The preceding recipe can be prepared for any number of guests. Here I break it down for a dinner for 8. Follow the recipe directions above.

*Baked Chicken Breasts in Filo served with Pink Madeira Sauce and garnished with watercress and tomato.*

# Champagne Rice Pilaf

When entertaining a crowd, one is always short of oven and stovetop space. I like to make rice in my electric fry pan, leaving my ovens and burners for other dishes. I'll precook the rice until it's three-quarters done, let it rest for several hours at room temperature, and then reheat just before serving. Rice with champagne? Not the usual marriage, but it turns out extraordinary.

1 pound (4 sticks) butter
6 cups long-grain white rice
4 cups fine noodles, such as vermicelli
8 cups chicken broth
4 cups champagne
1 tablespoon salt or to taste
1½ cups slivered blanched almonds sautéed in 4 tablespoons butter until golden

It's easiest to cook this large amount of rice in 2 separate saucepans. Melt butter in large wide saucepans, Dutch ovens, or electric fry pans. Add rice and noodles and sauté, stirring constantly, until rice is golden brown and makes a popping sound, about 7 to 10 minutes.

May be prepared several hours ahead to this point. Leave in pan at room temperature.

Bring chicken broth and champagne to a boil. Slowly pour over rice. Add salt. Bring to a boil, reduce heat to low, cover, and simmer slowly for 25 to 30 minutes or until all liquid is absorbed. Sprinkle with almonds.

Serves 24 to 30

*Variation:* Sauté rice as directed, transfer to ovenproof casseroles, and bake at 350° until liquid is absorbed, about 45 minutes to an hour.

## Veal au Vin with Quenelles

This veal dish, with fluffy meatballs in a currant-jelly and wine-flavored sauce, is the most elegant stew you'll ever find. Veal meatballs, called quenelles or forcemeat, are made like magic in the food processor. They are puréed veal, seasoned with shallots and fresh chives, and bound with egg whites and cream. This entrée is a good choice for a large crowd—it multiplies easily and improves in flavor when made ahead and refrigerated or frozen.

8 pounds good-quality stewing veal, cut into 1½-inch cubes
  Salt and pepper
4 tablespoons (½ stick) butter or margarine
2 tablespoons tomato paste
2 tablespoons instant beef soup base (beef-flavored bouillon)
10 tablespoons flour
6½ cups chicken broth
2 cups dry white wine
4 teaspoons currant jelly
2 large cloves garlic
¼ cup chopped shallots or onion
4 tablespoons chopped chives
¼ cup chopped parsley
2 pounds lean ground veal
8 unbeaten egg whites
2 cups whipping cream or half-and-half
2 teaspoons salt
1½ pounds fresh mushrooms, sliced

Sprinkle veal with salt and pepper. In a wide, heavy ovenproof saucepan or Dutch oven, melt the butter or margarine. Sauté the veal over high heat until lightly browned. This process will need to be done in batches; do not crowd the meat when browning. If butter begins to burn, reduce heat slightly. As meat browns, remove it to a large bowl or platter. To the drippings in the pan, add the tomato paste, beef soup base, and flour. Stir until incorporated; it will be thick and grainy. Add the broth, wine, and jelly. Cook, stirring constantly, scraping up all brown bits from the bottom of the pan, until mixture comes to a boil.

Taste for seasoning. Return meat and the juices to the pan. Preheat oven to 375°. Cover and bake for 1 to 1½ hours, basting occasionally. If juices are boiling too rapidly, reduce heat to 350°. Veal is done when it is easily pierced with a fork. (Pink veal or baby beef may take as long as 2½ hours.)

While veal cooks, make the meatballs: In food processor with metal blade, process half the garlic, shallots or onion, chives, and parsley; scrape down sides. Add half the veal and mix until blended. Add 4 egg whites. Process again. With machine running, pour 1 cup cream or half-and-half through the feed tube. Lastly mix in 1 teaspoon salt. Remove to bowl and repeat with remaining ingredients.

About 15 minutes before veal has completed cooking, dip 2 teaspoons or a meatball-size ice cream scoop into the hot gravy. Dip into meat mixture and drop a ball of the mixture into the stew. Repeat until all meat mixture is used. It will be necessary to drop the meat balls one on top of the other; don't be concerned—they will separate while cooking. Cover the pan and bake 20 minutes longer. If not serving immediately, cool completely.

✽ May be refrigerated for 2 days.

❅ May be frozen for 2 months.

Before serving, bring to room temperature. Stir in mushrooms. Reheat at 350°, stirring gently, until heated through, about 30 minutes. Veal may also be reheated on top of the stove, if desired.

Serves 24

## Veal au Vin with Quenelles for Twelve

4 pounds stewing veal
Salt and pepper
4 tablespoons butter or margarine
1 tablespoon tomato paste
1 tablespoon instant beef soup base (beef-flavored bouillon)
5 tablespoons flour
3¼ cups chicken broth
1 cup dry white wine
2 teaspoons currant jelly
1 large clove garlic
2 tablespoons chopped shallots or onion
2 tablespoons chopped chives, 4 parsley sprigs, or ¼ cup parsley leaves
1 pound ground veal
4 unbeaten egg whites
1 cup whipping cream or half-and-half
1 teaspoon salt
¾ pound small fresh mushrooms, sliced

The preceding recipe can be prepared for any number of guests. Here I break it down for a dinner for 12. Follow recipe directions above.

## Marinated Garden Feast

The beauty of this dish is that it looks like a bountiful, splendidly colorful garden feast. In contrast to a tossed salad, none of these ingredients will wilt sitting on a buffet. The fresh vegetables are slightly blanched to retain their bright colors and flavors. Proportions of the individual vegetables can be varied according to personal preference and the season of the year.

**2 pounds green beans**
**2 large heads cauliflower (about 5 pounds)**
**3 to 4 large bunches broccoli (about 3 pounds)**
**3 pounds carrots**
**Three 16-ounce bottles Italian salad dressing**
**Two 0.7-ounce packages dry Italian salad dressing mix**
**4 cloves garlic, crushed**
**1 cup chopped parsley**
**Three 8-ounce cans artichoke hearts**
**Lettuce leaves for garnish**
**Three 5½-ounce jars baby corn**
**4 cans (5 to 6 ounces dry weight) pitted black olives, drained**
**5 tomatoes, sliced into ¼-inch-thick slices**

Cut tips off green beans and cut into approximately 2-inch diagonal pieces. Cut stems off cauliflower and broccoli and break into serving-size flowerets, tapering ends slightly. Cut stems off carrots and peel. Using serrated cutter or knife, cut them into approximately 2-inch diagonal pieces.

Fill a large wide pot half full of water; bring to a boil. Add green beans. Bring water back to a boil and cook beans for 2 minutes. Remove with slotted spoon or strainer to a colander. Place in bowl of ice water to stop the cooking. Bring water in pot back to a boil. Repeat with remaining fresh vegetables, cooking each 3 minutes, except carrots, which, if large, may take 6 minutes. Cool completely.

To make marinade, mix bottled dressing, dry dressing, garlic, and parsley in large container or in 2 large jars. Marinade can be refrigerated up to a week and is excellent as a dressing for tossed salads or sliced tomatoes.

Place green beans, cauliflower, broccoli, and carrots in separate bowls or plastic bags.

✽ May be prepared one day in advance and refrigerated.

Pour ¾ to 1 cup marinade over each of the vegetables and refrigerate 4 to 6 hours. Drain artichoke hearts. Pour into plastic bag and add ¾ cup marinade. Turn bags over once or twice to distribute marinade.

Before serving, line one or two large platters with lettuce leaves. Remove vegetables from marinade and place decoratively on platter, keeping each kind separate. Place baby corn,

*Marinated Garden Feast.*

olives, and tomatoes on platter. Drizzle marinade over corn and tomatoes.

Serves 24

*Variation:* Zucchini, cucumbers, or asparagus may be added.

## *Chocolate Mousse Frangelico*

Frangelico is a hazelnut-flavored liqueur with the aroma and taste of these delicate and delicious nuts. The crust of the mousse is golden-colored, buttery, and nutty. The mousse itself is sweet, chocolaty, smooth, and fragrant with Frangelico.

½ **cup shelled hazelnuts, finely chopped (about 2 ounces)**
½ **cup all-purpose flour**
1 **tablespoon packed light, or golden, brown sugar**
6 **tablespoons cold unsalted butter**
1 **to 2 teaspoons ice water**

Make hazelnut crust: In food processor with metal blade or in medium bowl, mix nuts, flour, and brown sugar until blended. Cut butter into 6 pieces and process or cut into mixture until the consistency of coarse meal. Add 1 to 2 teaspoons ice water and mix just until mixture begins to hold together. Remove from bowl and

CHOCOLATE MOUSSE

**1 pound semisweet chocolate**
**2 large eggs, at room temperature**
**4 egg yolks, at room temperature**
**3 ounces Frangelico liqueur**
**6 egg whites, at room temperature**
**Dash of salt**
**Dash of cream of tartar**
**¼ cup powdered sugar**
**1 pint (2 cups) whipping cream**
**Chocolate Hearts and whipped cream for garnish (see following recipe; optional)**

press into the bottom of an ungreased 9-by-3-inch springform pan. Bake at 400° for 12 to 15 minutes or until lightly browned. Cool completely before filling.

❄ May be frozen.

Melt chocolate in double boiler over simmering water. Remove from heat and cool 10 minutes. With wooden spoon, mix in whole eggs one at a time. The mixture will be thick and stiff. Stir in egg yolks and Frangelico. In mixing bowl, beat egg whites until frothy. Add salt and cream of tartar and continue beating until soft peaks form. Beat in powdered sugar a tablespoon at a time, until stiff. In a separate bowl, whip cream until soft peaks form; do not overbeat. Fold chocolate and cream into whites. Pour into cooled crust. Cover and refrigerate at least 4 hours.

❄ May be refrigerated for 2 days.

❄ May be frozen. Defrost in refrigerator overnight.

Several hours before serving, place springform pan on a bowl which is smaller than the circumference of the springform. Slowly open sides of pan and let rim slip down. Smooth sides of mousse, if needed. Place mousse on serving platter. Decorate top with whipped cream piped through a pastry bag fitted with a large rosette tip. Garnish with chocolate hearts, if desired.

Serves 12

*Variations:* ½ cup almonds may be substituted for the hazelnuts in the crust. Two ounces Amaretto liqueur may be substituted for the 3 ounces Frangelico. Mousse may be served from a glass bowl instead of in a crust.

*Opposite page: Pull parchment off chocolate. Chocolate Mousse Frangelico is topped with whipped cream and chocolate hearts.*

## Chocolate Hearts

**4 ounces semisweet chocolate,
chopped**

*Spread chocolate on parchment hearts*

Use waxed paper or parchment to line a baking sheet which will fit in the refrigerator or freezer; set aside. Melt chocolate in a double boiler over hot water. Let sit off the heat for 3 to 4 minutes to thicken slightly. Draw a heart on heavy paper or cardboard; it can be any size you desire. Cut it out and trace it onto parchment or waxed paper, drawing as many hearts as desired, allowing extra for breakage. Cut out paper hearts.

With a small knife or spreader, spread chocolate on one side of paper. Place on prepared baking sheet. Refrigerate or freeze until firm.

❀ May be refrigerated several weeks.

❁ May be frozen.

Before using, carefully peel off paper, handling the chocolate as little as possible. Return to refrigerator or freezer. Use as desired to decorate desserts.

Makes 16 to 24 hearts

## Strawberries Romanoff

This dessert is the only one I know of that can be served next to a chocolate dessert and still get its own applause. It tastes so light it's like eating a cloud.

9 egg yolks
1½ cups sugar
½ cup Grand Marnier
1 pint (2 cups) whipping cream
5 pints strawberries

In mixing bowl, beat egg yolks and sugar until thick and creamy. Pour the mixture into the top of a double boiler and whisk over simmering water until smooth and thick, about 10 minutes. At first the custard will thin out, then as it cooks it will thicken. When it thickens and becomes hot to the touch, it is done. Do not let it boil, and do not be concerned if it feels granular.

Remove to a bowl and place in a larger bowl filled with ice water. Stir occasionally until cool. Stir in Grand Marnier. Whip cream until soft peaks form. Fold into custard.

❊ May be refrigerated covered overnight.

Wipe berries clean or wash, if you have to. (I don't.) Remove stems and cut large berries in half. Stir into custard. Pour into glass serving bowl.

❊ May be refrigerated 6 hours.

Serves 16

*Pipe ladyfingers onto baking sheet.*

*Place trimmed ladyfingers in sides of mold.*

## Lemon Bavarian

You don't have to be a lemon lover to love this dessert. These ladyfingers can't be compared to store-bought—the lemon in the batter tenderizes them to be the softest ones you've ever eaten. The lemon Bavarian filling is also light and lemony.

LEMON LADYFINGERS
- **3 large eggs, separated**
- **9 tablespoons sugar**
- **3 tablespoons lemon juice**
- **2 teaspoons finely grated lemon rind**
- **⅔ cup all-purpose flour**
  **Powdered sugar**

Make lemon ladyfingers: Line 2 baking sheets with parchment paper or grease and flour them. Preheat oven to 350°. Beat egg yolks and 6 tablespoons sugar until thick, light, and creamy. Mix in the lemon juice and rind. In a separate bowl, beat the egg whites until soft peaks form. Continue beating while adding the additional 3 tablespoons sugar, 1 tablespoon at a time, until stiff. Fold flour and whites alternately into yolks, beginning and ending with the flour.

Transfer the batter to a large pastry bag fitted with a ½-inch plain round tip. Squeeze fingers of batter approximately 1 inch wide and as long as the height of the mold you will use to hold the Bavarian. Space the fingers at least 1 inch apart. Sift powdered sugar lightly over the tops. Bake for 15 minutes or until golden.

❊ May be frozen.

Makes about 30 ladyfingers

## LEMON BAVARIAN

- **1 teaspoon unflavored gelatin**
- **⅓ cup lemon juice**
- **6 large egg yolks**
- **¾ cup sugar**
- **Grated rind of 2 small lemons**
- **1½ cups whipping cream**

GARNISH (optional)
**Lemon Peel Rose (see following recipe)**
**Whipped cream**

Make lemon Bavarian by softening the gelatin in the lemon juice for 5 minutes. In a mixing bowl, beat egg yolks and sugar until thick and light. Stir in lemon rind. Transfer mixture to a heavy saucepan and cook over medium heat, stirring constantly, until mixture is very thick and mounds slightly when dropped from a spoon, about 4 to 5 minutes. Remove the pan from the heat and immediately add the softened gelatin, stirring until dissolved. Pour into a bowl and set into a larger bowl of ice water; stir occasionally until cool. Meanwhile beat the cream until soft peaks form. Fold cream into cool lemon mixture and set aside while preparing the mold.

Line the sides of a 6-cup brioche or charlotte mold or an 8-inch springform pan with the ladyfingers, cutting them to fit as necessary. The bottom may also be lined with ladyfingers, if desired. Spoon in lemon Bavarian. Cover with plastic wrap and refrigerate for a minimum of 4 hours, or until firm.

✵ May be refrigerated for 2 days.

❀ May be frozen for 2 weeks. Defrost in refrigerator overnight.

Before serving, dip the mold into warm water. Invert onto serving plate. Refrigerate until ready to serve. Garnish with Lemon Peel Rose and whipped cream rosettes, if desired.

Serves 8

*Lemon Bavarian is decorated with piped whipped cream and topped with Lemon Peel Rose.*

## Lemon Peel Rose

**1 lemon**

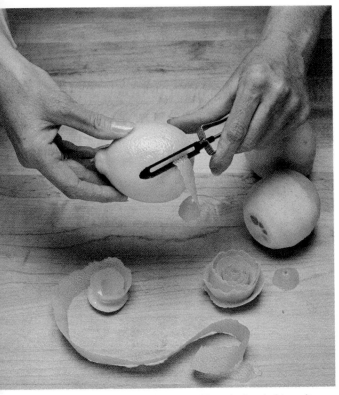

*Peel lemon with vegetable peeler in spiral to make rose.*

Peel the lemon, using a sharp vegetable peeler and cutting with a zigzag motion. Cut in a spiral, making a continuous strip about ½ inch wide. Lay peel out on a work surface yellow side down. Roll one end of the peel tightly to make the center of the rose. Loosely roll the remaining peel around, making it looser as it extends out.

❋ May be refrigerated overnight wrapped in wet paper towels and plastic wrap.

## Raspberry Almond Truffles

These truffles are almost like a bonbon candy. They're a little chewier from the raspberry jam and the chopped almonds, which means that you get to savor their flavor longer.

**Eight 1-ounce squares semisweet chocolate**
**6 tablespoons unsalted butter**
**½ cup seedless raspberry jam**
**½ cup chopped almonds**
**3 tablespoons crème de cassis**
**Powdered cocoa or chocolate sprinkles**

Melt semisweet chocolate and butter in the top of a double boiler over hot water, stirring until smooth. Remove from heat. Stir in jam, almonds, and crème de cassis. Remove to a bowl. Refrigerate covered until firm.

Scrape a teaspoon across the surface of the chocolate mixture. Press with fingertips into ¾-inch balls. Roll in cocoa or chocolate sprinkles. Place in bonbon papers, if desired. Store in airtight container in freezer. Serve directly from freezer, if desired.

❁ May be frozen for several months.

Makes about 36 truffles

## Orange Pecan Truffles

Orange lovers deserve their moment of triumph too. These creamy chocolate candies are bursting with orange essence and are crunchy with chopped pecans.

**Eight 1-ounce squares semisweet chocolate**
**6 tablespoons unsalted butter**
**½ cup orange marmalade**
**½ cup chopped pecans**
**2 tablespoons Grand Marnier**
**1 cup finely ground pecans**

Melt chocolate and butter in the top of double boiler over hot water, stirring until smooth. Remove from heat. Stir in marmalade, chopped pecans, and liqueur. Remove to a bowl. Refrigerate covered until firm.

Scrape a teaspoon across the surface of the chocolate mixture. Press with fingertips into ¾-inch balls. Roll in chopped pecans. Place in bonbon papers, if desired. Store in airtight containers in freezer. Serve directly from freezer, if desired.

❁ May be frozen for several months.

Makes about 36 truffles

## Pink Pastel Punch

A sweet, refreshing nonalcoholic punch. It freezes well before the ginger ale is added, so you might consider making an extra batch, freezing it in a decorative mold, and then unmolding it to float in the punch. Your punch will stay very cold and won't get diluted in flavor with melting ice.

**2 pints raspberry sherbet**
**12-ounce can pink lemonade concentrate, thawed**
**Two 10-ounce packages frozen raspberries in syrup, thawed**
**4 cups water**
**33.8-fluid-ounce bottle ginger ale or 7-Up, chilled**

Soften 1 pint raspberry sherbet. In punch bowl, combine softened sherbet and lemonade concentrate. Stir in frozen raspberries and water. Chill.

❉ May be refrigerated overnight.
❉ May be frozen.

Before serving, stir in ginger ale or 7-Up. Scoop remaining sherbet into balls and float on top of punch.

Makes 24 four-ounce servings

## Champagne Reception Punch

A wedding reception deserves a jubilant punch, and that's exactly what this not too sweet, yet not too dry, sparkling punch is. It's a great champagne stretcher, and its floating heart-shaped ice mold is quite romantic and colorful.

1 **bunch green grapes**
1 **box strawberries**
**25.4-fluid-ounce bottle sauterne**
1 **cup brandy**
¼ **cup sugar**
**32-ounce bottle club soda, chilled**
**Two 4/5-quart bottles dry**
   **champagne, chilled**

Make ice mold: Fill a heart mold or heart-shaped cake pan half full of water. Freeze solid. When frozen, place small clusters of grapes and strawberries over the top, covering the top almost completely. Carefully pour in enough water to half cover fruit. Return to freezer. When frozen, add more water, if needed. Freeze solid. To unmold, dip mold briefly in warm water and unmold onto freezer foil. Wrap in foil and freeze until ready to use. Repeat with second mold, if desired.

❀ May be frozen 1 month.

In a large bowl, combine sauterne, brandy, and sugar, stirring until sugar is dissolved.

❀ May be refrigerated overnight.

Before serving, pour sauterne mixture into a large punch bowl. Add ice mold. Pour in soda and champagne.

Makes 28 four-ounce servings

# 6

# PATRIOTIC
# PARTIES

# Fourth of July Barbecue

## MENU

SALMON SPREAD
BLUE CHEESE GARDEN DIP WITH
RAW VEGETABLES
GIN FIZZ COOLER

CHICKEN WITH PANHANDLE
BARBECUE SAUCE OR
FIRECRACKER BARBECUE SAUCE
MARINATED CHUCK ROAST
OLD-FASHIONED POTATO SALAD
RADISH SLAW
LITTLE PORKERS AND BEANS
HERBED GARLIC BREAD

STARS AND STRIPES CAKE
BLUEBERRY TORTE

*A warm summer sun and a soft breeze, combined with family, friends, and good food, make for a wonderful day. All the tried-and-true traditional favorites are here, with a few savory twists—chicken with a choice of sweet or spicy barbecue sauce, tender, marinated beef, a radish variation of coleslaw, and garlic bread drenched in herb butter. The Stars and Stripes Cake is a fitting tribute to Old Glory. Serve pitchers of the Gin Fizz Cooler to quench the summer thirst.*

*If you serve both the chicken and the beef, doubling the recipes for the beef and the garlic bread, the menu will serve 10 to 12. Don't forget that if you serve a large assortment of food, you won't need as much of any one kind.*

*Clockwise from lower lefthand corner: Radish Slaw, Old-Fashioned Potato Salad, Little Porkers and Beans, Gin Fizz Cooler, Herbed Garlic Bread, sliced Marinated Chuck Roast. In the center is the barbecued chicken with Panhandle Barbecue Sauce.*

## Salmon Spread

A spicy bright-pink spread that can just as easily be turned into a nut-studded or parsley-rolled salmon ball. The garnishment of stars and stripes accentuates the patriotic theme.

7¾-ounce can salmon, drained
8-ounce package cream cheese, at room temperature
1 tablespoon green onion dip mix
1½ tablespoons lemon juice
1 teaspoon Worcestershire sauce
1 small clove garlic, crushed
¼ cup finely chopped parsley
1 small green onion, finely chopped (about 1 tablespoon)
⅛ teaspoon pepper
1 whole pimiento or large pieces of pimiento (optional)
1 green onion (optional)
Crackers or bread rounds for serving

Drain salmon and set aside. In food processor with metal blade or in mixing bowl with electric mixer, mix cream cheese, dip mix, lemon juice, Worcestershire, garlic, parsley, chopped green onion, and pepper until blended. When smooth, add salmon and mix well. Line a 2-cup bowl with plastic wrap. Spoon salmon into the bowl, cover, and refrigerate until firm, at least 4 hours.

❋ May be refrigerated for 2 days.

Before serving, remove salmon from bowl, place on serving platter, and pull off paper. If you like, cut pimiento into stars, using small aspic cutter, cut top of green onion into thin strips, and place decoratively on top of spread.

Serve with crackers or bread rounds.

Makes 1⅔ cup; serves 8 to 10

## Blue Cheese Garden Dip with Raw Vegetables

Bits of radish, celery, onion, and pepper add texture and color to this simple, good spread. Serve with raw vegetables for dipping.

**3-ounce package cream cheese, at room temperature**
**½ cup small-curd cottage cheese**
**2 tablespoons sour cream**
**Tabasco sauce to taste**
**½ teaspoon dried dill**
**1 clove garlic, crushed**
**One ½-ounce package blue cheese dip mix**
**¼ cup finely chopped radishes**
**¼ cup finely chopped celery**
**¼ cup finely chopped green onion**
**¼ cup finely chopped green pepper**
**Assorted raw vegetables for dipping, such as carrots, celery, cauliflower, broccoli, zucchini, radishes, cherry tomatoes**

In mixing bowl or food processor with metal blade, mix cream cheese, cottage cheese, and sour cream until well blended. Add Tabasco sauce, dill, garlic, and dip mix. Stir in chopped vegetables. Refrigerate at least 4 hours before serving.

❀ May be refrigerated up to 3 days.

Serve with vegetables for dipping. If too thick, thin with additional sour cream.

Makes 1½ cups; serves 8

## Gin Fizz Cooler

It's great to have a beverage recipe that can be easily made on the patio for summertime entertaining. This cooler can be blended ahead, frozen, defrosted almost before serving, and still retain its sprightly, sparkling flavor.

**6-ounce can frozen lemonade concentrate, defrosted slightly**
**6-ounce can frozen pineapple concentrate, defrosted slightly**
**2 cups club soda, chilled**
**1½ cups gin**
**4 cups ice cubes**

Place half the ingredients at a time in blender; mix until thick and smooth. Repeat with remaining ingredients.

❀ Mixture may be frozen. Defrost for 1 hour at room temperature. Return to blender and process until smooth.

Makes twelve 4-ounce servings

## Chicken with Panhandle Barbecue Sauce
## or Firecracker Barbecue Sauce

Barbecueing chicken is no mean feat—it's a real challenge to get the inside cooked through without burning the outside. If you partially prebake the chicken and barbecue it, the results will be chicken that is moist and juicy on the inside and beautifully browned on the outside.

You will need whole broiler fryers cut up or select pieces of chicken such as legs, thighs, breasts, or wings. A 3½- to 4-pound broiler fryer, cut into 8 pieces, will serve 4, allowing 2 pieces of chicken per person.

Place chicken in shallow roasting pan or broiler pan. Sprinkle with salt and pepper. Bake at 375° for 30 minutes. (If making mainly thighs and legs, bake 5 minutes longer.) Remove from oven and brush chicken thickly with Panhandle Barbecue Sauce or Firecracker Barbecue Sauce (following recipes). Marinate for 4 to 6 hours in the refrigerator, covered with plastic wrap.

Before serving, bring chicken to room temperature. Brush with barbecue sauce and grill about 4 inches from hot coals for 20 to 25 minutes, turning and basting frequently. (The chicken may also be broiled indoors.) Remove chicken from heat and brush again lightly with sauce.

Serve immediately.

## Panhandle Barbecue Sauce

A well-balanced, all-purpose barbecue sauce that will give even oven-cooked meats a rich barbecue flavor. It's mellow, reddish brown in color, smooth in consistency, and much better than the bottled variety. All you need to do is measure the ingredients into a saucepan, simmer until thick enough to coat a spoon, and store in your refrigerator until ready to use.

10-ounce can tomato soup
8-ounce can tomato sauce
½ cup dark molasses
½ cup cider or white vinegar
½ cup light, or golden, brown sugar, packed
¼ cup vegetable oil
1 tablespoon instant minced onion
1 tablespoon seasoned salt
1 tablespoon dry mustard
1 tablespoon Worcestershire sauce
2 teaspoons paprika
½ teaspoon pepper
½ teaspoon garlic powder
1 teaspoon orange rind (optional)

In a medium saucepan, bring all ingredients to a boil. Simmer uncovered for 20 minutes, stirring occasionally. Cool and store in refrigerator.

❉ May be refrigerated for 6 months.

Use as directed in preceding chicken recipe.

Makes 1½ cups or enough for 2 to 3 chickens

## Firecracker Barbecue Sauce

Rich, robust, and spicy, a little of this sauce goes a long way. I like to make some chicken with this sauce and the rest with the milder Panhandle Barbecue Sauce (preceding recipe) so that everyone gets chicken that pleases his or her individual taste.

1 tablespoon catsup
2 tablespoons Worcestershire sauce
2 tablespoons soy sauce
4 tablespoons plum jam
1½ teaspoons salt
4 teaspoons sugar
2 teaspoons ground black pepper
2 teaspoons dry mustard
2 teaspoons ground ginger
1 teaspoon curry powder
4 tablespoons chutney
Dash of Tabasco

Mix all ingredients together in food processor with metal blade or in blender. Remove to medium saucepan and bring to a boil. Simmer 5 minutes. Cool and store in refrigerator.

✼ May be refrigerated for 6 months.

Use this sauce sparingly when basting, as it is very pungent.

Makes 1¼ cups or enough for 3 to 4 chickens

## Marinated Chuck Roast

The marinade works to tenderize as well as enhance the flavor of an economical cut of beef. It's a wee bit spicy but sweet-tinged, and the meat becomes crusty-brown on the outside yet pink and juicy on the inside.

1 medium onion, chopped
2 tablespoons vegetable oil
2 cloves garlic, crushed
¼ cup chopped fresh parsley
⅓ cup soy sauce
1 teaspoon powdered ginger
1 teaspoon ground allspice
1 teaspoon dried rosemary
3 tablespoons red wine vinegar
2 tablespoons light, or golden, brown sugar, packed
1¼ cups beef broth
2-to 3-pound boneless chuck roast, cut 1½ inches thick

To make marinade, sauté onion in a medium saucepan until soft but not brown. Add remaining ingredients (except roast) and bring to a boil. Remove from heat and cool.

✼ May be refrigerated for several months.

Place roast in deep glass or plastic container. (Do not marinate in aluminum.) Pour cooled marinade over roast and refrigerate covered; turn the roast in the marinade several times. Marinate for at least 5 hours, or preferably overnight. Remove roast from marinade and bring to room temperature. Barbecue or broil at high heat for 8 to 10 minutes per side, turning once. If using an instant read thermometer, it should register 120° to 125° for rare, 135° for medium, and 150° for well done. Slice roast at an angle into ¼-inch slices.

Serves 4 to 6

## Old-Fashioned Potato Salad

This salad will bring back memories of grandmother's hearty potato salad. It's what potato salad was meant to be. Serve it either warm or cool.

½ **pound bacon, cut into ½-inch pieces**
3 **pounds new potatoes (about 6 medium potatoes)**
3 **teaspoons salt**
6 **hard-boiled eggs, sliced**
½ **cup chopped green onions**
½ **cup chopped dill pickles**
1½ **teaspoons celery seed**
¼ **teaspoon pepper**
1 **teaspoon garlic salt**
1 **cup mayonnaise**
¼ **cup white wine vinegar**
¼ **cup hot water**
3 **tablespoons sugar**
2 **tablespoons Dijon mustard**

GARNISH (optional)
**Hard-boiled eggs, sliced or in wedges**
**Diced cooked bacon**
**Ripe olives**
**Parsley**

In a medium skillet, cook bacon over moderate heat, stirring occasionally, until crisp. Remove to paper towels; reserve ½ cup drippings and set aside.

Scrub potatoes and place in a large saucepan. Cover with water, add 2 teaspoons salt, and bring to a boil. Lower heat and boil gently until tender when pierced with a fork, about 25 minutes, depending on size. Drain, peel, and cut into ½-inch cubes. Place in a large bowl; add eggs, green onions, pickles, celery seed, 1 teaspoon salt, pepper, garlic salt, bacon, and mayonnaise. Toss gently until combined.

❊ May be refrigerated, covered, overnight.

In a small saucepan, heat reserved ½ cup bacon drippings, vinegar, hot water, sugar, and mustard. Bring to a boil, whisking constantly, and boil for 2 minutes. Pour over salad; toss gently. Serve warm or at room temperature.

❊ If serving at room temperature, the salad may be refrigerated overnight. Bring to room temperature 1 hour before serving.

Garnish with eggs cut into slices or wedges, bacon, and parsley, if desired.

Serves 8

## Radish Slaw

A gratifying change from serving coleslaw. Don't hesitate because of the unique ingredients—it's tart and refreshing. If you do not have a good light olive oil or walnut oil, substitute ¾ cup salad oil for the combination of the two. It will still be delicious and different.

2 pounds red radishes
1 pound shredded Swiss cheese (4 cups)
1 cup chopped green pimiento-stuffed olives, drained
½ cup chopped green onions, including tops
⅔ cup chopped fresh parsley
⅔ cup olive oil
¼ cup walnut oil or salad oil
6 tablespoons white wine vinegar
1 teaspoon salt
4 teaspoons Dijon mustard
Freshly ground pepper

Wash radishes and pat dry; cut a thin slice off both ends; shred or finely chop. Place radishes, cheese, olives, green onions, and parsley in a large bowl.

Make vinaigrette by mixing oils, vinegar, salt, mustard, and pepper together in a bowl or glass jar. Pour over slaw and refrigerate until ready to serve.

❉ May be refrigerated overnight.

Serves 10 to 12

## Little Porkers and Beans

Two kinds of beans are baked with bacon in a sweet-and-sour glaze that's bourbon-laced and beautifully browned. The "porkers" are optional.

**1 pound bacon, cut into 1-inch pieces**
**1 medium onion, chopped**
**Three 16-ounce cans brick oven baked beans**
**15-ounce can kidney beans, drained**
**2 tablespoons dark molasses**
**2 tablespoons either light or dark brown sugar, packed**
**⅓ cup bourbon**
**½ cup chili sauce**
**1 teaspoon dry mustard**
**Two 5½-ounce packages little cocktail wieners (about 32)**

In a large saucepan, cook bacon over moderate heat, stirring occasionally, until crisp. Remove to paper towels. Discard all but ¼ cup bacon drippings and sauté onion in drippings until soft. In large bowl, mix beans, bacon, onion, molasses, brown sugar, bourbon, chili sauce, dry mustard, and wieners. Pour into a 3-quart bean pot or casserole.

❉ May be refrigerated for 2 days.

Bake covered at 350° for 40 minutes. Uncover and bake 40 additional minutes, or until top is deep brown and bubbling. Let rest 15 minutes before serving.

Serves 14 to 16

## Herbed Garlic Bread

It's cheesy, crusty, and glazed on the outside and dripping in a golden herb butter on the inside.

**1-pound oval loaf French or
   sourdough bread, unsliced**
**12 tablespoons (1½ sticks) unsalted
   butter, at room temperature**
**¼ cup finely chopped parsley**
**¼ cup finely chopped chives or
   green onion tops**
**½ teaspoon salt**
**½ teaspoon dried basil**
**½ teaspoon dried thyme**
**2 medium cloves garlic, crushed**
**3 tablespoons grated Parmesan
   cheese**

Trim crusts from top and sides of bread. Cut 2-inch diagonal slices across bread, leaving bottom intact. Cut 2-inch diagonal slices in opposite direction, forming triangles. Combine butter, parsley, chives or green onions, salt, basil, thyme, and garlic in food processor with metal blade or in mixing bowl. Spread butter mixture in between cuts and over top and sides of loaf.

❋ May be wrapped in foil and refrigerated overnight.

❋ May be frozen.

Before serving, place on baking sheet and bring to room temperature. Sprinkle top with Parmesan cheese. Bake at 400° for 15 to 20 minutes or until golden brown.

Serves 6

## Blueberry Torte

*This old-fashioned rendition of a blueberry buckle is simply outstanding.*

PASTRY
1¾ cups all-purpose flour
⅓ cup sugar
Dash of salt
12 tablespoons (1½ sticks) cold
unsalted butter, cut into pieces
2 egg yolks

FILLING
4 cups blueberries
½ cup sugar
¼ cup quick-cooking tapioca
½ teaspoon grated lemon peel
¾ teaspoon ground cinnamon
⅛ teaspoon ground nutmeg

SOUR CREAM TOPPING
2 egg yolks
2 cups sour cream
½ cup sugar
1½ teaspoons vanilla extract

Make pastry: Place flour, sugar, and salt in food processor with metal blade or in mixing bowl. Add butter and mix until crumbly. Add egg yolks; mix until dough holds together and begins to form a ball. Press two-thirds of the pastry into the bottom of a 9-by-3-inch springform pan. Bake at 400° for 12 to 15 minutes or until lightly browned. Remove from oven and cool. Press remaining dough 1½ inches up the sides of the pan. (You may not use all of the dough.)

Make the filling: In a medium saucepan, combine blueberries, sugar, tapioca, lemon peel, cinnamon, and nutmeg. Let stand 15 minutes. Place saucepan over moderate heat and cook, stirring, until mixture reaches a full rolling boil. Remove from heat and cool slightly. Pour into pastry.

Make sour cream topping: In a small bowl mix egg yolks slightly. Stir in sour cream, sugar, and vanilla. Spoon over blueberries.

Bake torte at 350° for 45 minutes. Cool completely. Cover with foil and refrigerate, if desired.

❋ May be refrigerated for 2 days.

Before serving, place springform on a bowl which is smaller than the circumference of the springform. Open sides of pan and let rim slip down. Place torte on serving platter.

Serves 8 to 10

## Stars and Stripes Cake

What's more American than strawberry shortcake made into a flag? If you're not inclined to bake a made-from-scratch cake, use a packaged cake mix, following my timing and baking direction. Try the parchment paper if you can—it makes removing the cake a breeze.

*Stars and Stripes Cake with strawberry and whipped cream stripes and a blueberry background for whipped cream stars.*

*After cake has been filled, place toothpicks along top and bottom to outline form of flag. Cut around toothpicks.*

*Frost top and sides of cake.*

### SPONGE CAKE LAYERS

- **8 eggs, separated**
- **1½ cups sugar**
- **1 teaspoon vanilla extract**
  **Dash of cream of tartar**
- **1½ cups all-purpose flour**
- **2 teaspoons baking powder**
- **1 teaspoon salt**
- **¼ cup Grand Marnier or orange juice**

Grease two 15½-by-10½-by-1-inch jelly-roll pans. Line the pans with parchment or waxed paper. Grease the paper. If using waxed paper, dust with flour, shaking out the excess. Preheat oven to 375°. In mixing bowl with electric mixer, beat egg yolks until thick and light. Gradually beat in ½ cup sugar and vanilla. In separate bowl, beat egg whites until frothy. Add cream of tartar and beat until soft peaks form. Gradually add remaining 1 cup sugar, a tablespoon at a time, beating until stiff peaks form. Fold whites into yolks. Sift together flour, baking powder, and salt. Fold into egg mixture. Divide between pans, smoothing tops to make them even. Bake in center of oven for 12 minutes. If baking both pans in one oven, rotate them after 6 minutes. Cakes are done when the top springs back when lightly pressed with fingertip and top is pale golden. Do not overbake or cakes will be dry. Remove from oven and immediately invert onto racks or foil. Lift off pans and peel off paper. Cool.

May be wrapped in foil and stored at room temperature overnight.

❀ May be frozen.

Place cake layers on work surface. Sprinkle tops of cakes with Grand Marnier or orange juice. Place one layer on a large platter or cut a

## STRAWBERRY FILLING

**1 pint (1 box) strawberries**
**½ pint (1 cup) whipping cream**
**¼ cup powdered sugar**

## WHIPPED CREAM FROSTING

**1 pint (2 cups) whipping cream**
**⅓ cup powdered sugar**
**2 teaspoons vanilla extract**

## DECORATION

**2 pints (2 boxes) strawberries, the**
**smallest berries possible**
**1-pound 5-ounce can blueberry pie**
**filling, drained or 1 cup fresh**
**blueberries**

piece of heavy cardboard 1 inch larger than the cake and cover it with plastic-coated doilies.

Make strawberry filling: Clean, hull, and chop 1 pint strawberries. Beat cream until soft. Mix in powdered sugar and strawberries and beat until mixture turns pink. Spread filling over cake layer. Top with second layer. Cut cake as pictured to resemble a flag "waving."

Make whipped cream frosting: Whip cream until soft. Add powdered sugar and vanilla and beat until stiff. Frost top and sides of cake. Place remaining frosting in a pastry bag fitted with a ¼-inch star or ribbon tip. Slice strawberries, cutting from the top down. Using toothpicks, mark off a 5½-inch square on the upper left-hand corner of the cake. Alternate rows of overlapped sliced strawberries and piped whipped cream on rest of cake, making (hopefully) 13 stripes. (If you can't fit them all in, don't worry. By this time no one should be counting.) Fill the left-hand square with as much blueberry pie filling as needed or with fresh blueberries. Pipe desired number of whipped cream stars on the patch of blueberries.

❋ May be refrigerated 4 hours.

Serve proudly!

Serves 18 to 24

*Alternate layers of sliced strawberries and piped*
*whipped cream for the thirteen stripes.*

# Labor Day Picnic

MENU

CHILLED CUCUMBER AND
AVOCADO SOUP

PASTA SALAD WITH HAM AND PESTO
COLD STEAK SALAD
GOLDEN COUSCOUS
ARTICHOKE RICE MEDLEY

ASSORTED FRESH FRUIT
WITH TROPICAL DIPS
CREAMY PINEAPPLE DIP
STRAWBERRY GINGER DIP
CHEWY CHOCOLATE CARAMEL BARS
🦎

CITRUS ICED TEA

*Labor Day has come to signify the passing of summer and all its glory before the crisp days of autumn. Make your celebration a picnic to take advantage of the last warm days of the season. I've included here four of my favorite salad recipes. The pasta salad and the steak salad are wonderful ways to use leftover pasta and beef, and are versatile enough to appear both in a picnic basket and on a luncheon table. A cold couscous salad and artichoke hearts with curried rice provide a delightful change of pace from standard picnic fare. For dessert, there are two sweet, creamy dips for fresh fruit.*

*This menu for 8 is ideal for any outdoor meal on a sunny day.*

## Chilled Cucumber and Avocado Soup

The texture of this soup is of green velvet and its taste is subtle and mellow. If you can't find European or hot-house cucumbers, substitute regular ones. They must be peeled, seeded, and tasted to be sure they're not bitter. Cucumber soup should be eaten the day it is made—it turns bitter when left overnight. I serve this soup for a formal dinner party in shrimp cocktail glasses set over ice. Each bowl is topped with a cucumber round dolloped with sour cream and caviar.

1 large ripe avocado, peeled
6-to 8-ounce hot-house or European cucumber, or regular cucumber, seeded
1 large green onion, coarsely chopped
1½ cups chicken broth
3 tablespoons lemon juice
1 teaspoon dried dill or 1 tablespoon fresh chopped dill
Dash of sugar
½ cup sour cream
Salt and white pepper
Sour cream for garnish (optional)

Cut avocado into pieces and place them in food processor with metal blade or in blender; purée. Cut unpeeled cucumber into chunks. With the motor running, drop one piece of cucumber at a time through the feed tube. Add green onion and process until smooth. Add chicken broth, lemon juice, dill, sugar, and sour cream. Blend well. Season to taste with salt and pepper. Refrigerate until ready to serve or for several hours. Garnish with sour cream, if desired.

Serves 6

## Pasta Salad with Ham and Pesto

Pesto is growing more popular in America with the advent of the food processor and the availability of fresh basil. I add vinegar to a traditional pesto to turn it into a sensational salad dressing for leftover meat, rice, or vegetables.

1 pound penne or thin macaroni
12 ounces cooked ham, cut into 1-by-¼-inch strips (about 3 cups)
12 ounces Swiss cheese, cut into 1-by-¼-inch strips (about 3 cups)
½ cup sliced green onions
2 cups loosely packed fresh basil leaves
½ cup pine nuts or walnuts
½ cup grated Parmesan cheese
3 cloves garlic, peeled
¾ cup olive oil
½ cup white wine vinegar
Salt and pepper

Cook the penne or macaroni in 6 quarts boiling salted water until tender, but still firm to the bite. Drain and rinse with cold water to stop the cooking. Drain well. Place ham, cheese, green onions, and pasta in a large bowl.

To make pesto dressing, process basil, nuts, cheese, garlic, and oil in food processor with metal blade or in blender until mixture is well blended and smooth.

❋ Dressing may be refrigerated for 4 weeks in a jar with just enough olive oil over the top to seal it. Stir in olive oil before using.

❋ May be frozen.

Before using, stir in vinegar. Season to taste with salt and pepper.

Pour dressing over the salad and toss well. Cover and refrigerate for several hours for the flavors to blend.

❋ May be refrigerated overnight.

Serve at room temperature.

Serves 8

*Variation:* Chicken, beef, turkey, veal, or a combination of meats may be substituted for the ham.

## Cold Steak Salad

I chose to make this salad when I found out, with very little notice, that James Beard was coming to my school for lunch. It's so easy to make using the slicing blade of the food processor. A great way to use leftover roast, but certainly worth cooking a steak for. For a spicier dressing, add 1 to 2 teaspoons hot mustard to mustard vinaigrette.

**2-pound boneless sirloin steak, cut about 2 inches thick**
**Salt and freshly ground pepper**
½ **pound mushrooms, sliced**
½ **cup sliced green onions**
**14-ounce can hearts of palm, drained and sliced**
2 **tablespoons chopped chives**
2 **tablespoons chopped parsley**
2 **tablespoons chopped fresh dill or 2 teaspoons dried dill**
1 **egg**
⅓ **cup olive or salad oil**
3 **tablespoons tarragon vinegar or white wine vinegar**
4 **teaspoons Dijon mustard**
1 **teaspoon salt**
2 **teaspoons lemon juice**
1 **teaspoon Worcestershire sauce**
**Dash of Tabasco sauce**
2 **medium tomatoes, sliced (optional)**

Season both sides of the steak with salt and pepper. Broil or barbecue over high heat until medium rare, about 8 or 10 minutes per side. An instant read thermometer should register about 130°. Let the steak cool slightly. To slice in food processor, cut steak into pieces approximately as wide and as high as the feed tube. Place pieces on foil and freeze until just firm enough to be pierced with the tip of a knife. (Or freeze solid, and defrost to the right consistency.) Slice, using slicing disk of food processor. If slicing by hand, freeze steak slightly for ease in cutting. Slices should be about ⅛ inch thick. Place in large bowl.

Add the mushrooms, green onions, hearts of palm, chives, parsley, and dill. Make mustard vinaigrette by placing egg in food processor with metal blade or in blender. With machine running, slowly pour oil through the top. Add remaining ingredients (except tomatoes) and process until blended. Taste and adjust seasonings.

❋ Dressing may be refrigerated several days.

Pour dressing over salad and toss well.

❋ May be refrigerated for 6 to 8 hours.

Serve at room temperature. Garnish with tomato slices, if desired.

Serves 8

## Golden Couscous

Couscous is dry precooked semolina that is a delicious alternative to serving rice. My own version of this classic Moroccan dish is wonderful served hot and even better served cold as a salad. It draws its flavor from subtle hints of fragrant spices, dried fruits, and crisp vegetables and is perfect for buffet or picnic fare.

4 cups chicken broth
¼ cup plus 2 tablespoons olive oil
¼ teaspoon ground turmeric
¼ teaspoon ground cinnamon
¼ teaspoon powdered ginger
2 cups couscous
½ cup dark raisins
½ cup chopped dates
2 cups chopped zucchini (about 12 ounces)
1 cup chopped carrots
½ cup chopped onion
1 large tomato, seeded and chopped
15-ounce can chickpeas, drained
1½ tablespoons lemon juice
½ teaspoon salt
½ cup slivered almonds, toasted at 350° for 10 to 15 minutes and stirred occasionally

In a large saucepan, bring the broth, ¼ cup olive oil, turmeric, cinnamon, and ginger to a boil. Gradually stir in the couscous; boil for 1 to 2 minutes longer or until the liquid is absorbed. Remove from heat and stir in the raisins and dates. Cover tightly and let stand for 15 minutes.

Transfer couscous to a large mixing bowl and cool to room temperature. Stir in the zucchini, carrots, onion, tomato, and chickpeas. In a small bowl, combine the remaining 2 tablespoons olive oil, lemon juice, and salt. Pour over salad and toss well, breaking up any clumps. Cover and refrigerate 4 hours, for flavors to blend.

❊ May be refrigerated overnight.

Before serving, sprinkle with almonds.

Serves 8 to 10

## Artichoke Rice Medley

I doubt if you'll find this dish in India, but all its exotica can be tasted in this curry-flavored, amber-colored rice. The base of its dressing is the marinade for artichoke hearts, turned creamy with mayonnaise and zesty with seasonings.

**8-ounce box chicken-flavored Rice-A-Roni**
**Two 6-ounce jars marinated artichoke hearts**
**¼ cup chopped pimiento-stuffed olives**
**2 large green onions, sliced**
**8-ounce can water chestnuts, drained and coarsely chopped**
**⅓ cup mayonnaise**
**¼ teaspoon curry powder**
**¼ teaspoon salt**
**Freshly ground pepper**

Cook rice according to package directions. Remove to a large bowl. Drain artichoke hearts, reserving the marinade; chop coarsely. Add artichoke hearts, olives, onions, and water chestnuts to rice. In a small bowl, mix reserved artichoke marinade, mayonnaise, curry powder, salt, and pepper. Stir into warm rice. Serve warm or chilled.

✻ May be refrigerated for 2 days.

Serves 8

## Assorted Fresh Fruit with Tropical Dips

### Creamy Pineapple Dip

A blend of pineapple, lemon, and eggs is cooked to a silky custard, combined with whipping cream, and then chilled. It's easy to pack for a picnic, along with colorful fruit and cake cubes for dipping.

1 egg
1 egg yolk
¼ cup sugar
1½ teaspoons cornstarch
½ cup pineapple juice
2 tablespoons lemon juice
1 teaspoon grated lemon rind
½ cup whipping cream
Assorted fresh fruit for dipping, such as strawberries, peach slices, banana chunks, grapes, orange segments
Angel food, sponge, or pound cake cubes for dipping

In top of double boiler, mix egg, egg yolk, sugar, cornstarch, pineapple juice, lemon juice, and rind until well blended. Put over simmering water and cook, stirring constantly, until mixture just comes to a boil and thickens, about 20 minutes. Mixture will be very thick. Immediately remove from heat; cool. Whip cream to soft peaks and fold into pineapple mixture. Chill until ready to serve with fruit and cake cubes.

❉ Dip may be refrigerated for 2 days.

Makes 2 cups dip

### Strawberry Ginger Dip

Red ripe strawberries are puréed with a splash of Grand Marnier and simmered with melted marshmallows. Crystallized ginger is added for texture and special flavor, and it all turns a pretty pink color.

½ cup chopped strawberries
2 tablespoons Grand Marnier or orange juice
1 cup chopped whole or miniature marshmallows (about 2 ounces)
2 tablespoons finely diced crystallized ginger
¾ cup sour cream
Assorted fresh fruit for dipping, such as strawberries, peach slices, banana chunks, grapes, orange segments
Angel food, sponge, or pound cake cubes for dipping

In food processor with metal blade or in blender, process strawberries and Grand Marnier or orange juice until puréed. Remove to a small, heavy saucepan or double boiler. Add marshmallows. Cook, stirring over low heat or simmering water, until marshmallows are melted. Remove to bowl and stir in ginger. Cool; stir in sour cream. Refrigerate at least 4 hours before serving for flavors to blend.

❉ May be refrigerated for 4 days.
Serve with fruit and cake cubes.

Makes 1¼ cups dip

# *Chewy Chocolate Caramel Bars*

You can choose between the lighter German chocolate or the darker devil's food cake mix for the brownielike top and bottom layers. Sandwiched in between is a creamy sweet layer of melted caramel and chocolate chips.

**14-ounce package light-colored caramels (about 50)**
**⅔ cup evaporated milk**
**18½-ounce package German or devil's food chocolate cake mix**
**12 tablespoons (1½ sticks) butter, melted**
**1 cup chopped pecans or walnuts (about 4 ounces)**
**6-ounce package chocolate chips**

In a heavy, medium saucepan, combine caramels and ⅓ cup evaporated milk. Stir occasionally over low heat until melted.

In mixing bowl with electric mixer, beat cake mix, butter, and remaining ⅓ cup evaporated milk until dough is well mixed, about 1 minute; add nuts.

Grease a 9-by-13-inch baking pan. Press half the cake mixture into the pan. Bake at 350° for 10 minutes. Remove from oven; pour melted caramel over, and spread it evenly. Sprinkle chocolate chips on caramel. Using fingers, pinch handfuls of cake mixture together and drop pieces over the top. Spread lightly with a spatula, to cover the top as evenly as possible. Don't be concerned if the caramel is not completely covered. Return to oven and bake 20 to 25 minutes longer. Top should be crusty, but cake will look underdone; it will firm up as it cools. Refrigerate until firm enough to cut into bars.

❄ May be refrigerated for 1 week.

❆ May be frozen.

Serve cold or at room temperature.

Makes 32 bars

## Citrus Iced Tea

This lemon–orange tea is a refreshing thirst-quenching cross between lemonade, orangeade, and tea. Most tea tastes best freshly brewed, but the citrus juices in this tea keep it tasting fresh and fruity the following day.

  2 **quarts water**
 12 **single tea bags**
  1 **cup water**
 1⅓ **cups sugar**
  ½ **cup orange juice**
  1 **cup lemon juice**
    **Orange slices**
    **Lemon slices**
    **Ice cubes**

In medium saucepan, bring 2 quarts of water to a boil. Add tea bags and steep 10 minutes. Remove tea bags. In a small saucepan, slowly boil 1 cup water with sugar for 3 to 5 minutes or until sugar is dissolved. Add sugar syrup and citrus juices to tea. Remove to pitcher or bowl and refrigerate until chilled.

❋ May be refrigerated several hours.

Before serving, add fruit slices and ice cubes.

Makes 10 cups

# Election Returns Lap Party

## MENU

SAUCY SHRIMP
PUMPERNICKEL TOAST
WITH PARMESAN
❦

CHICKEN POT PIES
PEA SALAD WITH BACON
AND CASHEWS
WATERCRESS AND ORANGE SALAD
❦

CHOCOLATE MOCHA CHEESECAKE
❦

WINE RECOMMENDATION:
A SLIGHTLY SWEET, FRUITY
WINE SUCH AS A CHENIN BLANC

*Election Day evening is a great time for a casual dinner in front of the television set. Since all the dishes in this menu are spill-proof and require a minimum of silverware, they're perfect for eating off the lap.*

*Shrimp, onions, and black olives mingle flavors in a wine-vinegar marinade, and are served simply with toothpicks and napkins.*

*The savory chicken pies are my gourmet version of a freezer-to-oven "TV dinner": onions, carrots, mushrooms, and chicken breasts simmer in a white wine cream sauce, encased in golden puff pastry. The chocolate mocha cheesecake gets my vote as the evening's sure winner.*

*The recipes here serve 8.*

## Saucy Shrimp

Herbs, lemons, and olives complement shrimp in this robust and colorful marinade. Do not marinate the shrimp longer than four hours, for the flavors become too overpowering.

¼ cup salad oil
2 cloves garlic, crushed
1 tablespoon dry mustard
1 tablespoon salt
½ cup lemon juice
1 tablespoon red wine vinegar
1 bay leaf, crumbled
   Dash of cayenne pepper
1 lemon, thinly sliced
1 medium red onion, thinly sliced
1 cup pitted black olives or Greek olives, well drained
2 tablespoons chopped pimiento
2 tablespoons chopped fresh parsley
1½ to 2 pounds cooked medium or large shrimp

In a medium glass or plastic bowl, combine oil, garlic, dry mustard, salt, lemon juice, vinegar, bay leaf, and cayenne. Stir in lemon slices, onion slices, olives, pimiento, and parsley. Add shrimp, tossing until well coated. Refrigerate covered for 1 hour.

❋ May be refrigerated up to 4 hours.

Before serving, place all ingredients in a decorative glass serving bowl. Serve with frilly toothpicks.

Serves 8 to 10

## Pumpernickel Toast with Parmesan

Crispy brown rounds flavored with Parmesan are crunchy and good with Saucy Shrimp (preceding recipe), soup, salad, or any well-sauced hors d'oeuvre.

8-ounce package party-size pumpernickel bread (sliced ⅛ inch thick)
6 to 8 tablespoons butter, melted
½ cup grated Parmesan cheese

Place bread on baking sheet. Spread each side with melted butter. Sprinkle tops heavily with Parmesan cheese. Bake at 300° for 20 minutes. Bread will crisp as it cools. Leave uncovered at room temperature several hours or overnight before serving.

May be stored airtight in container for 1 week.

❋ May be frozen.

Makes about 20 slices

## Pea Salad with Bacon and Cashews

Bacon, celery, and cashews make this salad crispy, crunchy, and nutty while the sour cream binds it all together to rich smoothness.

10  slices bacon, diced
Two 10-ounce packages frozen peas,
    thawed
 1  cup chopped onion
 2  cups sliced celery
 1  pint (2 cups) sour cream
    Salt and pepper to taste
 1  cup salted cashews

In large skillet, cook bacon over moderate heat, stirring occasionally, until crisp. Drain on paper towels; set aside. In medium bowl, mix peas, onion, celery, and sour cream. Season with salt and pepper to taste. Refrigerate for several hours for flavors to blend.

❋ May be refrigerated overnight.

Before serving, stir in reserved bacon and cashews.

Serves 8

## Watercress and Orange Salad

Fresh fruit with salad greens provides a light, refreshing, and healthful change of pace. The distinctly sweet-and-sour dressing is a tangy addition to a colorful salad medley.

 2  heads Boston or butter lettuce
 1  cup watercress leaves
⅓  cup sugar
¼  cup red wine vinegar
1½ teaspoons lemon juice
¼  cup salad oil
 2  teaspoons chili sauce
½  teaspoon Worcestershire sauce
¼  teaspoon dry mustard
¼  teaspoon curry powder
    Few dashes of Tabasco sauce
 1  clove garlic, crushed
 2  oranges, peeled and cut into
    segments
 2  avocados, peeled and sliced
¾  cup coarsely chopped walnuts
    (optional)
    Salt and pepper

Wash lettuce and tear into bite-size pieces. Refrigerate until ready to use.

Make sweet-and-sour dressing: Mix sugar, vinegar, lemon juice, oil, chili sauce, Worcestershire, mustard, curry, Tabasco, and garlic in glass jar. Chill several hours before using. Shake well.

❋ Dressing may be refrigerated for 1 month. It is particularly good for any kind of fruit salad.

Before serving, mix lettuce, watercress, orange segments, avocado, and walnuts, if using, in a salad bowl. Toss with as much dressing as desired. You will have more dressing than you will need. Season to taste.

Serves 8

## Chicken Pot Pies

Don't let the long list of ingredients scare you off—the preparation time is relatively short because there is little precooking involved. Wine, cream, and chicken broth are the base of a creamy sauce topped with puff pastry that stays crispy and flaky. Puff pastry can usually be bought in the freezer section of supermarkets.

6 **whole chicken breasts, boned, skinned, and split (about 8 ounces each, net weight)**

¼ **pound (1 stick) butter or margarine**

½ **cup all-purpose flour**

1⅓ **cups chicken broth**

Cut chicken into 1-inch pieces; set aside. In large saucepan, melt butter. Stir in flour and cook over low heat, stirring, for 2 minutes. Remove from heat and whisk in chicken broth, wine, half-and-half, and lemon juice. Return to moderate heat and bring to a boil, whisking constantly. Remove from heat and stir in Tabas-

*Baked Chicken Pot Pies decorated with puff pastry leaves.*

1⅓ cups dry white wine or imported dry vermouth

1⅓ cups half-and-half

 4 tablespoons lemon juice

 ½ teaspoon Tabasco sauce

1½ teaspoons salt

 ½ teaspoon pepper

1½ teaspoons dried thyme

1½ teaspoons dried basil

 ½ cup chopped fresh parsley

1½ cups finely chopped carrots (about 8 ounces)

 1 pound mushrooms, coarsely chopped

1½ cups frozen whole onions (about 6 ounces)

 1 pound frozen puff pastry, defrosted in refrigerator

 1 egg mixed with 1 tablespoon water for wash

co sauce, salt, pepper, thyme, and basil. Taste for seasoning; cool. Stir in parsley, carrots, mushrooms, onions, and chicken. Divide among eight 12- to 16-ounce ovenproof casseroles or soup bowls.

On a lightly floured board, roll one sheet of pastry ¼ inch thick. Place one of the casseroles or soup bowls on pastry and cut a circle about 1 inch larger than the top rim of the bowl. Cut a ¼-inch hole in the center of the circle. (A small pastry tip works well for this.) Place pastry over top of bowl, pressing it over the sides to seal. Repeat with remaining pastry. Cut scraps of pastry into decorations, flowers, leaves, initials, etc.

When all of the bowls are covered, make "chimneys" out of freezer foil as pictured. Each "chimney" should be about 2 inches high and wide enough to cover the hole and extend about ½ inch into the pie. The foil chimneys will help keep the juices from spilling over onto the pies as they cook. Place decorations on top.

✳ May be refrigerated covered with foil overnight.

❄ May be frozen for 1 month. It is not necessary to defrost before baking.

Preheat oven to 400°. Place pies on rimmed baking sheets. Brush pastry with egg wash. Bake unfrozen pies for 20 to 25 minutes or until pastry is golden. Bake frozen pies for 35 to 40 minutes or until golden. Don't be concerned if some of the filling bubbles over onto the crust as they bake.

To keep pastry puffed, let pies sit 10 to 15 minutes before removing foil chimneys. They will still be very hot.

Serves 8

*Top left: Place filled bowls on puff pastry and cut out circles about one inch larger in diameter than top of bowls. Cut out small circle from center of each round. Brush rim of bowl with egg wash, place circles of dough on top and press dough onto sides of bowl.*

*Bottom left: Form chimneys of foil and insert into holes.*

## Chocolate Mocha Cheesecake

There's a mousselike consistency to this cheesecake which makes it much lighter than most yet it is still extremely rich. The top of the cheesecake is studded with chocolate chips, and the sparkle of Kahlúa enriches the deep chocolate flavor.

1½ packages (8½ ounces each) chocolate wafer cookies (about 60 cookies)

¼ pound (1 stick) unsalted butter, at room temperature for food processor, melted for mixing bowl

12-ounce package chocolate chips

Two 8-ounce packages cream cheese, at room temperature

1¼ cups sugar

6 large eggs

1 cup whipping cream

2 teaspoons vanilla extract

¼ cup Kahlúa or strong coffee

Make chocolate wafer crust: Crush cookies in food processor with metal blade or with rolling pin. Measure 3 cups crumbs. Return them to food processor or place them in a mixing bowl. Add butter and mix until blended. Press into bottom and three-fourths up the sides of a 9-by-3-inch springform pan. Refrigerate while preparing the filling.

❋ May be refrigerated several days.

❋ May be frozen.

Reserve ½ cup chocolate chips and set aside. Melt remaining chips in a double boiler over simmering water. In a mixing bowl with electric mixer, beat cream cheese and sugar until light and fluffy, scraping sides often. Add eggs one at a time, beating constantly. Mix in unwhipped cream, vanilla, Kahlúa or coffee, and melted chocolate. Mix well until blended, scraping sides once or twice. Pour filling into crust. Sprinkle reserved ½ cup chocolate chips over top. Bake at 350° for 1 hour. Turn off oven and leave cake in oven to cool, at least 2 hours. The cake will sink and crack as it cools. When completely cool, cover and refrigerate overnight before serving.

❋ May be refrigerated for 1 week.

❋ May be frozen. Defrost in refrigerator overnight.

Before serving, remove sides of springform pan by placing pan on a bowl which is smaller in circumference then the springform. Release sides and let them slip down. Leave cake on springform bottom and place on serving platter.

Serves 10 to 12

# 7

# FALL FARE

# Treats for Halloween

MENU

CARAMEL NUT CORN
SPICE COOKIE GOBLINS
CHOCOLATE-
ALMOND TOFFEE
ORANGE CANDIED NUTS
GINGER SPICE CAKE WITH
LEMON GLAZE

HOT MULLED WINE
WITCHES' BREW

*It's a cold, starless night and the wind is howling bitterly through the trees. Several black cats are crying into the night, and there is no sign of life on the street except for miniature masked goblins and wicked witches parading with neon orange shopping bags. Soon they'll be knocking on your door, crying out with little voices, "Trick or treat!"*

*Yes, it's Halloween, and unless you've got a trick up your sleeve you had best be armed with trays of delectable haunted and heavenly Caramel Nut Corn, Spice Cookie Goblins, and some devilishly delicious Chocolate-Almond Toffee.*

*Once the last troop of bounty-laden haunters has left your doorstep, treat yourself with some hot mulled wine and serve your own ghouls and goblins some warm spiced cider as they inspect the evening's take.*

*Clockwise from lower lefthand corner:*
*Spice Cookie Goblins, Ginger Spice Cake,*
*Orange Candied Nuts, Chocolate-Almond*
*Toffee, and Caramel Nut Corn.*

## Caramel Nut Corn

This is the real thing—crunchy, nutty, caramelized popcorn that's out of this world.

12 cups popped popcorn (½ cup
   unpopped corn)
½ pound (2 sticks) unsalted butter
2 cups light, or golden, brown
   sugar, packed
1 teaspoon salt
8 tablespoons light corn syrup
½ teaspoon baking soda
1 teaspoon vanilla extract
6 ounces whole unblanched
   almonds (1½ cups)
6 ounces pecan halves (1½ cups)

Place popcorn in a large shallow roasting pan or two 9-by-13-inch baking pans. Set aside.

In large heavy saucepan (about 4-quart), melt butter over low heat. Stir in brown sugar, salt, and corn syrup. Bring to a boil, stirring constantly. Insert candy thermometer and boil without stirring until thermometer reaches 285°, or syrup reaches the soft crack stage. Immediately remove from heat; stir in soda and vanilla. The baking soda will cause the mixture to foam up and become frothy.

Pour syrup over popped corn; using 2 wooden spoons, mix well. Bake at 250° for 15 minutes; stir well. Bake 15 minutes longer. Stir in nuts. Bake 30 more minutes, stirring well every 10 minutes. Turn out onto waxed paper. Cool completely. Break apart. Store in airtight containers.

May be stored in airtight containers for 3 months.

Makes 12 cups

## Spice Cookie Goblins

The delicately spiced cookie dough is fragrant with cinnamon, cloves, and ginger. The dough is rolled between sheets of waxed paper, placed in the freezer, then cut into shapes when frozen—it's much easier to cut out cookies from frozen cookie dough. Pint-sized volunteers love to help bake these cookies as well as eat them. This recipe is large and can easily be cut in half.

½ pound (2 sticks) butter or
  margarine, at room temperature
½ cup sugar
½ cup dark corn syrup
3 cups all-purpose flour
1½ teaspoons ground ginger
1½ teaspoons ground cinnamon
½ teaspoon ground cloves
  Pecan halves, sliced almonds,
  assorted nuts
  Mini chocolate chips
  Silver ball decorations
1 egg white, lightly beaten

Make cookie dough by creaming butter or margarine and sugar in large mixing bowl until light and fluffy. Mix in corn syrup. Turn mixer to low speed and slowly beat in the flour and spices. Remove to work surface and knead into a ball. Divide into three parts and shape each into a flat disc. Wrap in plastic wrap and refrigerate until well chilled.

❋ May be refrigerated for 5 days.

❊ May be frozen.

Remove a third of the dough from refrigerator about 5 minutes before rolling. Place a sheet of waxed paper on work surface. Lightly flour the paper. Place dough in center of paper. Lightly flour another sheet of waxed paper and place on top of dough. Roll dough between sheets of waxed paper until it is approximately ⅛ inch thick. Place dough and waxed paper in freezer. Repeat with remaining 2 balls of dough. When firm, remove one pastry sheet to work surface. Pull off top sheet of waxed paper. Turn over and pull off remaining waxed paper. Cut into desired shapes, using 2-inch to 4-inch cookie cutters. Decorate as desired, dabbing egg white on the back of decorations to hold them in place. Place cookies on baking sheets lined with parchment paper or greased. Repeat with remaining dough.

Bake cookies at 350° for 8 to 10 minutes, or until lightly browned. If baking 2 sheets at a time, reverse positions halfway through baking time. Cool slightly before removing from pans.

May be stored in airtight containers for 2 weeks.

❊ May be frozen.

Makes about 72 two-inch cookies

## Orange Candied Nuts

Pecans and almonds are coated with an orange-flavored sugar syrup accented by fresh orange peel.

 2 cups sugar
½ cup orange juice
 1 tablespoon white vinegar
¼ cup grated orange peel (from about 3 large oranges)
½ pound pecan halves
½ pound whole blanched almonds

Butter a 15½-by-10½-by-1-inch jelly-roll pan and set aside. Place the sugar and orange juice in a 3- to 4-quart saucepan. Bring the mixture to a boil over moderately high heat. Insert a candy thermometer, add the vinegar, and boil the syrup until it reaches 300° on a candy thermometer, or until the syrup reaches the hard crack stage. Remove from heat and add the orange peel and nuts to the syrup. Stir to coat nuts evenly. Press mixture into prepared pan, flattening with a spatula into a single layer. Cool to room temperature. Separate the nuts by breaking into pieces.

May be stored in airtight containers for several months.

Makes 4 cups nuts

## Ginger Spice Cake with Lemon Glaze

Imagine a cake with all the flavor of gingerbread, but with the texture of a spice cake. This cake is lighter in color than most gingerbreads, and it makes a morning cup of coffee or an afternoon cup of tea very special.

12 tablespoons (1½ sticks) unsalted butter
 1 cup light, or golden, brown sugar, packed
 ¾ cup dark molasses
 ¾ cup light corn syrup
 ½ cup milk
 1 teaspoon baking soda
 2 tablespoons hot water
2½ cups all-purpose flour
 1 teaspoon ground ginger
 1 teaspoon ground cloves
 1 teaspoon ground cinnamon
 2 large eggs
1½ cups powdered sugar
 2 to 4 tablespoons lemon juice
   Dash of yellow food coloring (optional)

Grease a 9-by-13-inch baking pan. Line bottom with waxed paper. Grease the paper. In a medium saucepan, heat butter, brown sugar, molasses, corn syrup, and milk until butter melts. In a small bowl, dissolve baking soda in hot water. Stir into butter mixture in saucepan. Place flour, ginger, cloves, cinnamon, and eggs in food processor with metal blade or in mixing bowl. Turn on motor and slowly pour in the warm butter mixture. Mix, scraping down sides, until well blended. Pour into prepared pan. Bake at 325° for 50 minutes or until skewer or toothpick inserted in center comes out clean. Cool 10 minutes. Invert cake onto cake rack, remove cake from pan, and cool thoroughly.

Make lemon glaze: Place powdered sugar in bowl. Stir in 2 tablespoons lemon juice. If too thick, add additional lemon juice a teaspoon at a time, until mixture is spreading consistency. Tint with food coloring if you like. Spread or drizzle glaze over smoothest side of cake.

May be stored in airtight container at room temperature for 1 week.

❀ May be frozen.

Serves 16

## Chocolate-Almond Toffee

Sandwiched between heavenly chocolate coated with toasted almonds is a rich, creamy, and crunchy caramel toffee. Be sure to use a *metal* baking pan only, so that you can bang it against the counter to remove the toffee.

½ **pound (2 sticks) unsalted butter**
½ **pound (2 sticks) unsalted margarine**
2 **cups sugar**
6 **tablespoons water**
2 **tablespoons light corn syrup**
1 **pound milk or semisweet chocolate, coarsely chopped**
2 **cups chopped almonds (8 ounces), toasted at 350° for 10 to 15 minutes and stirred occasionally**

Grease a 9-by-13-inch metal baking pan with butter or shortening. In a heavy medium saucepan (about 4-quart), combine butter, margarine, sugar, water, and corn syrup. Bring to a boil over moderate heat, stirring occasionally. Insert a candy thermometer and boil over moderately high heat until the thermometer reaches 300° or syrup reaches the hard crack stage. If the candy begins to turn dark around the sides of the pan, lower the heat. After the candy reaches 250°, it will be necessary to stir it often to prevent the bottom from scorching. Immediately pour the toffee into the prepared pan. Cool thoroughly.

When candy is firm, remove it from pan by turning the pan upside down and rapping it once or twice on a counter top. Melt the chocolate in a double boiler over hot water and spread half of it on one side of toffee. Sprinkle with half the almonds; press them in with the palm of your hand. Cool until chocolate hardens. Turn uncoated side up. Spread with remaining chocolate and press in remaining almonds. Refrigerate until chocolate hardens. Break into pieces by inserting the tip of a knife at the points where you want the candy to break. Store in airtight containers.

❋ May be stored at room temperature for 1 month or refrigerated for 3 months.

❋ May be frozen.

Makes 1½ pounds toffee

## Hot Mulled Wine

This is a popular recipe from my "Gifts from the Kitchen" classes. It makes a charming gift when given with a bottle of wine and a card inscribed with directions. It's easy and just the right idea for crisp fall weather.

MULLED WINE MIX
1½ **cups sugar**
1½ **teaspoons ground cinnamon**
½ **teaspoon ground cloves**
½ **teaspoon ground allspice**

Mix all ingredients together. Store in airtight container.

May be stored at room temperature indefinitely.

1½ **teaspoons Mulled Wine Mix**
⅓ **cup water**
⅔ **cup dry red wine**
  **Cinnamon stick**

FOR SINGLE SERVING
In small saucepan, bring mix and water to a boil. Add wine and heat until hot; do not boil. Serve in mug with cinnamon stick stirrer.

Makes 1 cup

¾ **cup Mulled Wine Mix**
3 **cups water**
1½-**liter bottle dry red wine**
  **Cinnamon sticks**

FOR PUNCH BOWL
In large saucepan, bring mix and water to a boil. Add wine and heat until hot; do not boil. Serve in punch cups or mugs with cinnamon stick stirrers.

Makes nine 1-cup servings

## Witches' Brew

Warm spiced cider is particularly satisfying after a cold night of trick-or-treating. Serve in hearty mugs in front of a roaring fireplace.

2 **quarts (8 cups) apple cider**
½ **cup light, or golden, brown sugar,**
  **packed**
1 **teaspoon whole allspice**
1 **teaspoon whole cloves**
¼ **teaspoon salt**
1 **lemon, sliced**
1 **orange, sliced**
1 **cinnamon stick**
1 **orange, cut into 8 wedges, studded**
  **with cloves**

In large saucepan, combine cider, brown sugar, allspice, cloves, salt, lemon and orange slices, and cinnamon stick. Slowly bring to a boil over moderate heat. Cover and simmer for 20 minutes. Strain.

❋ May be refrigerated overnight and reheated.

Pour warm cider into punch bowl or mugs. Garnish with clove-studded orange wedges.

Makes eight 1-cup servings

# A Bountiful Thanksgiving

MENU

HARVEST VEGETABLE PATCH WITH
BACON ALMOND DIP
❧

PURÉE OF PUMPKIN SOUP
❧

MARINATED ROAST TURKEY WITH
TRADITIONAL GIBLET GRAVY
❧

SAUSAGE APPLE STUFFING OR
DOUBLE NUT OYSTER STUFFING
❧

ORANGE PRALINE YAMS OR
APRICOT-GLAZED SWEET POTATOES
❧

CRANBERRY RASPBERRY RELISH OR
FRESH CRANBERRY SORBET
❧

SUGAR-AND-SPICE YAM MUFFINS
❧

GREEN BEANS WITH CASHEWS
❧

PUMPKIN CHEESE ROLL
CRANBERRY-PEAR TART
❧

WINE RECOMMENDATION:
A DRY AND SPICY WINE WITH A HINT
OF SWEETNESS, SUCH AS A
GEWÜRZTRAMINER—
OR SPARKLING APPLE CIDER

The very mention of Thanksgiving brings to mind a warm country kitchen and lots of good things to eat. The following menu is meant for overindulgence. The good, rich stuffings, sweet potatoes, muffins, and tarts might be more than we normally allow ourselves any other day of the year, but they are an indispensable part of Thanksgiving and its theme of abundance.

These recipes are some of my best. They reflect a creative approach to favorite Thanksgiving foods—a Fresh Cranberry Sorbet, for example, instead of cranberry sauce—while still maintaining the gracious traditions of this holiday.

Each individual recipe states the number of people that the recipe serves. However, if you are preparing every dish in the menu, the recipes will go a lot further. They can all be expanded or divided to accommodate the size of your guest list.

*Clockwise from lower lefthand corner: Apricot-Glazed Sweet Potatoes, Purée of Pumpkin Soup in pumpkin tureen, turkey stuffed with Sausage Apple Stuffing, Cranberry Raspberry Relish, Cranberry-Pear Tart, Sugar-and-Spice Yam Muffins, Pumpkin Cheese Roll, Fresh Cranberry Sorbet, Sausage Apple Stuffing.*

## Harvest Vegetable Patch

This is great fun and a sure way to bring smiles. To make the corn-on-the-cob scarecrow, buy 2 ears of corn, so you'll have extra husk and silk.

### VEGETABLES FOR DIPPING

**Carrots, peeled**
**Celery**
**Radishes**
**Cauliflower**
**Broccoli flowerets**
**Turnip or jicama, peeled**
**Green onions**

Cut into dipping-size pieces. Place in a bowl of ice water for at least 4 hours to crisp.

❋ May be refrigerated in ice water overnight.

Trimmed snowpeas and mushrooms, zucchini in slices or wedges, drained baby corn, and olives may also be used and require no soaking.

### EQUIPMENT FOR HARVEST VEGETABLE PATCH

**1 ear untrimmed corn on the cob**
  **Whole cloves**
  **String**
  **Wooden bamboo skewers**
**1 potato**
  **Toothpicks**
  **Large platter**
  **Seed packets (available from nurseries), such as carrot, zucchini, radish, etc.**
  **Fresh parsley**
  **Bacon Almond Dip (see following recipe)**

Remove outside layers of husk. Reserve leaves and some silk for arms. Pull silk down from one side of corn. Make a face in the corn, using cloves for eyes and mouth. Wrap pieces of husk around a piece of corn silk and a bamboo skewer, securing tightly with string to form each arm. Attach arms to corn with bamboo skewers. Slice a piece off the bottom and top of the potato so it lies flat. Using toothpicks, attach scarecrow to potato to stand it up. Place on large platter. Insert toothpicks into seed packets and anchor them into the potato, surrounding the scarecrow. Fill in spaces with parsley, covering the potato completely. Surround with assorted vegetables. Serve with dip.

*Pull off outer leaves of corn to use for arms. Pull silk down from one side of corn for face. Insert cloves for eyes, nose, and mouth. Place one or two leaves on counter. Place some silk hanging over one end. Insert wooden skewer and tightly roll leaves together. Tie with string. Attach arms to corn with skewers.*

*Bacon Almond Dip and cut raw vegetables with corn-on-the-cob scarecrow.*

## Bacon Almond Dip

This dip is really different, with the crunchy flavor of crispy bacon and toasted almonds. Try serving it in a scooped-out acorn squash.

1 pound bacon, chopped
Two 3-ounce packages cream cheese
   with chives, at room temperature
1 cup sour cream
2 tablespoons chili sauce
¼ teaspoon Tabasco sauce
   Freshly ground pepper
¼ cup chopped green onions
½ cup slivered almonds, toasted at
   350° for 10 to 15 minutes and
   stirred occasionally

In large skillet, cook bacon over moderate heat, stirring occasionally, until crisp. Drain on paper towels. In food processor with metal blade, or in mixing bowl, mix cream cheese, sour cream, chili sauce, Tabasco, and pepper to taste. Add green onions, bacon, and almonds and process or mix until blended but still chunky. Remove to a bowl and refrigerate until ready to serve.

✳ May be refrigerated for 2 days.

❄ May be frozen. Defrost in refrigerator.

If dip is too thick, stir in additional sour cream. Serve with vegetables.

Makes 2 cups; serves 8 to 10

## Purée of Pumpkin Soup

I have a friend and colleague who is a purist. He loves this soup, but keeps insisting it would be better with fresh pumpkin. One day I made two batches, one with canned and one with fresh, and took them to Elmer Dills, a popular Los Angeles restaurant critic who has a Sunday radio show. I asked him, on the air, which soup he liked best. He pointed to the canned pumpkin soup. For those skeptics who remain purists, a three-pound pumpkin, cut into cubes, cooked in water, and drained will yield one pound of pumpkin purée.

4 tablespoons (½ stick) butter or margarine
1 large onion, chopped
1 medium leek, white part only, chopped
1 pound canned or fresh pumpkin purée
4 cups chicken broth
1 teaspoon salt
½ teaspoon curry powder
¼ teaspoon ground nutmeg
¼ teaspoon ground white pepper
¼ teaspoon ground ginger
1 bay leaf
1 cup half-and-half

In medium soup pot, melt butter or margarine. Sauté onion and leek, stirring occasionally, until soft. Stir in pumpkin, chicken broth, salt, spices, and bay leaf. Bring to a boil. Lower heat and simmer, uncovered, for 15 minutes, stirring occasionally. Remove the bay leaf. Purée the mixture in batches in blender for a smoother texture or in food processor fitted with metal blade.

❋ May be refrigerated for 2 days.

❋ May be frozen.

Return to soup pot. Add half-and-half and cook over moderate heat, stirring occasionally, until heated through. Adjust seasonings.

Serves 6 to 8

## Marinated Roast Turkey

Before I knew much about cooking, I would get up at 6 A.M. Thanksgiving Day in order to get my 24-pound turkey stuffed and into a slow oven in order to get it out in time for dinner.

I have since learned that, no matter what method you use, the most important fact about roasting a turkey is not to overcook it—now I stay in bed until 8 A.M.! Most turkeys are cooked until the dark meat is done, which results in a dry breast. I am including a timetable, but a meat thermometer is more accurate, so cook your turkey until it registers 175°, 10° less than usually suggested. The dark meat will be done and the breast meat will still be moist and juicy.

I prefer to roast a turkey breast side down for the first half of baking time, and then turn it breast side up for the remainder. Juices will run into the breast and the meat will ultimately be juicier. But one year I tried to turn over a 24-pound turkey and it landed on the floor. Since the juices are better off in the turkey than on me, I roast the turkey breast side up if it's 16 pounds or larger.

12- to 20-pound turkey (allow
    approximately 1 pound per
    average serving)
1 cup vegetable oil
1 teaspoon poultry seasoning
2 cloves garlic, crushed
2 teaspoons seasoned salt
½ teaspoon pepper
    Sausage Apple Stuffing (see
      recipe below)
        or
    Double Nut Oyster Stuffing (see
      recipe below)
    Traditional Giblet Gravy (see
      following recipe)
    Parsley sprigs

Remove giblets and any fat from inside turkey cavity. Dry turkey inside and out with paper towels. In a small bowl, mix oil, poultry seasoning, garlic, seasoned salt, and pepper. Rub all over outside of turkey. Marinate in refrigerator several hours or overnight.

Remove from refrigerator at least 1 hour before cooking. Lightly spoon in desired stuffing; do not pack. Skewer cavity closed with turkey lacers or trussing needle. Tie legs together. Place turkey on rack in shallow roasting pan breast side up if 16 pounds or over and breast side down if smaller. Bake at 325° for approximately 20 minutes per pound for a bird up to 16 pounds; add 12 minutes per pound for each additional pound. Baste occasionally. If roasting breast side down, turn breast up halfway through the roasting time. If turkey gets too brown, cover loosely with a tent of foil, pressing it lightly into the drumstick and breast ends, making sure it does not touch the top and sides. Two-thirds through the roasting time, untie drumsticks so heat can reach the cavity. When you think turkey is almost done, insert an instant read thermometer into the thickest part of thigh, but not touching the bone. It should read 175°. Turkey is done when drumstick moves freely in its socket, and when the thickest part of the thigh is pierced, the juices run clear. There should be at least a cup or more of turkey juices in roasting pan when turkey is done. Remove turkey to carving board. Let rest for at least 20 minutes before carving.

While turkey rests, make giblet gravy. Remove skewers and string from turkey. Carve and place on serving platter. Serve with gravy.

TURKEY ROASTING TIMETABLE

For turkeys chilled and stuffed just before roasting. If unstuffed, subtract 30 minutes roasting time from birds over 12 pounds.

6 to 8 pounds: 3½ to 4 hours
8 to 12 pounds: 4 to 4½ hours
12 to 16 pounds: 4½ to 5½ hours
16 to 20 pounds: 5½ to 7 hours
20 to 26 pounds: 7 to 8½ hours

## Traditional Giblet Gravy

Thick gravies are out, along with thick waistlines. The proportions in my recipe give you "coat the spoon" gravy. If you prefer it thicker, use 2 tablespoons each of fat and flour per cup of liquid.

Gravymaking can send first-time or nervous cooks into a panic when their guests are waiting and the turkey's growing cold. To make your gravy ahead, substitute butter or oil for the fat skimmed from the turkey drippings, adding the juices from the roast turkey right before serving. Treat yourself to a great new gadget: a gravy separator that helps separate the fat from the drippings.

**Turkey giblets and neck**
**1 large onion, sliced (about 1 cup)**
**¼ cup celery leaves**
**½ cup sliced carrots**
**½ cup dry white wine**
**2 cups chicken broth**
**Turkey drippings**
**All-purpose or instant-blending flour**
**Salt and pepper**

Cut turkey neck and heart in half. If using liver, refrigerate until ready to use. Place giblets in medium saucepan. Add onion, celery leaves, carrots, wine, and chicken broth. Bring to a boil, lower heat, and simmer covered for 2 to 2½ hours or until gizzards are tender. If using liver, add it the last half hour. Strain, pressing on vegetables; reserve broth. Chop giblets, meat from neck, and liver, if using. Cover and set aside.

❋ May be made several hours ahead and refrigerated.

When turkey is done, pour drippings from roasting pan into gravy separator or pitcher. If using pitcher, place in freezer for 10 to 15 minutes for fat to rise to top; skim off fat. For each cup of gravy, measure 1 tablespoon fat back into roasting pan. Add 1 tablespoon flour for each tablespoon fat. Cook, stirring constantly over low heat, scraping up brown bits from bottom of the pan, until mixture is golden. Slowly whisk in pan juices and enough giblet broth to make 1 cup. Bring to a boil, stirring and scraping up all brown bits from bottom of the pan. Stir in chopped giblets and liver. Simmer 5 minutes and season to taste.

# Sausage Apple Stuffing

An old-fashioned stuffing that's soft and extra-smooth with sour cream, Madeira, and an enrichment of chicken livers. Apples and sausage add a little sugar and a little spice to this savory stuffing.

**24-ounce loaf egg bread**
**6 tablespoons butter or margarine**
**½ pound chicken livers, cleaned and cut in half**
**1 pound bulk pork sausage**
**2 cups chopped onion**
**½ cup finely chopped celery**
**2 medium apples, peeled, cored, and chopped (about 1½ cups)**
**3 cloves garlic, crushed**
**½ cup chopped fresh parsley**
**1 teaspoon dried thyme**
**¾ cup chopped pecans**
**2 eggs**
**½ pint (1 cup) sour cream**
**¼ cup Madeira wine**
**Salt and pepper**

Preheat oven to 200°. Cut crusts off bread and cut bread into ½-inch cubes. You should have 8 cups of bread cubes. Place on baking sheets and toast until cubes are dry, stirring occasionally, about 25 minutes. Remove to large bowl.

In a large skillet, melt 2 tablespoons butter or margarine. Sauté chicken livers until brown on the outside but still pink inside, about 3 to 5 minutes. Do not overcook. Remove livers with a slotted spoon; place on chopping board and chop fine. Add to bowl with bread cubes.

Add sausage to same skillet and cook, stirring, until all pink is gone from the meat. Place in bowl with bread cubes. Melt remaining 4 tablespoons butter or margarine in same skillet. Sauté onions, celery, apples, and garlic, stirring often until soft, about 8 minutes. Remove to bowl with bread cubes. Add parsley, thyme, and pecans.

In a small bowl, combine eggs, sour cream, and Madeira. Pour over stuffing and toss lightly but thoroughly. Season to taste.

❋ May be refrigerated covered overnight.

❋ May be frozen for 1 month.

Use to stuff turkey (see recipe). Or place in large shallow casserole. Bake covered at 350° for 30 to 45 minutes; uncover and bake 30 minutes longer or until top is crisp. Baste with turkey drippings, if desired.

Makes stuffing for a 14-pound turkey; serves 10 to 12

## Apricot-Glazed Sweet Potatoes

This casserole is not as sweet as the Orange Praline Yams (preceding recipe), but just as wonderful. The dried apricots add a slightly tart flavor as they are layered with the sweet potatoes. The top is richly glazed and studded with pecan halves.

**1 pound dried apricots**
**12-ounce can apricot nectar**
**1 cup water**
**4 pounds sweet potatoes or yams**
**½ cup light, or golden, brown sugar, packed**
**6 tablespoons butter or margarine, melted**
**2 tablespoons orange juice**
**1 tablespoon grated orange rind**
**½ cup pecan halves**

Place apricots in medium saucepan and cover with apricot nectar and water. Let stand 1 hour for fruit to soften. Place over moderate heat and simmer, uncovered, until apricots are very tender, about 40 minutes. Cool and drain well, reserving the liquid.

Scrub sweet potatoes or yams. Place on baking sheet and bake at 400° for 30 to 40 minutes or until tender when pierced with a fork. Cool; peel and cut into lengthwise slices about ¼ inch thick. Lightly grease a 2-quart (7 by 11 inches) shallow baking dish. Arrange a layer of sweet potatoes in the dish. Cover with a layer of apricots. Repeat, alternating layer of potatoes and apricots. Sprinkle top with brown sugar.

In a small bowl, mix ½ cup reserved apricot liquid with melted butter, orange juice, and orange rind. Pour mixture over the layers.

❋ May be refrigerated covered for 2 days.

Before serving, bring to room temperature. Bake uncovered at 375° for 40 minutes, basting occasionally with liquid in bottom of dish. Remove from oven and place pecan halves on top. Return to oven and bake until casserole is bubbling and top is well glazed, 5 to 10 minutes. Let stand 10 minutes before cutting into squares.

Serves 12 to 14

## Green Beans with Cashews

Green beans are at their best when parboiled in advance and then heated quickly on top of the stove just before serving. This is a sure way to retain the color and crispness that goes so splendidly with crunchy golden cashews.

3 **pounds fresh green beans**
**Salt**
¼ **pound (1 stick) butter or**
**margarine**
2 **teaspoons lemon juice**
1 **cup salted cashews**
**Salt and pepper**

Trim ends off beans. Bring a large pot of salted water to boil. Add beans, bring water back to a boil, and slowly boil the beans, uncovered, for 8 to 12 minutes, or until tender but still crunchy or firm to the bite. Immediately pour into colander and run under cold water for 3 to 4 minutes to stop the cooking. Remove to paper towels and dry.

❊ May be refrigerated covered overnight.

Before serving, bring to room temperature. Melt butter or margarine in large skillet or wok. Add beans, lemon juice, and cashews; cook over moderately high heat, stirring and tossing gently, until heated through. Season to taste with salt and pepper.

Serves 10

## Cranberry Raspberry Relish

Lift cranberries into the extraordinary with the fragrance of red raspberries. This extra-special relish is quickly assembled when a food processor chops the apples and the cranberries.

1 **pound fresh cranberries, finely**
**chopped**
2 **tart green apples, peeled, cored,**
**and finely diced**
1 **cup sugar**
½ **cup orange marmalade**
10-**ounce package frozen raspberries,**
**thawed and drained**
1 **teaspoon lemon juice or to taste**

Mix all ingredients in large bowl.

❊ May be refrigerated, covered, for 1 month.

Spoon relish into serving bowl.

Makes 6 cups; serves 12

## Fresh Cranberry Sorbet

This fresh cranberry sorbet is a briskly refreshing complement to a heavy Thanksgiving dinner. It soothes and reawakens taste buds to its tartly sweet and icy flavor. Frozen in ramekins and removed right before serving, it's easy and pretty.

**1 pound fresh cranberries (about 4 cups)**
**4 cups water**
**1¾ cups sugar**
**1 teaspoon lemon juice**

GARNISH
**Fresh cranberries**
**Sugar**
**Mint sprigs**

Wash the cranberries in a colander under cold running water. Place them in a medium saucepan with 4 cups water. Bring to a boil over high heat; reduce the heat to low, cover tightly, and simmer for 10 to 12 minutes or until they can be easily mashed against the side of the pan with a spoon. Stir in sugar and lemon juice.

Purée the cranberries and cooking liquid in batches in the food processor with metal blade. Strain into a bowl; discard the skins. Pour the mixture into 2 or 3 ice cube trays. Freeze until solid.

❈ May be frozen for one week.

Place a few cubes of cranberry ice into food processor with metal blade. Process until broken up and continue processing while dropping cubes one at a time through feed tube. You will need to do this step in batches. As each batch becomes finely puréed and snowy, remove to a bowl. Place in freezer. When all batches have been processed and sorbet has hardened somewhat, scoop into 8 small ramekins, custard cups, or soufflé dishes.

To garnish: Place cranberries on cake rack over cookie sheet. Brush cranberries lightly with water. Sprinkle lightly with sugar. Place on top of sorbet.

Cover loosely with foil and return to freezer.

❈ May be frozen overnight.

Before serving place a sprig of mint next to cranberries.

Makes about 1 quart; serves 8

## Sugar-and-Spice Yam Muffins

It wouldn't be Thanksgiving in my house if I didn't bake these muffins. They have a quick-bread texture, but the yams make them particularly moist, soft, and flavorful. Sweet potatoes can also be used. They're spicy with cinnamon and nutmeg and golden-brown on top.

¼ pound (1 stick) butter or margarine, at room temperature
1 cup sugar
1-pound can yams, drained, or 1¼ cups cooked mashed fresh yams or sweet potatoes
2 large eggs
1¼ cups milk
1 teaspoon lemon extract
2½ cups all-purpose flour
1½ tablespoons baking powder
¾ teaspoon ground nutmeg
½ teaspoon salt
1 heaping teaspoon ground cinnamon
½ cup chopped walnuts or pecans
¼ cup sugar mixed with 1 tablespoon ground cinnamon, for topping
Butter

In a mixing bowl or food processor with metal blade, cream butter and sugar until light and fluffy. Beat in yams or sweet potatoes. Add eggs one at a time, beating well after each addition. Mix in milk and lemon extract. Turn machine off and add flour, baking powder, nutmeg, salt, and cinnamon. Mix until incorporated; do not overmix. Stir in nuts.

Grease twenty-four 2½-inch muffin tins. Fill three-fourths full. Sprinkle sugar-cinnamon mixture over the tops. Bake at 400° for 20 to 25 minutes or until lightly browned and a skewer or toothpick inserted in center comes out clean. Turn out onto a rack and cool.

May be stored airtight for several days.

❀ May be frozen. Reheat before serving.

Serve warm with butter.

Makes 24 muffins

## *Pumpkin Cheese Roll*

All the flavors of pumpkin pie are baked into a cake that holds a sweet, creamy white filling. It's shaped into a roll, and when you cut it you'll see pretty swirls of creamy cheese inside the pumpkin cake.

PUMPKIN ROLL
- 3 **large eggs**
- 1 **cup sugar**
- ⅔ **cup mashed pumpkin, canned or fresh**
- 1 **teaspoon lemon juice**
- ¾ **cup all-purpose flour**
- 1 **teaspoon baking powder**
- 2 **teaspoons ground cinnamon**
- 1 **teaspoon ground ginger**
- ½ **teaspoon ground nutmeg**
- ½ **teaspoon salt**
- 1 **cup finely chopped walnuts**
  **Powdered sugar**

CHEESE FILLING
**Two 3-ounce packages cream cheese, at room temperature**
- 4 **tablespoons (½ stick) unsalted butter or margarine, at room temperature**
- 1 **cup powdered sugar**
- ½ **teaspoon vanilla extract**

Make pumpkin roll by first greasing a 15½-by-10½-by-1-inch jelly-roll pan. Line with parchment or waxed paper. Grease the paper. If using waxed paper, flour paper, shaking out the excess. Set aside.

In mixing bowl with electric mixer, beat eggs and sugar until thick, light, and creamy, about 3 to 4 minutes. Mix in pumpkin and lemon juice. In separate bowl, stir together flour, baking powder, cinnamon, ginger, nutmeg, and salt. Fold into pumpkin mixture. Pour into prepared pan; smooth top evenly. Sprinkle nuts over top. Bake at 375° for 12 to 15 minutes or until top springs back when lightly pressed with fingertip and cake begins to pull away from sides of the pan.

While cake is baking, place a clean dish towel on counter. Sprinkle powdered sugar through a strainer onto towel. Remove cake from oven and immediately turn it upside down onto towel. Remove cake pan and paper. Beginning at narrow end of cake, roll towel and cake together; set aside seam side down to cool. Make cheese filling: In a mixing bowl blend cream cheese and butter until light and fluffy. Slowly beat in sugar and vanilla extract.

When cake is cool, unroll and remove towel. Spread cheese filling over the top. Roll again. The nuts will be on the outside of the cake. Refrigerate for several hours.

❊ May be refrigerated covered overnight.

❊ May be frozen wrapped in foil for 1 month. Defrost in refrigerator overnight.

Serves 8 to 10

# Cranberry-Pear Tart

The perfect complement to any pumpkin dessert. A cookielike pastry dough contains an extra-creamy filling, rich with almond paste. Fresh cranberries cook up to release their juices and glaze the pears, tinting them a glistening pink. This dessert is too good to be just for Thanksgiving. Use any fresh fruit of the season and glaze it with strained apricot preserves.

SWEET TART PASTRY
- **12 tablespoons (1½ sticks) butter, at room temperature**
- **½ cup powdered sugar**
- **1¼ cups all-purpose flour**

FILLING
- **4 ounces almond paste**
- **8-ounce package cream cheese, at room temperature**
- **¼ cup sugar**
- **1 large egg**
- **½ teaspoon vanilla extract**
- **¼ teaspoon almond extract**

CRANBERRY PEAR TOPPING
- **1-pound 13-ounce can pear halves**
- **½ cup reserved pear syrup**
- **¾ cup sugar**
- **1 tablespoon cornstarch**
- **2 cups fresh cranberries**

Make sweet tart pastry: Preheat oven to 350°. In food processor with metal blade or in mixing bowl, blend butter, powdered sugar, and flour until mixture holds together. Press dough into the bottom and up the sides of an 11- or 12-inch tart pan with a removable bottom, an 11- or 12-inch quiche dish, or an 11- or 12-inch pizza pan. Prick bottom with a fork. Bake pastry for 20 minutes or until pale golden. The sides will shrink to form a slight rim. Remove from oven and cool completely before filling.

❀ May be frozen.

Make the filling: In food processor with metal blade or in mixing bowl, mix almond paste until it is broken up. Add cream cheese, sugar, egg, vanilla, and almond extract; mix until smooth. Pour into cooled pastry, spreading evenly. Bake at 375° for 10 minutes. Cool.

❀ May be refrigerated covered overnight.

❀ May be frozen for 1 month.

Make cranberry pear topping: Drain pears, reserving ½ cup syrup. Slice pears into thin slices; set aside. In a small saucepan, mix sugar and cornstarch. Slowly stir in pear syrup, mixing well. Bring to a boil, stirring constantly, and add ½ cup of the cranberries. Cook until cranberries pop and glaze turns pink. Stir in rest of the cranberries and cook just until they become soft, about 2 minutes.

Leaving a 1½-inch border around outer edge of tart for the cranberries, place pear slices overlapping in a circle. Fill outside border with cranberries. Spoon remaining cranberries in center of pears. Gently brush the pears with the cranberry juices remaining in the bottom of the pan. Refrigerate until firm.

❀ May be refrigerated uncovered several hours.

Serves 10 to 12

# Day-After-Thanksgiving Dinner

MENU

TURKEY VEGETABLE SOUP

TURKEY-SAUSAGE CASSEROLE OR
RANCH-STYLE TURKEY SALAD

APPLE BROWN BETTY

RECOMMENDED BEVERAGE:
LAST NIGHT'S LEFTOVER WINE

*The day after Thanksgiving you find your refrigerator full of good things to eat. Why try to recreate the Thanksgiving dinner when you have at hand the fixings for an entirely different, equally delicious meal?*

*The rich turkey stock for the Turkey Vegetable Soup is made with the carcass and any remaining stuffing and gravy. Both the soup and the Turkey-Sausage Casserole, a terrific combination of contrasting flavors, freeze beautifully for the cold winter nights ahead. These wonderful and versatile leftovers help extend the memorable pleasures of Thanksgiving.*

*This simple, economical meal serves 6.*

# Turkey Vegetable Soup

If you make this soup right, you'll never make it the same way again. It is a flavorful, hearty soup based upon leftovers, so you may add or subtract ingredients at will. If you prefer, add the stuffing near the end of the cooking time along with the vegetables and it will thicken the broth.

1 leftover turkey carcass with any remaining stuffing and gravy
2 onions with peel, quartered
½ cup celery leaves
2 carrots, unpeeled and sliced
1 teaspoon dried thyme
2 teaspoons dried marjoram
6 whole peppercorns
2 whole cloves
1 bay leaf
1 teaspoon salt
8 to 10 cups cold water, or enough to barely cover turkey bones
½ cup finely chopped peeled carrots
1 cup diced peeled potato
½ cup whole-kernel corn
½ cup diced green beans
½ cup diced zucchini
Pepper

On cutting board, cut carcass into 8 to 10 pieces. This is easiest to do with a cleaver or large chef's knife. Place carcass and any remaining stuffing and gravy in soup pot. Add onions, celery leaves, carrots, thyme, marjoram, peppercorns, cloves, bay leaf, salt, and enough water to barely cover the bones. Bring to a boil, lower heat, and simmer, covered, for 2 hours. Strain the soup into a container or clean soup pot. Pull meat off bones; discard bones and add meat to soup. Chill until fat rises to the top.

❋ May be refrigerated for 5 days.

Skim layer of fat off soup. Add vegetables. Simmer covered over moderate heat until all vegetables are tender, about 15 minutes. Season to taste with salt, pepper, and thyme.

❋ May be refrigerated overnight.
❋ May be frozen.

Serves 6 to 8

## Turkey-Sausage Casserole

This casserole makes a great family meal and is just as good made with chicken. It's creamy and cheesy, spiced with mustard and sausage, and if you have leftover stuffing, it can be sprinkled over all for a crisp and golden crust.

1 **pound sausage links**
¼ **pound (1 stick) butter or margarine**
¾ **pound mushrooms, sliced**
4 **tablespoons all-purpose flour**
1½ **cups chicken or turkey broth**
½ **cup whipping cream or half-and-half**
1 **cup shredded sharp Cheddar cheese (about 4 ounces)**
1 **teaspoon prepared mustard**
1 **teaspoon salt**
   **Freshly ground pepper**
3 **to 4 cups cooked turkey, cut into bite-size pieces**
1 **cup packaged herb-seasoned stuffing or leftover stuffing**

Place sausage in large skillet. Add ¼ inch of water, cover, and simmer for 10 minutes. Remove cover and simmer until water has evaporated and sausage browns. Turn and brown other side. Remove to paper towels and cool. Cut sausage into ¾-inch pieces.

In large saucepan, melt 4 tablespoons butter or margarine. Sauté mushrooms, stirring occasionally, until most of the liquid has evaporated. Sprinkle in flour and cook over low heat, stirring constantly, for 1 minute. Stir in chicken or turkey broth and cream or half-and-half. Cook over moderate heat, stirring constantly, until mixture comes to a boil. Cook for 1 minute. Remove from heat and stir in cheese, mustard, salt, pepper, turkey, and sausage. Pour into greased 7-by-11-inch (2-quart) casserole. Melt 4 tablespoons butter. If using dry herb-seasoned stuffing, place it in a small bowl and toss with butter. Sprinkle over casserole. If using leftover stuffing, sprinkle it over the casserole and sprinkle butter over the top.

✤ May be refrigerated, covered with foil, for 2 days.

❋ May be frozen for 1 month.

Bake uncovered at 350° for 20 minutes or until top is browned and sauce is bubbling.

Serves 6

## Ranch-Style Turkey Salad

I went to lunch at a café in Los Angeles and ordered their turkey salad. I was so impressed, I devised the recipe at home.

This hearty turkey salad is bursting with the flavor of bacon and healthful with colorful fresh-chopped vegetables.

1 pound bacon, cut into 1-inch pieces
1 head iceberg lettuce
0.4-ounce envelope Ranch Salad Dressing mix
1 cup buttermilk
1 cup mayonnaise
3 to 4 cups cooked turkey, cut into bite-size pieces
2 tomatoes, cut into wedges
2 avocados, peeled and cut into wedges
4 hard-boiled eggs, sliced
1 small red onion, thinly sliced
¼ pound mushrooms, sliced
1 zucchini, sliced
1 cup alfalfa sprouts

In large skillet cook bacon over moderate heat, stirring occasionally, until crisp. Drain on paper towels. Wash and tear lettuce into bite-size pieces. Refrigerate in plastic bags until ready to use. Make dressing according to package directions, using buttermilk and mayonnaise.

Before serving, place lettuce in large bowl. Add turkey, tomatoes, avocados, eggs, onion, mushrooms, zucchini, and alfalfa sprouts. Toss with approximately half the dressing, reserving remainder for another use.

Serves 6

*Variation:* 3 whole cooked chicken breasts may be substituted for the turkey.

*Tip:* Extra buttermilk may be frozen.

## Apple Brown Betty

This soothing old-fashioned dessert is amazingly simple to put together. Traditionally the crumbs are just on top, but I divide them between a top and bottom layer. The apple filling is soft and warm, and I like to serve it with icy-cold cream sauce or a scoop of ice cream for a contrast of taste sensations.

FILLING

- **2 pounds tart green cooking apples (about 4), peeled, cored, and sliced**
- **1 tablespoon lemon juice**
- **½ cup sugar**
- **1 teaspoon ground cinnamon**
- **½ teaspoon ground nutmeg**

CRUMB MIXTURE

- **¾ cup all-purpose flour**
- **½ cup graham cracker crumbs**
- **¼ cup rolled oats, instant or regular**
- **¾ cup light, or golden, brown sugar, packed**
- **¼ pound (1 stick) butter, cold and cut into 8 pieces**
- **½ cup chopped walnuts or pecans**

SOUR CREAM SAUCE (optional)

- **½ cup sour cream**
- **2 tablespoons powdered sugar**
- **½ teaspoon vanilla extract**

In a large bowl, toss apples with lemon juice, sugar, cinnamon, and nutmeg.

Make crumb mixture: In food processor with metal blade or in mixing bowl, mix flour, graham cracker crumbs, oats, and brown sugar. Add butter and mix until crumbly. Stir in nuts. Divide crumbs in half. Sprinkle half in the bottom of a 9½- or 10-inch pie dish. Layer apples over crumbs and top with remaining crumbs. Bake at 375° for 30 minutes or until top is crisp and golden and apples are tender. Serve warm.

Make sour cream sauce, if desired, by mixing all sauce ingredients in a small bowl. Serve cold with warm dessert.

✳ May be refrigerated overnight and reheated.

Serves 8

# 8
# SEASON'S GREETINGS

# A Christmas Banquet

MENU

CHEESE TREES
CHESTNUT SOUP

CORNISH GAME HENS WITH
APRICOT RICE STUFFING
VEGETABLE CHARTREUSE OR
DOUBLE MUSHROOM TIMBALES
TOMATO AND CHEESE PLATTER WITH
SPINACH VINAIGRETTE OR
MARINATED BRUSSELS SPROUT AND
TOMATO SALAD

FLAMING FUDGE ALASKA

WINE RECOMMENDATION:
AN ELEGANT, DRY CHARDONNAY WITH
A GOOD BALANCE OF FRUIT AND OAK

*A holiday as significant and important as Christmas deserves a real banquet. Though duck or goose is the traditional Christmas fare, I prefer Cornish hens because they're so elegant and easy to prepare. They are stuffed with a splendid, moist apricot-rice stuffing and served with either a gorgeous, multicolored vegetable mold or individual creamy mushroom timbales. I offer a choice of two festive red and green salads to enliven your Christmas table. The Flaming Fudge Alaska can be completely made ahead, frozen, and then popped in the oven to warm and brown the meringue just before serving; at the last minute, ignite the brandy and present the flaming dessert at the table.*

*This banquet serves 8 and can be planned either as a sit-down dinner or a buffet.*

## Cheese Trees

Have fun cutting a flaky, rich cheese dough into Christmas trees or other holiday shapes. They freeze beautifully and are a perfect accompaniment to soup or salad as well as hors d'oeuvre for drinks. Try varying the topping—instead of sesame seeds, use poppy or caraway.

10 tablespoons (1¼ sticks) unsalted butter, at room temperature
1⅔ cups shredded Gruyère or Emmenthal cheese
2 cups all-purpose flour
1 heaping teaspoon salt
1 heaping teaspoon paprika
½ teaspoon baking powder
½ cup whipping cream
1 egg yolk mixed with 2 teaspoons water for wash
Sesame seeds

Blend butter and cheese in large mixing bowl of an electric mixer. Mix in flour, salt, paprika, and baking powder. Add cream and mix until blended. Divide dough in half. Shape into two flat balls; flatten and wrap in plastic wrap. Refrigerate until cold enough to roll, several hours or overnight.

❋ May be refrigerated for 5 days.

❋ May be frozen.

On a lightly floured surface, roll out each ball of dough ¼ inch thick. Cut out trees with Christmas tree cookie cutter. Reroll and cut scraps once or twice. Place cut-outs on parchment-lined or greased baking sheets. Brush tops lightly with egg yolk mixed with water. Sprinkle with sesame seeds. Bake at 375° for 10 to 12 minutes or until lightly browned. If baking two sheets in one oven, rotate their positions halfway through the baking time.

May be stored airtight for 1 week.

❋ May be frozen. Reheat at 375° for 5 minutes.

Makes 60 two-inch trees, or about 30 four-inch trees

## *Chestnut Soup*

This is an outstanding soup, made from an inspired blend of vegetables, herbs, chestnuts, and a splash of Madeira. It calls for canned chestnuts, which may be purchased from the gourmet section of most supermarkets, often by the French name, *marrons*. Fresh chestnuts may be substituted, but must be peeled. Cut an X into the flat end and roast or boil them until hot. Peel while still hot.

6 tablespoons butter or margarine
1 cup chopped celery
1 cup chopped carrot
1 cup chopped onion
¾ pound potatoes, peeled and chopped (about 2 medium potatoes)
3 cups chicken broth
2½ cups beef broth
¼ cup chopped fresh parsley
1 teaspoon dried thyme
1 teaspoon dried sage
1 teaspoon dried basil
One 15½-ounce can chestnuts in water, drained, or 1 pound fresh, peeled chestnuts
½ cup dry Madeira
1 cup whipping cream
Salt and white pepper to taste

In a large soup pot, melt butter or margarine. Add celery, carrot, onion, and potatoes; cook covered over moderately low heat, stirring occasionally, for 20 minutes or until vegetables are very soft but not brown. Stir in chicken and beef broth, parsley, thyme, sage, and basil. Reserve ½ cup chestnuts for garnish. Add remaining chestnuts to soup. Simmer covered for 20 minutes. Cool slightly; purée in blender for a smoother soup or in batches in food processor with metal blade.

❋ May be refrigerated for 2 days.
❊ May be frozen.

Place in soup pot. Add Madeira and cream; simmer 5 minutes. Season to taste with salt and pepper. Sprinkle reserved crumbled chestnuts over each serving.

Serves 10 to 12

# Double Mushroom Timbales

Cream and mushrooms seem created just for each other. This custard is delicate, light as a cloud.

½ ounce dried mushrooms
2 tablespoons butter or margarine
¾ pound fresh mushrooms, sliced
¼ cup chopped shallots or onion
3 eggs
3 egg yolks
2½ cups whipping cream
1 teaspoon salt
Dash of cayenne pepper
¼ teaspoon ground nutmeg
8 whole mushrooms, sautéed (optional)

Place dried mushrooms in a small bowl; cover with hot water and let sit for 30 minutes to soften. Drain, squeeze dry, and cut off tough stems. Chop the mushrooms into small pieces.

In a medium skillet, melt butter or margarine. Sauté sliced fresh mushrooms, dried mushrooms, and shallots or onion until soft and all moisture has evaporated. Cool slightly.

In a medium bowl, mix eggs, yolks, cream, salt, cayenne, and nutmeg. Stir in mushrooms. Butter eight to ten ½- to ¾-cup timbale molds or soufflé dishes. Line the bottom with parchment or waxed paper; grease the paper. Lightly sprinkle ground nutmeg in the bottom of each mold. Pour custard into molds.

❈ May be refrigerated covered overnight.

Place molds in shallow baking pan. Place pan in middle rack of oven and pour in enough hot water to come halfway up sides of the molds. Bake at 325° for 30 to 45 minutes, or until knife inserted in center comes out clean. Timing will depend on size of mold. Let rest 5 to 10 minutes. Run tip of knife around edge of molds. Invert onto plate. Garnish with whole sautéed mushrooms, if desired.

Serves 8 to 10

# *Cornish Game Hens with Apricot Rice Stuffing*

This entrée works equally well if the hens are not deboned, but it is magnificent if they are (many butchers will bone them for you). This savory stuffing is perfumed with apricots, cinnamon, and currants. The hens become incredibly tender in the marinade, which in turn enhances the flavor of a delicious Grand Marnier orange sauce. Since the hens marinate for 24 hours, be sure to start this a day ahead.

**8 Cornish game hens (weighing approximately 1 to 1¼ pounds each)**
**Seasoned salt**
**¼ pound (1 stick) butter or margarine, at room temperature**
**Parsley for garnish**

APRICOT RICE STUFFING
**2 ounces dried apricots, chopped (about ⅓ cup)**
**3 tablespoons currants or chopped raisins**
**2 tablespoons Grand Marnier**
**5-ounce box brown and wild rice mix**
**¼ teaspoon ground cinnamon**
**Salt and pepper**

Remove giblets from cavity of hens. Dry hens well with paper towels. If boning, place hens breast side down on flat surface. Make a cut down each side of the center of the backbone. Scrape meat away from bone with the edge of a sharp knife. Continue to pull meat away from bone with fingers, working and pulling it away from bone on each side. Cut joint at wing tips and legs, leaving wings and drumsticks attached to meat. Turn over and carefully cut flesh away from breastbone. Lay boned hens opened out, skin side down. Sprinkle lightly with seasoned salt.

Make apricot rice stuffing: Soak apricots and currants or raisins in Grand Marnier for several hours; or heat Grand Marnier until hot and soak fruit for 30 minutes. Make rice according to package directions. Stir in dried fruit, cinnamon, and salt and pepper to taste. Cool completely before using.

❄ Stuffing may be refrigerated for 2 days.

❅ May be frozen.

Divide cooled stuffing equally among the hens, mounding in the center of each hen. Fold each side of hen over stuffing, overlapping slightly. With hands, push into original shape. Skewer or truss closed. Tie legs together with string. Place a metal skewer through wings to hold them in place.

If not boning, stuff apricot rice stuffing inside cavity of hen. Skewer or truss cavity closed.

*Stuffed Cornish game hens garnished with watercress and orange slices.*

## ORANGE-FLAVORED MARINADE

- **2 cups orange juice**
- **1 cup lemon juice**
- **2 teaspoons salt**
- **4 teaspoons powdered ginger**
- **1 large bay leaf, crumbled**
- **1 large onion, thinly sliced**
- **2 large cloves garlic, thinly sliced**

## SAUCE BIGARADE

- **4 tablespoons sugar**
- **2 tablespoons red wine vinegar**
- **2 cups beef broth**
- **2 tablespoons cornstarch or arrowroot**
- **1 beef bouillon cube, crumbled**
- **4 tablespoons cold water**
- **1¼ cups reserved orange-flavored marinade**
- **3 to 4 tablespoons Grand Marnier**
- **1 tablespoon orange marmalade or apricot preserves**
  **Salt and pepper**

Make orange-flavored marinade by mixing all marinade ingredients in a medium bowl. Place marinade in a shallow glass or plastic dish into which the hens fit snugly. Place hens in marinade; turn to coat all sides.

❄ Refrigerate covered for 24 hours, turning once.

Several hours before serving, remove hens from marinade and dry thoroughly. Reserve 1¼ cups marinade for sauce. Let hens sit at room temperature for 1 hour before baking.

Make sauce bigarade: In medium saucepan, mix sugar and vinegar. Bring to boil over moderate heat. Boil for about 3 minutes, until sugar is dissolved and caramelizes into a thick brown syrup. Be careful not to let it burn. Immediately pour in the broth. Bring to a boil and simmer slowly, stirring occasionally, until caramel dissolves.

❄ Sauce may be refrigerated overnight.

After removing hens from marinade, strain 1¼ cups marinade into sauce. Simmer 10 minutes. Remove sauce from heat. Mix cornstarch or arrowroot, beef bouillon cube, and water in a small bowl until dissolved; stir into sauce. Return to heat and bring to boil, stirring constantly until thickened. Stir in Grand Marnier and preserves. Season to taste with salt and pepper.

Sprinkle hens with seasoned salt. Spread each hen with about 1 tablespoon butter. Place hens breast side down on rack in shallow roasting or broiler pan. For boned hens, bake at 375° for 20 minutes. Turn and bake breast side up 20 to 25 minutes longer, basting occasionally. For unboned hens, bake at 400° for 30 minutes on each side. If hens are not brown enough at the end of baking time, place under broiler for several minutes. Hens are done when drumstick moves easily in its socket and juices run clear when thigh is pierced. Place hens on serving platter. Remove skewers and string. Serve with sauce bigarade.

Serves 8, allowing 1 hen per person

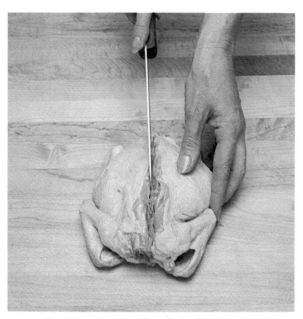

*Cut down along each side of the backbone.*

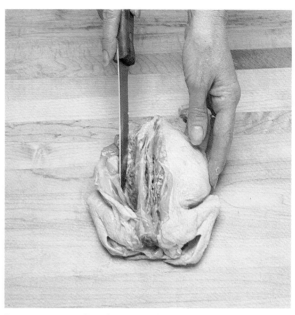

*Scrape meat away from bone toward sides of bird.*

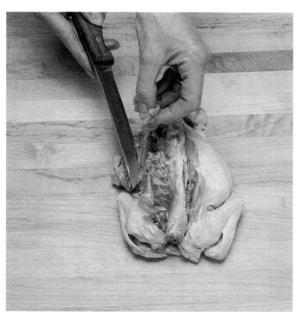

*Scrape meat down from thigh bone.*

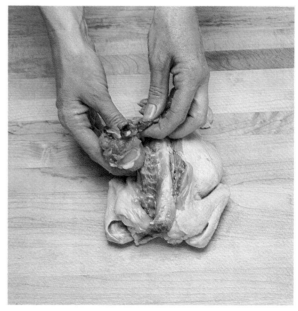

*Pop out thigh bone at joint.*

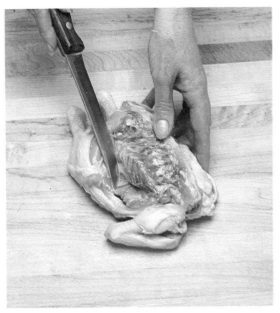

*Exposed bones after both sides have been cut loose.*

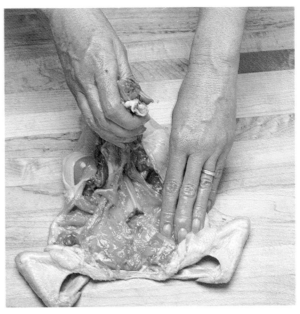

*Pull out breast bone.*

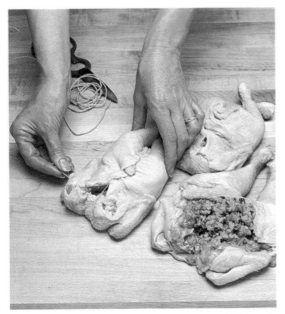

*Stuffed bird in the lower right-hand corner, trussed bird on the left.*

*Tie drumsticks together with string.*

*Vegetable Chartreuse is served on a silver cake platter.*

## Vegetable Chartreuse

In the early 1900s the great chef Antonin Carême created a spectacular dish by arranging an assortment of beautifully cut vegetables inside an oval mold. He then filled the mold with layers of cabbage and boned partridge. When unmolded, it looked like a beautiful vegetable mosaic. He called it a Chartreuse of Partridge. This dish is my own version, with thanks to Carême.

**Two 1-pound cans yams, drained, or**
**   2 pounds fresh yams or sweet**
**   potatoes**
**¼ cup whipping cream**
**¼ cup grated Parmesan cheese**

If using fresh yams or potatoes, bake at 400° for 30 to 40 minutes or until tender when pierced with a fork. Cool and peel. Place yams or potatoes in mixing bowl with electric mixer or in food processor with metal blade. Mix until

½ teaspoon salt
Freshly ground pepper to taste
1 pound green beans, ends trimmed
2 large carrots, peeled
2 small zucchini, thinly sliced
1 cup fresh broccoli flowerets
1 cup fresh cauliflower flowerets
¼ cup fresh or frozen peas
12 tablespoons (1½ sticks) butter
2 cloves garlic, crushed
1½ cups shredded Swiss cheese
   (about 6 ounces)

smooth. Add whipping cream, Parmesan cheese, salt, and pepper to taste. Set aside.

Grease a 2-quart (8-cup) charlotte mold. Line the bottom with a round of parchment or waxed paper; grease the paper and set aside.

Trim the beans to the height of the charlotte mold. Cut the carrots the same length as the beans. Then cut them into strips ¼-inch thick and ¼-inch wide. Slice any short pieces into ¼-inch rounds.

Fill a medium saucepan half full of salted water. Bring to a boil and cook each type of vegetable except peas separately until crisp tender. Remove with slotted spoon to a bowl of ice water for 1 to 2 minutes to stop the cooking. Remove to paper towels to dry, keeping the vegetables separate. Season with salt and pepper.

Melt the butter over low heat; stir in the garlic.

Arrange a layer of cut vegetables in an attractive pattern on the bottom of the charlotte mold, as pictured. Spread one fourth of the yams over the vegetables. Arrange beans and carrot sticks upright around the side of the mold, using some of the yam mixture around the bottom to help hold them in place. Drizzle 2 to 3 tablespoons of the garlic butter over the yams and sprinkle with ¼ cup Swiss cheese. Continue to fill the mold, alterating layers of vegetables, cheese, yams, and garlic butter. You should have two thin layers of yams in the mold. Spread the remaining quarter of yams on top, and sprinkle with the remaining garlic butter and cheese.

❉ May be refrigerated covered with plastic wrap and foil overnight.

Before serving, bring to room temperature. Bake uncovered at 350° for 40 to 45 minutes or until heated through. Run a knife around the inside edge of the mold and invert onto a serving plate. Serve with a spatula and large spoon, cutting and scooping out portions.

Serves 8

*Place vegetables on bottom of paper-lined charlotte mold. Alternating carrots and green beans, lay vegetables upright along sides of mold, using yams to hold them in place. Continue layering until mold is full.*

# Tomato and Cheese Platter with Spinach Vinaigrette

A red-and-green platter is just right for the Christmas spirit. Overlapping slices of tomatoes, red onions, and cheese form a ring that is bathed in a spinach and basil vinaigrette. This very green, very thick vinaigrette is slightly nutty and slightly cheesy.

SPINACH VINAIGRETTE
¼ cup olive oil
½ cup salad oil
¼ cup walnuts
3 cloves garlic, crushed
⅓ cup dried basil or 1 cup fresh basil leaves, chopped
⅓ cup torn spinach leaves, packed
⅓ cup chopped fresh parsley, packed
¼ cup grated Parmesan cheese
¼ cup plus 2 tablespoons white wine vinegar
1 teaspoon salt
Freshly ground pepper

8 ripe but firm tomatoes
Lettuce leaves for platter
2 small red onions (same size as tomatoes, if possible), peeled and thinly sliced
1 pound provolone or mozzarella cheese, sliced

Make spinach vinaigrette: In food processor with metal blade or in blender, process all vinaigrette ingredients until blended, seasoning to taste with salt, pepper, and additional vinegar or oil, if needed. Leftover vinaigrette is delicious on cold meats and cheese.

❋ May be refrigerated covered overnight.

Peel tomatoes by plunging them into a pot of boiling water for 10 seconds. Drain and run under cold water to stop the cooking. Peel and slice into ¼-inch-thick slices. Cover a round platter with lettuce leaves. Overlap alternating slices of tomatoes, onions, and cheese.

❋ May be refrigerated covered with plastic wrap for several hours.

Before serving, pour desired amount of spinach vinaigrette over salad.

Serves 8 to 10

*Tip:* Refrigerate whole onions overnight for a milder taste.

*Variation:* Substitute sliced cucumbers for onions.

## Marinated Brussels Sprout and Tomato Salad

Although this salad portrays the perfect colors for your Christmas dinner, it's exceptional all year round. Brussels sprouts are one of our most underrated vegetables. They'll delectably absorb this tangy marinade that's just right for their unique flavor. Crushed red chilies are available in spice jars in most supermarkets, but you can substitute Tabasco.

VINAIGRETTE MARINADE
- 1 cup salad or olive oil
- ¼ cup lemon juice
- ¼ cup white wine vinegar
- 2 cloves garlic, crushed
- 2 teaspoons seasoned salt
- 1 teaspoon sugar
- ½ teaspoon dry mustard
- ½ teaspoon salt
- ¼ teaspoon crushed dry red chilies or Tabasco sauce

- 1 pound fresh Brussels sprout (about 2 cups)
- 1½ pounds zucchini (about 3 medium), sliced
- ¼ cup sliced green onions
- 1 pound cherry tomatoes
- 1 head Boston or red leaf lettuce

Make vinaigrette marinade: Mix all marinade ingredients together in glass jar or food processor with metal blade.

❊ Marinade may be refrigerated up to 2 days.

In a medium saucepan, bring a small amount of salted water to boil. Add Brussels sprout, return to a boil, and simmer until tender but still crisp, about 5 minutes. Do not overcook, as they will continue to cook in the marinade. Plunge immediately into a bowl of ice water to stop the cooking. Drain well; slice into 4 or 5 slices each. Toss with zucchini and onions.

Pour marinade over vegetables and refrigerate covered for at least 12 hours, stirring occasionally.

❊ May be refrigerated overnight.

One hour before serving, add tomatoes to marinade. Line a serving platter with lettuce leaves. Spoon vegetables onto lettuce leaves.

Serves 8

## Flaming Fudge Alaska

Any two flavors of ice cream will do, but my personal favorites are available at chain ice cream stores. The fudgy, moist, dark-chocolate base is topped by a bowlful of ice cream and swirled with crème de cacao meringue. An egg shell is buried in the meringue, warm brandy is poured in and ignited, and this dessert appears at the table like an erupting volcano.

FUDGE CAKE
**Three 1-ounce squares unsweetened chocolate**
**¼ pound (1 stick) butter or margarine**
**1 cup sugar**
**2 large eggs**
**½ cup all-purpose flour**
**Pinch of salt**
**1 teaspoon vanilla extract**
**½ cup chopped pecans (optional)**

ICE CREAM AND TOPPING
**2 pints mint chocolate chip ice cream**
**2 pints mocha almond fudge ice cream**
**5 egg whites, at room temperature**
**Dash of cream of tartar**
**¾ cup sugar**
**1 tablespoon crème de cacao**
**Half an empty egg shell**
**2 sugar cubes**
**2 tablespoons brandy, warmed**
**Fudgy Fudge Sauce (see recipe in Saluting the Graduate menu)**

Make fudge cake: Melt chocolate and butter or margarine in medium saucepan over low heat. Remove from heat and cool slightly. In mixing bowl with electric mixer, beat sugar and eggs until light and fluffy. Mix in flour, salt, vanilla, nuts (if using), and chocolate. Pour into a greased 8-inch springform pan. Bake at 325° for 20 minutes; cake will be soft but will firm up as it cools. Remove to rack and cool completely before removing from pan.

✱ May be refrigerated or stored airtight for 1 week.

✱ May be frozen.

Line a 1½-quart (6-cup) metal bowl with plastic wrap. Stir mint chocolate chip ice cream to soften slightly; spread a layer about 1 inch thick over bottom and sides of foil. Place bowl in freezer while softening mocha almond fudge ice cream slightly; pack into center of bowl. Cover top with foil; press with hands to even and smooth the top of the ice cream. Freeze firm.

In large mixing bowl with electric mixer, beat egg whites until frothy. Add cream of tartar and beat until soft peaks form. Gradually add sugar, 1 tablespoon at a time, beating well after each addition, until mixture is satiny and the consistency of marshmallow cream. Beat in crème de cacao. Remove foil from top of ice cream. Place fudge cake on ovenproof platter. Invert ice cream onto cake. Pull off plastic wrap. Quickly cover ice cream and fudge base with meringue, swirling it into peaks. Place half an egg shell into top. The top of the egg shell should be even with the top of the meringue.

❀ May be frozen overnight.

Preheat oven to 500°. Bake Alaska in lower third of oven for 3 minutes or until lightly browned. Soak sugar cubes in brandy for 2 to 3 minutes and remove. Heat brandy just until hot; do not let it boil. Pour small amount into egg shell, filling one-third full. Add sugar cubes. Stand back and carefully ignite, and bring dessert to the table flaming. Serve with Fudgy Fudge Sauce.

Serves 12 to 14

# Holiday Open House

## MENU

AVOCADO CASHEW WREATH
SMOKED OYSTER ROLL
SALMON SOUFFLÉ TORTE
POTTED EDAM CHEESE
CHRISTMAS PEPPERS AND DILL DIP

SWEET-AND-SOUR CHICKEN WINGS
MINTED MEATBALLS
WITH CUCUMBER YOGURT SAUCE
ON THE RITZ
HOLIDAY FIESTA CHIPS

COLD HAM WITH
TANGY MUSTARD OR
PECAN-STUFFED HONEY-GLAZED HAM
WALDORF CINNAMON MOLD
LAYERED WINTER SALAD

SPIRITED PUNCH BOWL
CHRISTMAS PUNCH WITH
CRANBERRY ICE WREATH

YULE LOG
LEMON TARTS
HOLIDAY BREAD PUDDING WITH
BRANDY CREAM SAUCE
COLD CHESTNUT SOUFFLÉ

An open house buffet can truly be a pleasure to host. Once you've captured the Christmas spirit—with flickering candlelight, the scent of pine in the air, the table laden with holiday food and all the work behind you—you are free to bask in the pleasure of greeting old friends and new.

This is an extensive menu, with a sensational variety of hors d'oeuvres both hot and cold—some to pass to guests, some to adorn the buffet table. All of the cold hors d'oeuvres are in festive shades of red and green. I offer a choice of two hams: one a fruit-glazed baked ham, marbled with a jellied mustard and served cold; the second stuffed with pecans and cornbread and served hot. The dessert table of luscious holiday offerings includes a traditional Christmas yule log cake, an old-fashioned bread pudding with a brandied cream sauce, and a cold coffee-and-rum-laced chestnut soufflé.

This open house buffet menu serves 16 to 24.

*Clockwise from left: Avocado Cashew Wreath, Christmas Peppers and Dill Dip, Christmas Punch, Salmon Soufflé Torte, Smoked Oyster Roll.*

## Avocado Cashew Wreath

This "wreath," with "bows" of red pimientos, is a festive change of pace from traditional guacamole.

3 **medium avocados**
Two **8-ounce packages cream cheese, at room temperature**
2 **cups finely chopped cashew nuts (about 8 ounces), toasted at 350° for 10 minutes and stirred occasionally**
1 **cup shredded sharp Cheddar cheese (about 4 ounces)**
2 **tablespoons lemon juice**
2 **cloves garlic, crushed**
4-**ounce can diced green chilies**
¼ **cup finely chopped onion**
2 **teaspoons Worcestershire sauce**
1 **teaspoon salt**
**Pepper to taste**
**Green food coloring (optional)**
**Chopped parsley for garnish**
1 **whole pimiento or pimiento pieces for garnish**
**Crackers or bread rounds for serving**

In food processor with metal blade, mash avocados. Remove and measure 2 cups. Process avocado and remaining ingredients in two batches. Mix until well blended. Stir in a few drops of green food coloring, if needed.

❀ May be refrigerated overnight in bowl with avocado pit, covered with plastic wrap directly on spread to prevent it from turning dark.

❅ May be frozen.

Before serving, stir well. Spoon onto platter in the shape of a wreath, as pictured. Sprinkle with chopped parsley and strips of pimiento shaped into a bow. Serve with crackers or bread rounds.

Makes 4 cups spread; serves 12 to 16

*Variation:* Mixture may be divided into 4 logs, each approximately 1½ inches thick. Roll logs in toasted cashews, chopped parsley, or paprika.

## Potted Edam Cheese

This cheese spread has a most beguiling taste. After it's potted for a week, you cannot distinguish one intriguing flavor from another. Be sure to wait at least one week, so the ingredients can commingle.

**2-pound round Edam cheese**
**1 cup port wine**
**1 tablespoon caraway seeds**
**1 teaspoon dry mustard**
**¼ teaspoon cayenne pepper**
**1 teaspoon dry cumin**
   **Plain water biscuits or wheat crackers**

Slice the top off the cheese and scoop out the inside, leaving the shell intact. Shred the cheese. In food processor with metal blade or in mixing bowl, mix cheese, wine, and spices until mixture is blended into a fairly smooth paste. Pack the cheese back into the cheese shell. Replace the lid and wrap the cheese in plastic wrap. Refrigerate for at least one week for flavors to blend.

❋ May be refrigerated for 1 month.

Serve at room temperature with biscuits or crackers.

Makes 5½ cups; serves about 20

## Christmas Peppers and Dill Dip

Deck the buffet table with green and red peppers. These vegetables are cut into strips and molded around a dish to form a container for a dip flavored with Dijon mustard and fresh dill. It's colorful, festive, and tastes good too.

**2 cups mayonnaise**
**½ cup sour cream**
**2 tablespoons Dijon mustard**
**2 tablespoons chopped fresh dill or 2 teaspoons dried dill**
**2 teaspoons lemon juice**
   **Red peppers, sliced into ½-inch strips**
   **Green peppers, sliced into ½-inch strips**
   **Sprigs of fresh dill for garnish**
   **Cherry tomatoes**
   **Cucumber spears**

In a medium bowl, combine mayonnaise, sour cream, mustard, dill, and lemon juice. Refrigerate covered for at least 4 hours.

❋ May be refrigerated for 2 days.

Before serving, spoon dip into glass serving dish. Alternate strips of red and green peppers around edge of bowl so dip looks as if it were inside the pepper. Garnish with fresh dill. Serve with cherry tomatoes and cucumber spears for dipping.

Makes 2½ cups dip; serves 14 to 16

## Salmon Soufflé Torte

Sandwiched between two light layers of soufflé base is a filling of dill-flavored cream cheese and smoked salmon. It's frosted like a cake with a fluffy sour cream frosting and decorated with dainty bouquets of salmon flowers.

### SOUFFLÉ LAYERS
4 tablespoons (½ stick) butter or margarine
½ cup all-purpose flour
2 cups milk
4 egg yolks
1 teaspoon sugar
Dash of salt
4 egg whites
Dash of cream of tartar

### SMOKED SALMON FILLING
8-ounce package cream cheese, at room temperature
½ cup sour cream
2 tablespoons lemon juice
4 tablespoons chopped green onions
¼ pound smoked salmon, shredded
4 tablespoons peeled and chopped cucumber
¼ teaspoon dried dill or 1 tablespoon fresh dill

### SOUR CREAM FROSTING
½ pint (1 cup) sour cream
1 teaspoon onion powder
1 tablespoon lemon juice

### GARNISH
1 slice smoked salmon (reserved from the ¼ pound in filling, if desired)
Pitted black olives, sliced
Chives or green onion tops, cut into thin strips for stems
Chives or green onion tops, cut for leaves
Sprigs of fresh dill or parsley

Make soufflé layers by melting butter or margarine in a small saucepan. Stir in flour and cook over low heat until well blended, about 2 minutes; do not brown. Whisk in milk and continue cooking and stirring until sauce comes to a boil and thickens. In a small bowl, lightly whisk egg yolks, sugar, and salt. Stir a small amount of hot mixture into the yolks; return to saucepan. Cook for 1 minute, stirring constantly. Remove from heat. Meanwhile beat egg whites until frothy. Add cream of tartar and beat until mixture forms stiff but not dry peaks. Fold sauce into whites.

Line the bottoms of two 9-inch layer cake pans with rounds of parchment or waxed paper; grease the paper and the sides of the pan. Divide soufflé mixture between the pans, spreading it evenly. Bake at 350° for 35 to 40 minutes or until lightly browned and top springs back when pressed lightly with fingertip. If baking in one oven, rotate positions halfway through the baking time. Cool in pans for 10 minutes. Invert layers onto cake racks and pull off paper. Cool completely.

✼ May be refrigerated overnight, wrapped in foil.

✼ May be frozen for 1 month. Wrap individually. Defrost in refrigerator.

Make salmon filling: In bowl with electric mixer, beat cream cheese, sour cream, and lemon juice until smooth. Mix in remaining filling ingredients until blended.

Place one soufflé layer on serving platter. Spread with filling. Place second layer on filling.

✼ May be covered with plastic wrap and refrigerated for 2 days.

Several hours before serving, make sour cream frosting by mixing all frosting ingredients together in a small bowl. Frost torte, and decorate top with flowers cut from smoked salmon and olives. Make stems and leaves from chives and green onions. Garnish with sprigs of fresh dill or parsley. Serve cut into wedges like a pie.

Serves 12

## Smoked Oyster Roll

A layer of puréed smoked oysters is spread over a layer of garlic-flavored cream cheese. It's rolled up, pinwheel fashion, and sliced into rounds of pretty brown and white spirals. It's an oyster-lover's delight, but even those who say they don't like oysters will love this spread—the texture of the oysters changes here and their flavor is muted.

1 medium clove garlic, crushed
1 medium shallot, chopped, or 1 tablespoon finely chopped onion
Two 8-ounce packages cream cheese, at room temperature
2 tablespoons mayonnaise
2 teaspoons Worcestershire sauce
¼ teaspoon salt
⅛ teaspoon white pepper
Dash of Tabasco sauce
Two 3¾-ounce cans smoked oysters, drained
½ cup finely chopped pistachio nuts, pecans, or walnuts
Pimiento strips for garnish (optional)
Parsley sprigs for garnish (optional)
Crackers or bread rounds for serving

In food processor with metal blade or in mixing bowl, mix garlic, shallot or onion, cream cheese, mayonnaise, Worcestershire sauce, salt, pepper, and Tabasco sauce until blended. Spread mixture onto a piece of aluminum foil into a rectangle approximately 8 by 10 inches.

In same bowl, purée or mash oysters. Spread over cream cheese. Cover loosely with plastic wrap and refrigerate for several hours or until firm.

❋ May be refrigerated overnight.

Using a long, narrow spatula to help release cream cheese from foil, roll up like a jelly roll. Don't be concerned if it breaks and cracks. Shape into a long log; roll in nuts, covering log completely.

❋ May be refrigerated wrapped in plastic wrap for 3 days.

Garnish with pimiento and parsley, if desired. Serve with crackers or bread rounds.

Serves 8 to 10

## Sweet-and-Sour Chicken Wing Drumsticks

If you take the thickest and meatiest bone of the wing and push all the meat to the top, you have what is called a chicken wing drumstick. If you are unable to purchase wing drumsticks and don't wish to make them yourself, ordinary chicken wings may easily be substituted. They make great finger food for a large cocktail party, but do supply plenty of napkins. This sweet-and-sour sauce is thick, dark, and delicious. The drumsticks cook for a long time so they become very crisp and deeply glazed with the sauce.

**60 chicken wing drumsticks**
**12-ounce bottle chili sauce**
**10-ounce jar grape jelly**
**2 tablespoons lemon juice**
**½ teaspoon garlic powder**
**16-ounce can sweet-and-sour sauce**
**7½-ounce jar junior baby food peaches**
**¼ teaspoon powdered ginger**

Line a large shallow roasting pan with heavy foil. Place wing drumsticks in pan. In a medium saucepan, bring remaining ingredients to a boil, stirring occasionally, until jelly is melted. Pour three-fourths of the sauce over the drumsticks. Bake at 350° for 1½ to 2 hours or until brown and crispy, basting and turning often.

✱ May be refrigerated covered for 2 days. Refrigerate extra sauce separately.

❀ May be frozen. Sauce may be frozen. Bring to room temperature.

Brush drumsticks with reserved sauce. Bake at 350° for 20 to 30 minutes or until heated through.

Makes 60 drumsticks

*Variation*: Panhandle Barbecue Sauce or Firecracker Barbecue Sauce (see recipes in Fourth of July menu) both are delicious on drumsticks.

# Minted Meatballs with Cucumber Yogurt Sauce

A very dear friend of mine is Jimmy Nassikas, president of the Stanford Court Hotel in San Francisco. These wonderful Greek meatballs are adapted from his mother's recipe. The Cucumber Yogurt Sauce can be used as a dip for the meatballs or spooned over the meatballs in pita pockets.

**1** large onion, finely chopped
**½** cup fresh chopped mint leaves, packed
**3** slices white bread with crusts, toasted and crumbled
**3** large cloves garlic, crushed
**2** large eggs
**2** heaping tablespoons tomato paste
**½** pound ground lamb
**½** pound lean ground beef
**1** teaspoon salt
**¼** teaspoon ground black pepper
    Toaster-size pita bread, cut in half, for serving (optional)

In food processor with metal blade or in large mixing bowl with electric mixer, combine onion, mint, toast, garlic, eggs, and tomato paste. Mix until well blended. Remove to a large bowl and mix in meat with hands. Season with salt and pepper. Shape into 1-inch balls. Preheat oven to 400°. Place meatballs on greased shallow rimmed baking sheets and bake for 12 to 15 minutes or until golden brown.

✻ May be refrigerated overnight. Underbake slightly. Reheat at 400° until heated through.

✻ May be frozen. Underbake slightly. Defrost on baking sheet and reheat at 400° until heated through.

Serve with toothpicks and Cucumber Yogurt Sauce for dipping or spooning into pita, if desired.

Makes about 40 meatballs

## Cucumber Yogurt Sauce

**1** cucumber
**½** teaspoon salt
**1** cup plain yogurt
**1** small onion, chopped
**1** tablespoon chopped fresh mint
    Salt and pepper to taste

Peel, seed, and grate cucumber. Place in colander in sink, sprinkle with salt, and allow to drain for one hour or longer. Squeeze in dish towel to remove excess juices. In a medium bowl mix ¾ cup yogurt, onion, and mint. Stir in cucumber and refrigerate for at least 1 hour.

✻ May be refrigerated overnight.

Before serving, drain off any excess liquid. Stir in remaining ¼ cup yogurt.

Makes about 2 cups

## *On the Ritz*

This is a baked cracker sandwich with a sweet cheese filling. It's dipped in eggs, fried, and then baked until the outside is golden brown and the filling is melted and creamy.

½ **pound ricotta cheese**
2 **tablespoons sugar**
2 **tablespoons lemon juice**
¼ **teaspoon salt**
1 **large egg yolk**
16-**ounce box Ritz crackers**
4 **to 5 eggs**
¼ **pound (1 stick) butter**
1 **pint sour cream, for dipping (optional)**

Make cheese filling by mixing the ricotta cheese, sugar, lemon juice, salt, and egg yolk in a small bowl with a fork. Set aside.

Fill a medium bowl with lukewarm water. Dip each cracker into the water to soften; do not let them get so wet they fall apart. Place them in rows on a clean dish towel. Spread half of the crackers with 1 heaping teaspoon cheese filling. Top with other half of the crackers. Crimp edges with fingers to seal; they will not close completely.

In a medium bowl, mix 4 eggs. Dip each cracker sandwich into the eggs. Use additional egg, if needed. Melt 4 tablespoons butter in a large skillet and fry the sandwiches over moderate heat, a few at a time, until golden on each side. Watch carefully when frying, as they brown quickly. Add additional butter as needed. Remove to paper towels to drain.

❊ May be refrigerated overnight in one layer. Do not pile one on the other.

❊ May be frozen for 3 months. Freeze uncovered on baking sheets until solid. Remove to covered containers. Defrost on baking sheets.

Before serving, bake at 375° for 20 minutes or until golden brown and crispy. If baking one sheet beneath the other, rotate their positions halfway through the baking time. Pass sour cream for dipping, if desired.

Makes about 50 sandwiches

## Holiday Fiesta Chips

Crunchy chips sprinkled with cheese and glistening with spoonfuls of bright red and green jelly—a simple but tasty way of saying Christmas.

1 pound hot pepper Monterey Jack cheese, shredded
¼ pound Cheddar cheese, shredded
Two 8-ounce packages tostitos or tortilla chips
8-to 10-ounce jar red jalapeno jelly
8-to 10-ounce jar green jalapeno jelly

In a small bowl mix Jack and Cheddar cheeses. Place chips on baking sheet or ovenproof serving platter. Sprinkle a small amount of cheese in the center of each chip. Spoon a scant teaspoon of red and green jelly on top of the cheese.

❊ May be refrigerated covered overnight.

Before serving, broil until cheese is melted and bubbling.

Makes about 96 chips

*Mustard-marbled ham topped with cranberry sauce and studded with kumquats.*

## Cold Ham with Tangy Mustard

Cold ham never looked so good. A spicy mustard with a hint of sweetness is marbled throughout the ham. It holds up majestically on a buffet table and is great to serve when your ovens are busy heating up hors d'oeuvre. If the mustard is too spicy for your taste, you can serve it separately as a sauce—just eliminate the gelatin and lemon juice.

**6-to 8-pound boneless fully cooked ham**
¼ **cup lemon juice**
1 **envelope unflavored gelatin**
⅓ **cup dry mustard**
⅔ **cup white vinegar**
3 **eggs**
4 **tablespoons Dijon mustard**
½ **cup sugar**

Remove all skin and fat from ham. Using a zucchini or apple corer, make deep cuts at about 2-inch intervals all over the ham. Cutting down as far as possible toward the bottom of the ham, cut out pieces of ham from the holes. (Save ham scraps for another use.)

Make jelled mustard: In a measuring cup, mix lemon juice and gelatin; let sit 5 minutes for gelatin to soften. In small, heavy saucepan, mix

**8-ounce can whole-berry cranberry
sauce**
**8 to 12 glazed or preserved
kumquats (optional)**
**1-pound bag whole cranberries,
strung with needle and thread
(optional)**
**Parsley for garnish**

dry mustard and vinegar; let sit 5 minutes.
Whisk in eggs, Dijon mustard, sugar, and softened gelatin. Cook over moderate heat, stirring
constantly, until mixture thickens slightly. Do
not boil. Refrigerate mustard until slightly
thickened. Using a funnel, pour mustard into
the holes of the ham. If excess mustard spills
onto the top of the ham, spread it smoothly
over the top. Refrigerate until mustard is set,
about 45 minutes. Turn over and repeat process,
making and filling more holes on the bottom of
the ham. Refrigerate until firm.

❋ May be refrigerated covered for 2 days.

Before serving, spread cranberry sauce over
top of ham. If desired, decorate by placing kumquats on toothpicks and inserting around sides
of ham. Drape strung cranberries over kumquats. Refrigerate until serving time. Slice as
needed. Or slice and place overlapping on a
platter. Ham may sit at room temperature for 4
to 6 hours before the jelled mustard becomes
soft.

Serves 18 to 24

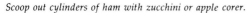

*Scoop out cylinders of ham with zucchini or apple corer.*

*Pour slightly thickened mustard sauce through funnel into holes.*

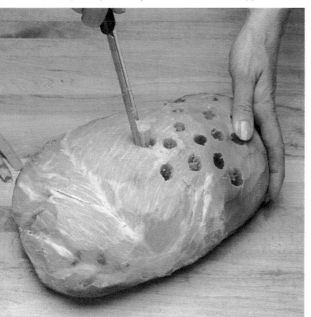

## Pecan-Stuffed Honey-Glazed Ham

A tunnel is cut through the center of a ham, and it's packed with crunchy cornbread and pecan stuffing. Glazed with golden honey and orange juice, this ham is then topped with the remaining stuffing mixture.

**6-to 8-pound boneless ham, fully cooked**

**2½ cups chopped onion**

**¼ pound (1 stick) butter or margarine**

**1½ cups packaged cornbread stuffing mix**

**¾ cup chopped fresh parsley**

**2½ cups coarsely chopped pecans**

**3 teaspoons prepared mustard**

**3 eggs, lightly beaten**

**¾ cup honey**

**3 tablespoons frozen orange juice concentrate, thawed**

Cut all skin and fat from ham. Make a cavity in the ham by cutting a 2-inch-diameter cylinder through the length of the ham, beginning in the front and working toward the back. Remove ham from cylinder, leaving a 2-inch tunnel. (Save the center scraps of ham for another use.)

Make pecan stuffing: In large skillet, sauté onion in butter or margarine until soft. Remove to bowl and add cornbread stuffing mix, parsley, pecans, mustard, and egg; toss lightly. Stuff cavity of ham with two thirds of the stuffing, packing it in lightly. Score top of ham in diamond pattern, cutting about ¼ inch deep.

✲ May be refrigerated for 2 days. Refrigerate remaining stuffing in covered bowl.

Bring to room temperature. Preheat oven to 325°. Place ham on rack in roasting pan. Bake for 1½ hours.

While ham is baking, make glaze by mixing honey and orange juice concentrate in bowl. After 1½ hours, pour glaze over ham; bake 20 minutes. Remove ham from oven and spread the remaining stuffing evenly over the top. Baste with pan juices. Return to oven and bake 20 to 30 more minutes or until top is brown and crusty.

Serves 18 to 24

Cut a two-inch cylindrical tunnel through center of ham. Remove ham and spoon in stuffing.

Pecan-stuffed ham topped with a honey-glazed stuffing.

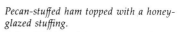

## Waldorf Cinnamon Mold

This red molded salad has a sweet cinnamon flavor highlighted by fresh apples and oranges. A beautiful and refreshing complement to ham.

½ cup red hot cinnamon candies
¼ cup sugar
6-ounce package cherry gelatin
2 cups diced peeled apple
1 cup diced peeled orange
½ cup chopped walnuts or pecans

In a medium saucepan, bring red hots, sugar, and 2 cups water to a boil, stirring occasionally until melted. Place gelatin in large bowl. Pour boiling mixture over gelatin and stir to dissolve. Stir in 2 cups cold water. Chill until partially set. Stir in apple, orange, and nuts. Pour into a 6-cup mold. Refrigerate until firm.

❋ May be refrigerated covered with plastic wrap for 2 days.

Before serving, go around edge of mold with sharp knife. Dip in warm water several times and invert onto serving plate.

Serves 12 to 14

## Layered Winter Salad

Using the ingredients for summer gazpacho, you can have a winter salad resplendent with tomatoes, cucumbers, mushrooms, and red onions. It's all coated with an herb-scented vinaigrette and festively garnished. The right salad for a buffet—it can sit for hours and won't wilt.

BASIL VINAIGRETTE
½ cup olive oil
¼ cup white wine vinegar
2 tablespoons dried basil or ¼ cup chopped fresh basil
¼ cup chopped fresh parsley
1 clove garlic, crushed
2 tablespoons lemon juice
4 drops Tabasco sauce
Salt and pepper to taste

SALAD
1 large hot-house or European cucumber, thinly sliced
1 teaspoon salt
½ pound mushrooms, thinly sliced
1 green pepper, seeded and sliced into thin strips
1 medium red onion, thinly sliced
3 medium tomatoes, thinly sliced

GARNISH (optional)
**Tomato wedges**
**Green pepper**
**Black olives, pitted and halved**

Make basil vinaigrette: Combine all vinaigrette ingredients together in food processor with metal blade or in blender.

❋ Vinaigrette may be refrigerated 4 days.

Place the cucumber slices in a colander in the sink. Sprinkle with salt, toss lightly, and let them drain for 1 hour. Dry them with paper towels.

In a large glass salad bowl, layer cucumber, mushrooms, pepper, and onions.

Sprinkle half the vinaigrette over the vegetables. Layer the tomato slices on top and pour on the remaining dressing. Cover with plastic wrap and refrigerate for several hours.

❋ May be refrigerated overnight.

Before serving, place tomato wedges around top of salad. Cut the pepper into triangles to resemble leaves; arrange them on each side of tomatoes. Place olives around the outer edge; insert a strip of green pepper into each olive center.

Serves 8

## Christmas Punch with Cranberry Ice Wreath

This sweet nonalcoholic punch is a sparkling Christmas red color. A cheery wreath made from cranberry juice is garnished with whole cranberries and green leaves and floats atop the punch.

3-ounce package cherry-flavored gelatin
1 cup boiling water
6-ounce can frozen lemonade concentrate
3 cups cold water
1-quart bottle cranberry juice cocktail, chilled
Cranberry Ice Wreath (see following recipe)
1-pint 12-ounce bottle ginger ale, chilled

Dissolve cherry-flavored gelatin in boiling water. Stir in lemonade concentrate. Add the cold water and the cranberry juice cocktail.

✻ May be refrigerated overnight.

Place cranberry ice wreath in a large punch bowl. Pour punch over ice. Slowly pour in chilled ginger ale.

Makes about 25 4-ounce servings

## Cranberry Ice Wreath

3 cups cranberry juice
2 cups water
10 to 12 fresh garden leaves, such as lemon or camellia (optional)

Mix cranberry juice and water. Pour half of it into a 6-cup ring mold. Freeze solid. Remove from freezer; place leaves shiny side up on frozen ring. Carefully pour a small amount of remaining cranberry water over leaves. Return to freezer until frozen. Add more cranberry water to fill mold to the top, if necessary. Freeze overnight or until solid.

Before serving, unmold ice ring by dipping bottom of mold in cold water; turn out on heavy foil. Wrap ring securely in foil. Return to freezer.

✻ May be frozen for 1 month.

Makes 1 ice ring

## Spirited Punch Bowl

A great way to make punch for a bunch. The fruit juice base can be frozen in one-quart milk cartons and then defrosted before serving right in your punch bowl. Chop up slightly, add the 7-Up and the alcohol, and you have a very easy spirited punch.

1½ cups water
 1 cup sugar
24-ounce can pineapple juice
 ¼ cup lemon juice
1½ cups orange juice
 2 ripe bananas, mashed
 1-liter bottle 7-Up, chilled
 1 cup vodka
 1 cup dark rum
   Ice cubes or Ice Mold (see following recipe)

Make sugar syrup by placing water and sugar in small saucepan; bring to a boil and simmer, stirring occasionally, for 3 minutes or until sugar is dissolved. Cool.

❋ May be refrigerated indefinitely.

In large container, combine sugar syrup, pineapple juice, lemon juice, orange juice, and bananas.

❋ May be refrigerated 2 days.

❋ May be frozen for several months. Remove from freezer 2 to 3 hours before serving.

Place fruit mixture in punch bowl. Stir in 7-Up, vodka, and rum before serving. Add ice or ice mold.

Makes 32 four-ounce servings

## Ice Mold

Follow directions for the ice mold in the Champagne Reception Punch (see recipe in the Wedding Reception menu), using a ring mold and green and red grapes.

## *Lemon Tarts*

This rich cream cheese pastry is one of the easiest and best in the world. It's baked into shells and filled with a sparkling sweet and tart lemon curd. The same recipe also makes lime tarts, and it's pretty to alternate the colors on a serving platter.

**FLAKY PASTRY**
- **¼ pound (1 stick) butter, cold and cut into pieces for food processor; at room temperature for mixer**
- **3-ounce package cream cheese, cold and cut into pieces for food processor; at room temperature for mixer**
- **1 cup all-purpose flour**

**LEMON FILLING**
- **2 large eggs**
- **½ cup sugar**
- **¼ cup lemon juice (about 3 lemons)**
- **2 teaspoons grated lemon rind**
- **4 tablespoons (½ stick) butter, at room temperature**

**GARNISH** (optional)
- **½ pint whipping cream, whipped**

Make flaky pastry: In food processor with metal blade or in mixing bowl, mix butter and cream cheese until blended. Add flour and continue mixing until well incorporated. Divide into small balls of dough. Press into the bottom and up the sides of 1½-inch ungreased miniature muffin tins, making a thin shell. Bake at 375° for 30 minutes or until golden. Remove to rack and cool completely. Remove from tins by inserting the tip of a small knife into an edge and inverting.

May be stored airtight for several days.

❄ May be frozen

Make lemon filling by placing eggs, sugar, lemon juice, and lemon rind in top of double boiler. Whisk until well blended. Place over simmering water and cook, stirring constantly, until mixture becomes thick and shiny and comes just to a boil. Immediately remove from heat; stir in butter and cool. Spoon into cooled pastry shells. Refrigerate for several hours for filling to become firm and flavors to blend.

❄ May be refrigerated overnight.

❄ May be frozen for 1 month. Defrost in single layers in refrigerator.

Garnish with small rosettes of whipped cream piped through a ½-inch rosette tip, if desired.

Makes 24 tarts

*Variation*: Lime Tarts: Lime filling is made the same way as lemon filling. Substitute ¼ cup lime juice and 2 teaspoons lime rind for the lemon juice and rind. The remaining ingredients remain the same. Add a few drops of green food coloring to filling.

*Yule Log is decorated with colored butter cream frosting to resemble a cut log.*

## Yule Log

No Christmas is complete without the classically elegant Bûche de Noël. But besides having a reputation for being traditional, it also has a reputation for being a lot of hard work to make. My Christmas present to you is a Bûche de Noël made easy. A lot of time-consuming steps are eliminated but none of its flavor or beauty. The chocolate cake is moist and fine-textured, and the butter cream is buttery, rich, and chocolaty; it easily serves as the filling, the frosting, and even the base for the decorations.

## CAKE

- 6 **egg yolks**
- 1 **cup powdered sugar**
- ½ **cup unsweetened cocoa**
- 6 **egg whites, at room temperature**
  **Dash of cream of tartar**
  **Dash of salt**

## BUTTER CREAM FROSTING

- 3 **egg whites, at room temperature**
  **Dash of salt**
  **Dash of cream of tartar**
- 1⅓ **cups sugar**
- ⅓ **cup water**
- ½ **pound (2 sticks) unsalted butter, at room temperature, cut into small pieces**
- 1 **tablespoon vanilla extract**

**Eight 1-ounce squares semisweet chocolate, melted in top of double boiler**
- 2 **tablespoons rum or strong coffee**

## GARNISH (optional)
**Green food coloring**
**Red food coloring**

*Immediately upon removing cake from oven, roll as tightly as possible in dish towel sprinkled with powdered sugar.*

Grease a 10½-by-15½-by-1-inch baking pan. Line bottom with parchment or waxed paper. Grease the paper; set aside. In a large mixing bowl with electric mixer, beat egg yolks until very thick and light. Sift powdered sugar and cocoa into a bowl; gradually add to egg yolks, beating constantly. Beat egg whites until frothy; add cream of tartar and salt and beat until stiff peaks form. Fold whites into chocolate mixture. Spread evenly into prepared pan. Bake at 350° in center of oven for 12 to 15 minutes or until top springs back when lightly touched with fingertip.

While cake bakes, place a clean dish towel on counter. Sprinkle powdered sugar through a strainer onto towel. Remove cake from oven and immediately invert onto towel. Remove cake pan and pull off paper. Roll cake and towel together lengthwise as tightly as possible; set aside seam side down to cool completely.

Make butter cream frosting: In a large mixing bowl with electric mixer, beat egg whites until frothy. Add salt and cream of tartar and beat until stiff. Meanwhile, dissolve sugar and water in a medium saucepan. Turn up heat and cook, without stirring, until sugar reaches the soft ball stage, 236° to 238° on a candy thermometer. Mixing constantly, slowly pour sugar syrup into whites. Do not be concerned with the syrup that splatters onto the sides of the bowl. Continue beating until mixture feels cool to the touch, approximately 10 minutes. When cool, beat in the butter a small piece at a time. Add vanilla. Remove ¾ cup butter cream to a small bowl. Beat chocolate and rum or coffee into remaining butter cream.

Unroll cool cake. Spread cake with half the chocolate butter cream. Reroll as tightly as possible. Roll cake onto heavy foil. Wrap cake in the foil and refrigerate or freeze until well chilled, about 1 hour. It is easier to frost when it is very cold. Leave remaining chocolate and plain butter cream at room temperature.

Place chilled cake on a serving platter lined with strips of waxed paper. Refrigerate plain butter cream for 15 minutes, while frosting and

*Unroll cake and spread with filling.*

*Cut off ends and place them on top to simulate log stumps. Frost with butter cream; decorate with pink and green butter cream, melted chocolate, and plain butter cream.*

decorating the cake. Cut a small diagonal piece off each end of the cake. Place these pieces on top of log to make stumps. Frost entire cake, except ends of logs and stumps, with chocolate butter cream. Run tines of fork along the frosting to resemble bark. Spread a layer of plain cream on ends of logs and stumps.

Place butter cream in pastry bag fitted with small writing tip. Pipe in circles on ends of logs and stumps to resemble age rings. Blur slightly with toothpicks.

Divide remaining butter cream into two bowls. Stir a few drops of green food coloring into one to tint green for leaves and vine. Place in pastry bag. Using small writing tip, pipe vine onto yule log. Change to leaf tip and pipe leaves on vine.

Tint remaining butter cream with a few drops of red food coloring. Use small writing tip to pipe berries around leaves.

Refrigerate until firm.

❄ May be refrigerated overnight.

Carefully remove strips of waxed paper. Bring to room temperature one hour before serving.

Serves 12

## Holiday Bread Pudding with Brandy Cream Sauce

A rich egg custard is studded with brandy-soaked raisins and poured over triangles of toasted bread. During baking, the bread rises to the top to form a crust. The brandy cream sauce complements not only this delicious bread pudding, but provides a perfect topping for any holiday pudding, or for fresh or stewed fruit.

PUDDING

  2 tablespoons brandy
⅔ cup seedless dark raisins
12 slices white sandwich bread, crusts removed
  5 eggs
  4 egg yolks
  1 cup sugar
  1 cup whipping cream
  4 cups (1 quart) milk
  2 teaspoons vanilla extract
1¼ teaspoons ground cinnamon
¼ teaspoon ground nutmeg
  4 tablespoons (½ stick) butter or margarine, melted

BRANDY CREAM SAUCE

  3 egg yolks
  1 tablespoon cornstarch
¼ cup water
¾ cup sugar
1½ cups milk
2-3 tablespoons brandy
  1 teaspoon vanilla extract

Make the pudding: Pour brandy over raisins and let sit for 4 hours or longer. Or heat brandy, pour over raisins, and let sit 30 minutes. Cut bread slices in half to form triangles; set aside. In a large mixing bowl with electric mixer, beat eggs and yolks with sugar until light and creamy. Add cream, milk, vanilla, cinnamon, nutmeg, and melted butter or margarine. Mix until well blended.

Butter a 7-by-11-inch baking dish. Sprinkle raisins on bottom of dish. Arrange bread slices overlapping in rows across the width of the baking dish. Carefully pour custard over bread. Place casserole in a shallow baking pan and place on middle shelf of oven. Pour enough hot water into baking pan to come halfway up sides of casserole. Bake at 350° for 50 to 60 minutes or until knife inserted in center comes out clean and top is golden brown. Best served warm the same day or at room temperature.

❊ May be refrigerated covered overnight. Do not reheat. Bring to room temperature before serving.

Make brandy cream sauce: In a medium saucepan, lightly beat the egg yolks. In a measuring cup, dissolve cornstarch in water and add to yolks. Stir in sugar and milk; blend well. Cook over low heat, stirring constantly, until sauce comes to a boil and thickens. Remove from heat and stir in brandy and vanilla.

❊ Sauce may be refrigerated for 1 month.

Serve sauce at room temperature with pudding.

Serves 12

## Cold Chestnut Soufflé

This soft and creamy soufflé is similar to a mousse in consistency. The addition of coffee brings out the good, rich chestnut flavor.

*Separate chocolate from leaves by gently pulling back on leaf. Top Cold Chestnut Soufflé with whipped cream and decorate with green chocolate leaves.*

SOUFFLÉ

    ½ cup dark rum
    1 envelope unflavored gelatin
    1 teaspoon instant coffee granules
    8 egg yolks
    ¾ cup sugar
15½-ounce can sweetened chestnut
        purée or spread
    1½ cups whipping cream
    8 egg whites, at room temperature
        Dash of salt
        Dash of cream of tartar

GARNISH

    ½ pint (1 cup) whipping cream
        Green Chocolate Leaves (see
        following recipe)

Prepare a 1½-quart (6-cup) soufflé dish by wrapping a double thickness of foil around dish, letting it extend 2 inches above top of dish, forming a collar. Secure with Scotch tape. Set aside.

Place rum, unflavored gelatin, and coffee in a measuring cup. Stir to mix; set aside for 5 minutes for gelatin to soften.

In mixing bowl with electric mixer, beat egg yolks and sugar until thick and creamy. Pour into a medium saucepan and cook over low heat, stirring constantly, until mixture feels hot to the touch and sugar is dissolved. Stir rum-coffee mixture into yolks. Heat until gelatin and coffee are completely dissolved; do not boil. Remove pan from heat. Process or mix chestnut purée until smooth; whisk into gelatin. Transfer mixture to a large bowl and refrigerate or stir over a bowl of ice water until cool.

In mixing bowl, beat 1½ cups whipping cream until soft peaks form; do not beat stiff. In another bowl, beat egg whites until frothy. Add salt and cream of tartar and beat stiff. Fold cream and whites into chestnut mixture. Pour into prepared soufflé dish, smoothing the top. Refrigerate until firm. When firm, cover top with plastic wrap.

✻ May be refrigerated overnight.

❈ May be frozen for 2 weeks. Defrost in refrigerator overnight.

Before serving, remove collar by going around edge of foil with point of sharp knife. Carefully pull off foil. For garnish, whip cream until stiff. Pipe or spoon rosettes of cream around the top. Decorate with green chocolate leaves.

Serves 12

## Green Chocolate Leaves

Green chocolate is obtained by slowly melting white chocolate over hot water and tinting it green. Not all white chocolate melts, so be sure to look for Toblerone or chocolate for dipping or melting. You spread the chocolate on the leaf, and when it's firm, you peel it off. At Christmastime, the most festive leaf to use is holly.

I'll never forget a humiliating experience I had many years ago when I was making chocolate holly leaves for a large cooking demonstration that was a fund-raiser for a children's hospital. I heard a voice from the audience say, "I'm a doctor and I wonder if you're aware that holly leaves are poisonous." I must have turned as red as a holly berry as I stammered, "No, I didn't. After all these years of eating them, I guess I'm lucky to be alive."

I ran home and called every university botany department I could get hold of. The reason I live to tell the story is that although the leaves are poisonous, if you wash them well and don't eat the leaves themselves, the poison does not penetrate the coating. So please don't eat the real leaves, just the green chocolate ones.

**24 garden leaves, such as lemon, camellia, or holly, with small stem attached**
**4 ounces white chocolate, chopped**
**Green food coloring**

Wash leaves and dry well. Line a baking sheet which will fit in the refrigerator with waxed paper. In the top of a double boiler, melt white chocolate over hot water, stirring until smooth. Stir 1 to 2 drops green food coloring into the chocolate to tint leaf green. Using a small knife or spreader and holding the leaf by the stem, spread the underside of the leaf with the chocolate. Place leaves chocolate side up on baking sheet. Refrigerate until firm.

✿ May be refrigerated 1 week. Place in airtight container when solid.

❄ May be frozen in airtight container.

To remove the leaf from the chocolate, grasp the leaf's stem and gently pull back on the leaf, separating it from the chocolate.

✿ May be refrigerated several days.

❄ May be frozen.

Makes about 24 leaves

*Spread leaves with chocolate on one side. Place on baking sheet and refrigerate until firm.*

# Cookies for Carolers

### MENU

MARSHMALLOW TURTLE COOKIES
WREATH COOKIES
LINZER COOKIES
JAM LOGS AND THUMBPRINTS
ENGLISH CURRANT TARTS
CANDY-DECORATED
ALMOND COOKIES
HOLIDAY FRUIT BARS
❧

CANDY CANE PUNCH

*Cookies are an ever popular dessert, but never so in demand as they are during the Christmas season. They're terrific for gifts, wonderful to have on hand for company, and deliciously rewarding for neighborhood carolers.*

*Three basic doughs will make several varieties of cookies. If you bake your cookies on parchment-lined baking trays, it makes the job much simpler and ensures even baking, by keeping the bottoms from burning before the tops are done. I cut several sheets of parchment so that I can get an assembly line going: drop the cookie dough onto the parchment and when a tray of baked cookies comes out of the oven, slide the sheet of baked cookies off, set an already prepared sheet on the tray and slide it back into the oven. This is a sure-fire way to bake dozens of cookies in a matter of minutes. If you dab shortening in each corner of the baking sheet it will hold the parchment in place and keep it from curling.*

*Whenever I make cookie dough that needs to be rolled out, I roll it between two sheets of waxed paper, then freeze it until hard, since it's so much easier to cut dough into shapes when it's frozen.*

*Clockwise from lower lefthand corner: Christmas Wreath Cookie, Linzer Cookies on upper plate, Holiday Fruit Bars on lower plate, Candy Cane Punch, chocolate Wreath Cookie, Jam Logs and Thumbprints (in center), Marshmallow Turtle Cookies, English Currant Tarts.*

## Brown Sugar Cookie Dough

This is a rich but not overly sweet pastry that lends itself well to cookies which will be frosted or decorated. Use it for Marshmallow Turtle Cookies and Wreath Cookies, neither of which have to be rolled out—this pastry shapes easily with your hands.

10 tablespoons (1¼ sticks) butter or margarine
⅔ cup light, or golden, brown sugar, firmly packed
 1 large egg
 1 teaspoon vanilla extract
 ¼ teaspoon salt
1¾ cups all-purpose flour
 ½ teaspoon baking powder
 ½ teaspoon baking soda

In mixing bowl with electric mixer, cream butter and sugar until light and fluffy. Beat in egg and vanilla. Add salt, flour, baking powder, and baking soda, mixing until blended.

Use as directed in following recipes, or wrap in plastic wrap and refrigerate or freeze.

❉ May be refrigerated for 1 week.

❉ May be frozen.

## Marshmallow Turtle Cookies

The base of the turtle is brown sugar cookie dough, which is placed upon "legs" of pecan halves. It's baked, topped with marshmallows, and returned to the oven just long enough for the marshmallows to slightly melt. The marshmallow top is coated with dark chocolate and you've got a deliciously edible turtle.

 1 recipe Brown Sugar Cookie Dough (see preceding recipe)
10-ounce package pecan halves (about 2½ cups)
20 marshmallows, cut in half horizontally
 6 ounces semisweet chocolate

Make brown sugar cookie dough. Place 4 pecan halves in clusters on parchment-lined or greased baking sheets. Break off small pieces of dough and roll into 1-inch balls. Place a ball in the center of each of the 4 pecans. Lightly press dough into pecans. Bake at 325° for 10 to 15 minutes or until bottoms are lightly browned. Remove from oven. Top each cookie with a marshmallow half, cut side down. Return to oven for 1 minute. Immediately press marshmallow down lightly. Remove to racks to cool.

Melt chocolate in top of double boiler. Dip cookies into the chocolate to cover the marshmallow. Cool until chocolate has hardened.

❉ May be refrigerated or stored airtight for several weeks in cool place.

❉ May be frozen. Defrost in single layer.

Makes 36 to 40 cookies

## Wreath Cookies

These wreaths are made by joining 12 cookies together in a circle. When they bake, they spread into a lovely round and fluted wreath. Cut cardboard rounds a little smaller than the wreaths and cover them with attractive doilies. Then you can easily store these wreaths in the freezer, ready to pull out at a moment's notice.

1 recipe **Brown Sugar Cookie Dough**
    (see recipe above)
6 ounces **semisweet chocolate,**
    **melted**
    **Powdered sugar**
    **Milk**
    **Pecan halves, silver ball**
    **decorations, sliced almonds,**
    **and/or glacéed cherries**

Line baking sheets with parchment paper or grease them. Make brown sugar cookie dough. Divide into 3 equal parts. Working with one-third of the dough at a time, break off 12 pieces of dough and roll them into twelve 1-inch balls. Place balls one-half inch apart on a baking sheet, forming a 6-inch circle. Flatten slightly. Repeat with remaining two-thirds of the dough, making 2 more circles. Bake at 325° for 15 minutes or until bottoms are lightly browned. If baking 2 cookie sheets in one oven, rotate their positions halfway through the baking time. Cool 15 minutes and remove from baking sheet. Do not be concerned if they break. The frosting will cover any cracks. Wreaths may be frosted with melted chocolate or powdered sugar mixed with just enough milk to make a spreading consistency. Before frosting sets, decorate with nuts, silver balls, and/or glacéed cherries.

May be stored airtight for several weeks in a cool place.

❋ May be frozen. Defrost in single layer.

Makes 3 wreaths

*Note:* To tie a bow through the top, make 2 holes using handle of wooden spoon in the center of two of the balls of dough. Bake 10 minutes; press the holes again. When cool, tie colored ribbon through holes.

## Linzer Cookies

A variation of the Linzer torte in the Christmas spirit. Two cookies are sandwiched together with jam and topped with a flurry of powdered sugar.

**1 recipe spice cookie dough (see Spice Cookie Goblins in Treats for Halloween menu)**
**¾ cup seedless red raspberry jam or currant jelly**
**Powdered sugar**

Make and roll spice cookie dough as directed in recipe. Remove one sheet of dough from freezer and pull off waxed paper, as directed. Cut into 2-inch rounds, using cookie cutter. Place on baking sheets lined with parchment paper or greased. Using an aspic cutter—tree, bell, circle, or other shape—cut out a design from the center of half the cookies. Repeat with remaining dough. Reroll and cut scraps.

Bake at 350° for 8 to 10 minutes or until lightly browned. If baking 2 cookie sheets in one oven, reverse positions halfway through the baking time. Cool slightly and remove from pan to racks and cool completely.

Place uncut cookies on work surface; spread with a layer of jam. Place cut-outs on racks over baking sheets. Place powdered sugar in a fine strainer and sprinkle over cookies. Gently press powdered sugar cookies onto jam cookies.

May be stored in airtight containers for 2 weeks. Layer carefully with waxed paper between layers.

❉ May be frozen. Layer with waxed paper between layers.

Makes 36 cookies

## *Almond Cookie Dough*

This is a sweet and rich dough that will make Jam Logs and Thumbprints, Candy-Decorated Almond Cookies, and English Currant Tarts, all from the same batter. The added almonds give it an extra crunch. You will be using one-third of the dough for each type of cookie, or you can use it all for any one type of cookie.

½ **pound (2 sticks) unsalted butter, at room temperature**
½ **cup powdered sugar**
½ **teaspoon vanilla extract**
½ **teaspoon almond extract**
2 **cups all-purpose flour**
¼ **teaspoon salt**
½ **cup finely chopped almonds**

In mixing bowl with electric mixer, beat butter and sugar until light and fluffy. Add vanilla and almond extract, beating well. Mix in flour, salt, and almonds. When well blended, divide dough into thirds. Wrap in plastic wrap and refrigerate until chilled.

❋ May be refrigerated up to 5 days.
❋ May be frozen.

## *Jam Logs and Thumbprints*

If you've ever tried baking cookies with jam on them, you probably ended up with more jam on the baking sheets than in the indentations where it was placed. These cookies are filled with jam after they're baked, but while they are still warm. The jam rests like a jewel on top of the cookie as the heat of the cookie sets it right where it belongs.

⅓ **recipe prepared Almond Cookie Dough (preceding recipe)**
1 **egg white**
¾ **cup finely chopped almonds**
**Seedless raspberry or apricot preserves**

Preheat oven to 325°. Divide dough into approximately 1-inch pieces. Dip each piece into slightly beaten egg white; then roll in chopped almonds. Place on parchment-lined or greased baking sheets. Using a wooden spoon, press an indentation across the center of each cookie, forming a log, or in the center, forming a thumbprint. Bake 5 minutes; remove from oven and press indentation again. Bake 12 to 15 minutes longer or until lightly golden. Remove to racks and spoon preserves into indentations while cookies are still warm.

May be stored airtight at room temperature for 2 weeks.
❋ May be frozen.

Makes 20 to 24 cookies

## English Currant Tarts

The English are known for "high tea," and these delicious pastries would certainly elevate anyone's tea. If you have problems obtaining currants, you may substitute chopped seedless dark raisins. These rich and fruity tarts are easy to make, as the filling bakes right along with the pastry. They're also easy to remove from the pans once they are completely cooled.

⅓ **recipe prepared Almond Cookie Dough (above)**
1 **egg**
⅛ **teaspoon salt**
2 **tablespoons unsalted butter or margarine**
¼ **cup finely chopped dates (about 8)**
½ **cup currants**
¼ **cup diced pecans**
½ **cup sugar**
½ **teaspoon vanilla extract**
   **Glacéed cherries for garnish**

Divide dough into 16 pieces. Press into bottom and up sides of greased 1½-inch miniature muffin pans. Set aside.

Preheat oven to 325°. In food processor with metal blade or in mixing bowl, mix all ingredients except cherries until well blended. Spoon into tart shells. Top each with half a glacéed cherry. Bake for 25 minutes. Cool completely in pans. Insert tip of a knife into tarts and remove from pan.

✽ May be stored airtight at room temperature or in refrigerator for 2 weeks.

❄ May be frozen.

Makes 16 tarts

## Candy-Decorated Almond Cookies

The crowning decoration on these cookies is the colored chocolate, melted over water, and spread into plastic candy molds, available at most candymaking or cake-decorating stores. If you are using two or three different colors of chocolate at a time, it is easiest to melt them in egg poachers.

⅓ **recipe prepared Almond Cookie Dough (above)**
   **Colored chocolate, such as red, green, yellow, blue**

On floured board, roll pastry ⅛-inch thick. Cut out rounds using a 2-inch cookie cutter. Place on parchment-lined or greased baking sheets, about 1 inch apart. Bake at 325° for 12 to 18 minutes or until edges begin to brown slightly. If baking two sheets in one oven, rotate their positions halfway through the baking time. Cool 10 minutes before removing from baking sheets.

*Use chocolate to attach candy to cookies.*

Melt chocolate in top of double boiler over hot water. Spread into small plastic candy molds. Freeze until set. Remove chocolate from molds by inverting molds and flexing plastic. Dab a small amount of melted chocolate on back of mold and press onto cookie.

May be stored airtight at room temperature for 2 weeks.

❋ May be frozen.

Makes about 24 cookies

*Melt different colored chocolates in an egg poacher over simmering water. Using toothpicks, place first layer of colored chocolate into molds. Freeze until firm. Repeat with remaining layers; freeze after each color is added. When finished, flex mold and pop out candies.*

## Holiday Fruit Bars

These wonderful fruit-filled bars are much moister than most and keep beautifully. The marmalade contributes to their rich flavor and smooth texture. One recipe goes a long way—it fills a jelly-roll pan that will cut into 48 bars.

¾ cup good-quality orange
   marmalade
2 teaspoons grated orange rind
½ cup chopped dates
½ cup seedless dark raisins
1 cup chopped walnuts
1 cup dark brown sugar, packed
8 tablespoons (1 stick) unsalted
   butter or margarine
1 teaspoon vanilla extract
2 eggs
1¾ cups all-purpose flour
1 teaspoon baking soda
½ teaspoon salt
1½ cups powdered sugar for glaze
3 to 4 teaspoons milk for glaze

In a medium bowl, combine marmalade, orange rind, dates, raisins, and walnuts; set aside. In mixing bowl with electric mixer, cream together brown sugar, butter, and vanilla until fluffy. Add eggs; beat well. Stir in flour, baking soda, and salt; mix until incorporated. Mix in marmalade mixture. Spread into greased and floured 15½-by-10½-by-1-inch baking pan. Bake at 350° for 25 to 30 minutes or until top is set and golden. Cool in pan. Cut into 1¼-by-2½-inch bars. Remove to wire racks set over baking pans. Mix powdered sugar with enough milk to make a thick glaze; drizzle over bars.

❊ May be stored airtight or refrigerated for several days.

❉ May be frozen.

Makes 48 bars

## Candy Cane Punch

This berry-red fruit punch makes a festive addition to any holiday table. Serve hot or cold topped with ice cream.

Two 10-ounce packages frozen
   raspberries in syrup
1 quart cranberry apple drink
3 tablespoons lemon juice
1 quart peppermint stick or
   burgundy cherry ice cream
   Candy canes for stirrers

Slightly thaw the berries. Combine berries, cranberry apple drink, and lemon juice in a medium saucepan. Simmer 10 minutes. Pour mixture through a strainer, pressing on fruit to release as much of the juices as possible. Serve hot or cold in mugs, topped with a scoop of ice cream and a candy cane stirrer.

Makes 9 cups; serves 10 to 12

# Hanukkah Candle Lighting Party

## MENU

HERRING SALAD SPREAD
POTATO PANCAKES (LATKES)
PINK CINNAMON APPLESAUCE
VEGETARIAN CHEESE CASSEROLE
BLUEBERRY STAR MOLD

🦎

COOKIE MENORAH
HANUKKAH COOKIES
HANUKKAH STARS
HANUKKAH CUT-OUTS

🦎

WINE RECOMMENDATION:
A LIGHT, MEDIUM-DRY WHITE
WINE SUCH AS A CHENIN
BLANC OR RIESLING

*Hanukkah is one of the prettiest and most festive of the Jewish celebrations, and I hope that my dinner menu adds to your holiday joy. The eight days of Hanukkah are celebrated by lighting candles on a menorah, one on the first day, two on the second day, and so on, until eight candles are lit.*

*Potato pancakes, or latkes, are a traditional Hanukkah food. These crisp, light pancakes are served with a vegetarian casserole and a striking blueberry mold. This menu is light but filling, and can be prepared in accordance with Jewish dietary restrictions. If you want to serve a heavier meal, you can easily substitute the brisket recipe from the Passover menu.*

*The colorful cookie menorah helps carry out the Hanukkah theme. Placed on a platter and surrounded by other holiday cookies, it makes a lovely edible centerpiece.*

*This menu serves 10 to 12.*

## Potato Pancakes (Latkes)

Every year I am invited to a large Hanukkah party. And every year I hear a friend groaning about the potato pancakes: she stood an entire day making them, and now they taste like soggy brown mashed potato cakes. No wonder. They were being reheated four layers deep, and instead of crisping they were steaming. People constantly ask me if you can freeze potato pancakes. Yes, but that depends on how you reheat them. For best results, they should be frozen on baking sheets in single layers; then they can be piled atop each other. Before reheating, return them frozen to baking sheets and bake them at high heat in single layers. It only takes a few minutes to heat them, no longer than if you pile them.

I don't advise doubling the recipe, as the last of the raw potato batter gets too starchy and brown when it sits too long. It's really not much harder to make two or three batches. You will probably be surprised by my addition of vitamin C. Ascorbic acid helps prevent potatoes and fruit from turning dark. I defy anyone to tell me which crispy, melt-in-your-mouth pancake was made first and which made last.

1 **vitamin C tablet**
2½ **pounds baking potatoes (about 4 large potatoes)**
½ **onion**
2 **eggs, lightly beaten**
1 **teaspoon salt**
¼ **teaspoon baking powder**
2 **tablespoons flour or matzoh meal**
**Vegetable oil**
**Pink Cinnamon Applesauce for serving (see following recipe) or regular applesauce**
**Sour cream**

Place vitamin C tablet in a small bowl with 2 tablespoons water to dissolve. Shred potatoes, using shredding blade of food processor or by hand; place in a bowl. If shreds are large, return to food processor with metal blade and process in batches to chop slightly. Remove to bowl and stir in dissolved vitamin C. Shred or finely chop onion. Add to potatoes. Add eggs, salt, baking powder, and flour or matzoh meal; mix well.

In a large skillet, heat ½ inch oil over moderately high heat. Using a slotted spoon, place about 2 tablespoons of batter into hot oil for each pancake. Do not crowd pancakes in pan.

Flatten slightly with the back of the spoon and fry pancakes until golden on both sides, turning once. As you reach the end, squeeze batter lightly to remove excess liquid. After frying, remove to paper towels to drain. Pancakes may be kept warm in low oven in single layer.

❀ May be frozen. Freeze on baking sheets in single layers. When solid, place in container. Before defrosting, return to baking sheets. Bake at 450° for 5 to 10 minutes or until crisp and bubbling.

Serve with applesauce and sour cream, if desired.

Makes about 24 pancakes

## Pink Cinnamon Applesauce

This is one of those recipes that you can taste just one bite of and know it's homemade: apples simmer to a soft purée as they become pink and cinnamony.

**1 pound cooking apples, peeled, cored, and cut into pieces**
**¼ cup red hot cinnamon candies**
**½ cup water**
**2 tablespoons lemon juice**

Place all ingredients in medium saucepan. Bring to a boil. Reduce heat and simmer covered, stirring occasionally, for 20 minutes or until apples are soft enough to mash with a fork or potato masher to desired consistency, smooth or chunky.

Makes 1½ cups; serves 6 to 8

## Herring Salad Spread

Herring generously shares the spotlight with crunchy apples and green peppers. This spread is bound with eggs, sour cream, and mayonnaise and is so smooth it can be formed into a mold. The herring flavor is mild but just rich enough to tantalize your taste buds.

**1-pound jar herring fillets**
**2 green apples, peeled**
**½ cup chopped onion**
**½ cup chopped green pepper**
**2 hard-boiled eggs, coarsely chopped**
**½ cup sour cream**
**½ cup mayonnaise**
**Cocktail rye rounds or rye bread cut into quarters, for serving**

GARNISH (optional)
**2 egg yolks, sieved**
**2 egg whites, sieved**
**½ cup finely minced parsley**

Drain herring well, reserving onion slices. Chop herring, reserved onion slices, and apples into small pieces in food processor with metal blade or by hand. Place in medium bowl and add chopped fresh onion, green pepper, and hard-boiled eggs. Mix in mayonnaise and sour cream, stirring until blended. Line a 4-cup mold or bowl with plastic wrap. Pour into mold.

❀ May be refrigerated overnight.

Before serving, invert spread onto serving plate. Remove plastic wrap. Garnish with rows of sieved egg yolks, whites, and parsley. Serve with rye bread.

Makes 4 cups; serves about 12

## *Vegetarian Cheese Casserole*

This casserole can be served as a main dish or a side dish. It's marbled throughout with tomato sauce, eggplant, zucchini, and mushrooms, and its scent of herbs will waft invitingly throughout your house. It's so light and cheesy it's like a vegetable custard.

**1 small eggplant (about 1 pound), peeled**
**½ cup vegetable oil**
**½ pound fresh mushrooms, sliced**
**12 ounces zucchini (about 2 medium), sliced**
**2 onions, chopped**
**4 cloves garlic, crushed**
**Two 28-ounce cans Italian tomatoes, drained and chopped**
**1½ teaspoons dried basil**
**1½ teaspoons dried oregano**
**1 teaspoon salt**
**¼ teaspoon freshly ground pepper**
**8 large eggs**
**¼ cup all-purpose flour**
**1 cup grated Parmesan cheese (about 4 ounces)**
**1 pound mozzarella cheese, shredded (about 2 cups)**
**Paprika**

Slice eggplant into ½-inch slices and then into ½-inch cubes. In a large skillet, heat ¼ cup oil. Add eggplant and mushrooms and sauté over moderate heat, stirring occasionally, until mixture is very dry, about 10 minutes. Remove to a large bowl. In skillet, sauté zucchini for 3 to 4 minutes to soften slightly; remove to bowl with eggplant. Add remaining ¼ cup oil to skillet; sauté onion and garlic until soft. Stir in tomatoes, basil, oregano, salt, and pepper. Cook, stirring occasionally, until liquid has evaporated, about 30 minutes; remove to bowl with vegetables. Stir well.

In separate bowl, beat eggs, flour, and ½ cup Parmesan cheese until blended. Stir into vegetables. Pour half the mixture into a buttered 9-by-13-inch baking dish. Sprinkle with half the mozzarella cheese. Top with remaining vegetables, spreading top evenly. Sprinkle top with remaining Parmesan and mozzarella cheeses. Lightly sprinkle with paprika.

❋ May be refrigerated covered with plastic wrap overnight.

Bring to room temperature before baking. Bake at 400° for 25 to 30 minutes or until puffed and golden.

Serves 10 to 12

## Cookie Menorah

The dough for this clever centerpiece cookie is shaped with your hands—no rolling required.

½ recipe prepared spice sugar cookie dough (see recipe for Spice Cookie Goblins in Treats for Halloween)
1 egg white, lightly beaten
¼ cup powdered sugar
1 to 2 teaspoons milk
Yellow and orange food coloring for flames
Multicolored candy decors

*Draw menorah on paper. Roll dough into pencil-thin candles, tapering ends into flames. Make wider rolls for the base of the menorah.*

Divide cookie dough in half. Refrigerate half. Line a baking sheet with parchment paper or foil. Draw a diagram of a menorah approximately 12 inches across on the paper, as pictured. Break off one piece of dough and roll with hands into a base for the menorah. Place on paper on baking sheet. Roll dough with hands into a thicker cylinder to form a stand for the menorah. Attach to base. Flatten bottom slightly. Break off small balls of dough and roll them into 9 pencil-thin candles. Place on menorah; pinch top ends into shape of flame. Make one longer candle for the center. Brush menorah with lightly beaten egg white. (It is not necessary to brush the candles as they will be frosted.)

Preheat oven to 350°. Bake menorah for 12 to 18 minutes or until bottom is lightly browned. Cool completely before removing from paper. Repeat with remaining dough.

Place menorah on a cake rack over a cookie sheet. Do not be concerned if it breaks. It can easily be patched together on serving platter. In a small bowl, mix powdered sugar with enough milk to make a thick frosting. Remove a small amount to a bowl and tint yellow-orange for flames. Thin remaining frosting by adding a few drops of milk and spread frosting on candles. It does not have to be thick or spread smoothly as it will be covered. Sprinkle candles with multicolored candy decors. Spread yellow frosting on flames. Carefully transfer to serving platter.

May be stored in airtight containers for 2 weeks.

❋ May be frozen.

Makes 2 menorahs

*Cookie Menorah decorated with multicolored cookie decors, Hannukkah Stars, and Hanukkah Cookie Cut-outs.*

## Blueberry Star Mold

Everyone who celebrates Hanukkah knows how difficult it is to decorate food for this holiday—there is certainly not much blue food around. When I created this recipe, I was terribly excited, because I had never before cut decorations out of one mold and embedded them in another. But now I had lovely six-pointed white stars set into a shimmering blueberry mold.

A friend stopped over and I excitedly showed her the mold and asked her what holiday it was for.

"It's obvious," she answered confidently; "Fourth of July."

SOUR CREAM LAYER
  1 envelope unflavored gelatin
  ¼ cup water
  1 cup half-and-half
  ½ cup sugar
  ½ pint (1 cup) sour cream
  1 teaspoon vanilla extract

BLUEBERRY MOLD
  6-ounce package lemon gelatin
15-ounce can blueberries, undrained
  2 cups pineapple juice
  1 tablespoon sugar
  ½ cup water

Make sour cream layer: Place unflavored gelatin and water in measuring cup; set aside to soften for 5 minutes. In a small saucepan, bring half-and-half to a simmer. Add sugar and softened gelatin mixture; stir until dissolved. Remove from heat and cool completely. In a medium bowl, stir sour cream; add cooled gelatin and vanilla. Pour into a 9-inch-square greased baking pan. Refrigerate until set.

Make blueberry mold by placing lemon gelatin in large bowl. Strain blueberries, reserving the juice. In a small saucepan, heat pineapple juice, 1 cup reserved blueberry juice, sugar, and water until boiling. Pour over gelatin; stir until gelatin is dissolved. Chill in refrigerator or over a large bowl of ice water, stirring occasionally, until mixture thickens and is almost set. Fold in blueberries.

Using a cookie cutter, cut stars out of sour cream layer in pan. Place as many stars as desired on the bottom of a 5-cup mold. Carefully spoon thickened blueberry mold over stars. Chill until firm.

❋ May be refrigerated, covered with plastic wrap, overnight.

Before serving, go around edge of mold with tip of a knife. Dip in warm water several times and invert onto serving platter.

Serves 8 to 10

*Variation*: Instead of sour cream layer, make blueberry mold as directed, leaving out the ½ cup water and adding 1 cup sour cream and 1 ripe mashed banana.

# Hanukkah Cookies

For the Hanukkah Stars cookies you will need blue chocolate, or white chocolate tinted with blue food coloring, and a plastic mold with Jewish stars, available in many candymaking or cake-decorating stores. The Hanukkah Cut-outs are decorated with a simple powdered sugar frosting. Preparing Hanukkah cookies should be, and can be, just as festive and as much fun as baking Christmas ones!

## Hanukkah Stars

**2 recipes prepared Almond Cookie Dough (see recipe in Cookies for Carolers menu)**
**Blue chocolate**

Make and bake candy-decorated Almond Cookie Dough as directed. Decorate following directions, using blue chocolate and Jewish star molds.

Makes about 30 cookies

## Hanukkah Cut-outs

**½ recipe prepared Almond Cookie Dough (see Cookies for Carolers)**
**½ cup powdered sugar**
**Milk**
**Blue food coloring**

Divide dough in half. On a floured board, roll half the dough at a time, approximately ⅛-inch thick. Cut into desired shapes using cookie cutters. Place on parchment-lined or greased baking sheets. Repeat with remaining dough, rerolling and cutting scraps. Bake at 325° for 12 to 15 minutes, or until sides begin to turn golden. If baking two cookie sheets in the same oven, rotate their positions halfway through the baking time. Cool slightly, and remove from cookie sheets to cool completely.

Make powdered sugar frosting by placing sugar in a small bowl. Stir in milk, a few drops at a time, until a thick spreading consistency is obtained. Remove a small amount to another bowl and tint blue. Frost and decorate cookies as desired.

Makes about 30 cookies

# Gifts from the Kitchen

MENU

DRIED FRUIT FRUITCAKE
GREATEST GRANOLA
AN APPLE-FOR-THE-TEACHER BREAD
VEGETABLE JARDINIÈRE
CHOCOLATE SPICE CANDLE CAKE
CAPPUCINO

I've been teaching a "Gifts from the Kitchen" class for ten years now, and each year the demand for the class grows bigger and bigger. Many of us prefer to stay away from the stores and are turning to homemade gifts as a way of avoiding excessive commercialism, frantic holiday crowds, and extravagant prices.

Gifts from the kitchen are given all year long, and many recipes throughout this book make loving presents. The additions in this chapter help to round out the selection.

All of these recipes have wonderful keeping qualities and are a creative twist on the traditional. They're wonderful to have on hand for at-home entertaining, any time of the year. However you choose to use these recipes, consider them my gifts to you.

*Clockwise from left: Apple-for-the-Teacher Bread, Vegetable Jardinière (packed in jars), Chocolate Spice Candle Cake, Dried Fruit Fruitcake.*

## Greatest Granola

This may be the greatest gift you can give yourself or your family. There's nothing like it on the grocer's shelves. It's great for a snack, in milk, or baked in cookies, and it's terrific sprinkled on ice cream or yogurt.

2½ cups regular rolled oats
½ cup sliced almonds
½ cup sunflower seeds
½ cup sesame seeds
½ cup shredded coconut
¼ cup wheat germ
¼ cup all-purpose flour or soy flour
¼ cup nonfat dry milk
2 tablespoons light, or golden, brown sugar, packed
½ teaspoon ground cinnamon
½ cup vegetable oil
½ cup honey
½ teaspoon salt
½ cup seedless dark raisins

In a large bowl, combine oats, almonds, sunflower seeds, sesame seeds, coconut, wheat germ, flour, dry milk, brown sugar, and cinnamon. In a small bowl, mix oil, honey, and salt; pour over dry ingredients. Mix thoroughly. Spread in a rimmed baking pan and bake at 350° for 40 to 45 minutes, stirring every 10 minutes. Stir in the raisins the last 10 minutes. Remove from oven and cool. Store in airtight container.

May be stored at room temperature several months.

❀ May be frozen.

Makes 5 cups

## Vegetable Jardinière

Layers of lightly pickled vegetables make a fresh bouquet of colors and tastes that are both sweet and spicy.

2½ cups water
2½ cups white vinegar
1½ cups sugar
1½ teaspoons salt
1 clove garlic, peeled and cut in half
1 bay leaf
¼ cup mixed pickling spices
1 teaspoon dried tarragon
2 bunches broccoli (about 3 pounds)
2 heads cauliflower (about 4 pounds)
10 stalks celery, sliced into 1-inch diagonal pieces

Make pickling solution: In a large heavy pot, not aluminum or iron, combine water, vinegar, sugar, salt, garlic, bay leaf, pickling spices, and tarragon; bring to a boil. Reduce heat, cover, and simmer for 5 minutes.

Cut stems off broccoli and cauliflower; discard stems. Separate into flowerets. Add half the vegetables to the pickling solution. Cover pot, bring to a boil, and cook 15 minutes, stirring once or twice. Using slotted spoon, remove vegetables to a rimmed baking sheet; cool. Repeat with second half of vegetables. Strain liquid into a pitcher or bowl. Layer alternating rows of vegetables into glass jars. Place the most attractive pieces against the sides of the jar. Fill

6 large carrots, peeled and sliced into ¼-inch diagonal pieces or rounds
3 to 4 red peppers, seeded and cut into quarters

the center with the less attractive or broken pieces. Pour pickling solution into the jars, covering the vegetables completely. If you need more liquid, make solution in same proportions, omitting the bay leaf, pickling spices, and tarragon. Let cool, then add to jars. Cover jars and store in the refrigerator.

❋ May be refrigerated up to 2 months.

Makes about 4 quarts

## An Apple-for-the-Teacher Bread

Not a true apple bread, for the moistness and sweet flavor comes from applesauce. It's golden brown, fragrant with spices, and baked in custard cups to resemble apples.

1 cup sugar
½ cup vegetable oil
2 eggs
3 tablespoons milk
1¼ cups applesauce
2 cups all-purpose flour
½ teaspoon baking powder
1 teaspoon baking soda
½ teaspoon ground cinnamon
¼ teaspoon salt
¼ teaspoon ground nutmeg
¼ teaspoon ground allspice
½ cup seedless dark raisins
Cinnamon stick for garnish
4 small candied mint leaves or garden leaves for garnish

In a mixing bowl with electric mixer, beat sugar, oil, eggs, milk, and applesauce until blended. Add remaining ingredients and mix until blended. Grease four 10-ounce custard cups. Divide batter among the cups. Bake at 350° for 40 to 45 minutes or until cake tester or toothpick inserted in center comes out clean. Cool 10 minutes; invert onto racks, turn right side up, and cool completely.

❋ May be refrigerated for 1 week.

❋ May be frozen.

Before giving as a gift, place ½-inch cinnamon stick into center of bread for apple's stem. Insert candied or real leaf next to stem.

Makes four loaves

*Variation:* Bread may be baked in a greased 9-by-5-by-3-inch loaf pan. Bake for 50 to 60 minutes or until tests done.

## Dried Fruit Fruitcake

Fruit cakes are traditional for the holidays, but I have yet to meet the person who has preferred the traditional glacéed fruit variety to this dried fruit cake. It's very moist, full of an assortment of good spices, and soaked in brandy and Grand Marnier. I like to make these in small aluminum pans available at the supermarket—they are inexpensive and just the perfect size. If you wrap the cakes with the bows on the sides of the packages instead of on the tops, you will be able to stack the cakes all wrapped and ready to go in the refrigerator or in the freezer. Cakes do not need to be wrapped in cheesecloth. They will keep for several weeks in the refrigerator in foil or may be frozen.

½ **pound (2 sticks) unsalted butter or margarine, at room temperature**
1 **cup light, or golden, brown sugar, packed**
½ **cup honey**
5 **large eggs**
½ **cup apricot nectar**
¼ **cup half-and-half**
2 **cups all-purpose flour**
1 **teaspoon baking powder**
1¼ **teaspoons ground cinnamon**
½ **teaspoon ground allspice**
½ **teaspoon salt**
¾ **pound dried apricots, coarsely chopped**
¾ **pound pitted dates, chopped**
½ **pound golden raisins**
1 **pound coarsely chopped walnuts or pecans**
¼ **cup brandy**
¼ **cup Grand Marnier or other orange-flavor liqueur**

In large mixing bowl with electric mixer, cream butter or margarine, sugar, and honey until light and fluffy. Beat in eggs one at a time. Add apricot nectar and half-and-half. Mix in flour, baking powder, cinnamon, allspice, and salt. Blend well. Transfer to large bowl and stir in dried fruit and nuts. Grease and flour six 5-by-3-by-2-inch aluminum loaf pans. Divide the batter among the pans. Bake at 300° for 1 hour and 15 minutes or until cake tester or toothpick inserted in center comes out clean. Remove to racks and cool in pans.

In a small bowl, combine the brandy and Grand Marnier or orange liqueur. Sprinkle each cake with some of the mixture and let the cakes stand for 1 hour. Remove the cakes from the pans. Wrap them in cheesecloth soaked with brandy and then in foil. Refrigerate for at least 2 weeks.

❋ May be refrigerated for 6 months. Cheesecloth should be resoaked when dry, about once a month.

❋ May be frozen.

Makes 6 small loaves

*Variation:* Cake may be baked in two 9-by-5-inch loaf pans.

## Chocolate Spice Candle Cake

This moist cake is aromatic with spices and rum. Because it's baked in coffee cans, it resembles a candle with a sweet white glaze dripping thickly down it like candle wax.

Unsweetened cocoa
2 cups all-purpose flour
1¼ cups sugar
2 teaspoons baking soda
Pinch of salt
½ teaspoon ground nutmeg
1 teaspoon ground cinnamon
½ teaspoon ground allspice
4 tablespoons unsweetened cocoa
1½ cups applesauce
½ cup milk
¼ pound (1 stick) butter or margarine, melted
¼ cup plus 2 tablespoons dark rum
1 cup seedless dark raisins, chopped
1 cup chopped pecans
2 cups powdered sugar
2 tablespoons milk
1 pecan half, split lengthwise, for garnish

Grease two 1-pound coffee cans and dust with cocoa; shake out excess.

Sift flour, sugar, baking soda, salt, nutmeg, cinnamon, allspice, and cocoa into a large bowl. Add applesauce, milk, butter or margarine, and 2 tablespoons rum. Stir until well blended. Stir in raisins and pecans. Divide between the prepared cans. Place in center of oven and bake at 350° for 50 to 55 minutes or until a cake tester inserted in center comes out clean and top springs back when pressed with fingertip. Cool in cans for 30 minutes. Invert onto cake racks, turn right side up, and cool completely.

Sprinkle each cake with ⅛ cup rum, pouring it slowly over the top and sides. Wrap in foil. Or, wrap cakes in cheesecloth soaked in rum.

❋ May be refrigerated for 2 weeks.

❊ May be frozen.

Make glaze: Put powdered sugar in small bowl. Stir in milk. If too thick, add more milk, drop by drop, until glaze thickly drops from a spoon. Drizzle it over the top of the cake, letting it drip over the sides of the cake like melted wax on a candle. Insert split pecan into the top for a wick. Refrigerate until set. Wrap in plastic wrap before wrapping as a gift.

❋ May be refrigerated for 1 week.

❊ May be frozen.

Makes 2 cakes

*Tip:* Dried fruits may be chopped in food processor with a little flour from the recipe.

*Variation:* Recipe may be doubled and baked in a 9-by-13-inch baking pan.

## *Cappucino*

Everybody loves cappucino, and you'll love how easy it is to make a cappucino gift package. One part is the frozen mix, a triple-rich blend of chocolate, whipping cream, and brandy. The other is a blend of sweet liqueurs and dark rum. Place the mixes in a pretty basket with directions (keep some for yourself—it tastes wonderful on a cold winter's night).

FROZEN CAPPUCINO MIX

**¼ cup sugar**
**⅓ cup water**
**Two 1-ounce squares unsweetened chocolate**
**1-ounce square semisweet chocolate**
**2 egg yolks**
**3 tablespoons brandy**
**1½ pints (3 cups) whipping cream**
**⅓ cup instant espresso coffee powder**

CAPPUCINO LIQUEUR MIX

**⅓ cup dark rum**
**½ cup Amaretto liqueur**
**1 cup Kahlúa**

To make frozen cappucino mix: In a small saucepan, bring sugar and water to a boil over moderate heat. Boil for 3 minutes. Meanwhile, in food processor with metal blade, chop chocolate. With motor running, pour hot sugar syrup into chocolate; blend for 10 seconds. Add egg yolks; mix for 10 seconds and add brandy. Mix well.

In mixing bowl, whip cream and instant espresso coffee until thick. Add the chocolate mixture and mix well. Pour into containers. Store in freezer.

❀ May be frozen indefinitely.

Makes 3 pints

To make cappucino liqueur mix: Mix all ingredients and pour into clean bottles.

To make cappucino, add a heaping tablespoon frozen mix and ½ to 1 ounce liqueur mix to a cup of hot coffee. Stir well. Top with a dollop of whipping cream, if desired.

# INDEX

Alaska, flaming fudge, 244–245
almond(s):
  bacon almond dip, 212
  Brie, baked, with pita petals, 98
  chocolate chip almond torte, 93
  chocolate-almond toffee, 206
  chunky chicken salad, 125
  cookie dough, 227
  cookies, candy decorated, 278–279
  maple almond omelet soufflé, 78–79
  orange candied, 204
  raspberry almond truffles, 165
  variation for hazelnut crust, 159
almond paste: tart filling, 225
Amaretto:
  apricot cake, 130
  butter, 19
  bacon Amaretto dressing, 85
  spinach Amaretto salad, 85
antipasto salad, 116
appetizers:
  artichokes, marinated, 33
  avocado cashew wreath, 248
  avocado onion dip, 134
  bacon almond dip, 212
  blini cups with caviar, 5
  blue cheese dip, 173
  Brie, baked, with pita petals, 98
  Brie en croûte, 96–97
  cheese trees, 233
  chicken wing drumsticks, sweet-and-sour, 252
  chips, holiday fiesta, 255
  chutney-frosted cheese spread, 149
  confetti cheese spread, 4
  crunchy appetizer pie, 84
  currant-studded pâté, 148
  dill dip, 249
  Easter egg spread, molded, 44
  Edam cheese, potted, 249
  feta shrimp triangles, 145
  filo artichoke pie, 123
  Green Goddess cucumber cups, 32
  ham biscuits, 6
  ham, cheese and green peppercorn pâté, 44

appetizers (cont'd)
  herring salad spread, 284
  meatballs, minted, with cucumber yogurt sauce, 253
  mushroom tartlets, 146–147
  nuts, seasoned, 23
  pumpernickel toast with Parmesan, 194
  Reubens, miniature, 34
  Ritz cracker sandwiches, 254
  salmon soufflé torte, 250–251
  salmon spread, 172
  sausage rings, golden, 144
  shrimp, saucy, 194
  smoked oyster roll, 251
  smoked salmon spread, 96
  toast hearts, 24–25
  tuna pâté, 4
  vegetables for dipping, 210
apple(s):
  brown Betty, 230
  butterscotch baked, 39
  cheese apple muffins, 81
  cinnamon applesauce, pink, 283
  cranberry raspberry relish, 221
  haroset, 62
  matzah fruit kugel, 69
  sausage apple stuffing, 217
  Waldorf cinnamon mold, 260
apple-for-the-teacher bread, 293
apricot cake baby carriage, 130–131
apricot rice stuffing, 236
apricot-glazed sweet potatoes, 220
artichoke(s):
  filo artichoke pie, 123
  marinated, 33, 156–157
  mushroom artichoke filling, 26
  rice artichoke medley, 189
ascorbic acid, to preserve color, 282
asparagus:
  au gratin, 91
  with lemon matzah sauce, 68
  variation for marinated garden feast, 157
avocado(s):
  cashew avocado wreath, 248
  and cucumber soup, chilled, 185

avocado(s) (cont'd)
  Mexican omelet, 77
  mixed-up salad, 138
  onion avocado dip, 134
  turkey salad, ranch style, 229
  watercress and orange salad, 195

baby carriage apricot cake, 130–131
bacon:
  almond bacon dip, 212
  Amaretto bacon dressing, 85
  beans, baked, 178
  pea salad with cashews and, 195
  potato salad, old-fashioned, 176
  turkey salad, ranch style, 229
  variation for mushroom ham quiche cups, 136
baked apples, butterscotch, 39
baked Brie with pita petals, 98
baked fish in lemon yogurt sauce, 87
banana(s):
  banana split pie, 141
  gin fizz cooler, 173
  Mother's eye-opener, 82
  pancakes, 79
  strawberry banana daiquiris, 23
  variation for blueberry star mold, 288
  variation for pink stork cocktail, 122
banquet menu, 238
barbecue menu, 171
barbecue sauces for chicken, 174–175
barley mushroom soup, 13
bars:
  chewy chocolate caramel bars, 191
  holiday fruit bars, 280
basil vinaigrette, 261
Bavarian, lemon, 162–163
beans, baked, 178
beans, green:
  with cashews, 221
  marinated garden feast, 156–157
  vegetable chartreuse, 240–241
Beard, James, 187
beer:
  green, 37

beer *(cont'd)*
  lemon beer marinade, 86
  rye beer bread, 18
beef:
  brisket, with broccoli farfel stuff-
    ing, 66–67
  chuck, marinated, barbecued, 175
  fillets of, chasseur, 99
  ground:
    cheesy spaghetti, 109
    meatballs, minted, with cucum-
      ber yogurt sauce, 253
    quick, deep-dish pizza, 114
  steak, cold salad, 187
Betty, apple, 230
beverages:
  candy cane punch, 280
  cappucino, 296
  cassis champagne with raspberry
    cubes, 9
  champagne reception punch, 167
  Christmas punch with cranberry
    ice wreath, 262
  citrus iced tea, 192
  gin fizz cooler, 173
  golden celebration punch, 109
  green beer, 37
  hot mulled wine, 207
  Irish coffee, 40
  Mother's eye-opener, 82
  pineapple-coconut frappes, 134
  pink pastel punch, 166
  pink stork cocktail, 122
  spirited punch bowl, 263
  strawberry banana daiquiris, 23
  witches' brew, 207
bigarade sauce, 237
biscuits, ham, 6
bisque, seafood, 12–13
  *See also* soups
blini cups with caviar, 5
blue cheese:
  confetti cheese spread, 4
  dip, with raw vegetables, 173
blueberry sauce, 119
blueberry star mold, 288
blueberry torte, 180
Bolognese sauce with pasta, 112
boning of Cornish game hens, 236,
  238–239
Boston lettuce and walnut salad, 102
bouquet garni, for fruited rice pilaf,
  48
Boursin:
  Brie en croûte, 96–97
  molded Easter egg spread, 44
Bracer, Flo, 146
bran pineapple muffins, 82
brandy:
  cream sauce for bread pudding,
    268
  crêpes made with, 135
  pink stork cocktail, 122
bread "bowls" for Irish stew, 36
bread pudding with brandy cream
    sauce, 268

breads:
  apple cheese muffins, 81
  apple-for-the-teacher bread, 293
  banana pancakes, 79
  beer rye bread, 18
  Easter nest bread, 52–53
  herbed garlic bread, 178
  honey wheat bread, 15
  onion poppy seed bread, 16–17
  peanut butter and jelly muffins, 81
  pineapple bran muffins, 82
  sugar-and-spice yam muffins, 223
  zucchini bread, 139
breakfast dishes, 75–82
Brie:
  baked, with pita petals, 98
  confetti cheese spread, 4
  en croûte, 96–97
brisket of beef, stuffed, 66–67
broccoli:
  bouquets, 25
  broccoli-farfel stuffing, 66–67
  gratin sauce for, 91
  marinated garden feast, 156–157
  sauce, pasta with, 111
  variation for spinach gratin, 7
brown sugar cookie dough, 274
brunch menu, 121
brussels sprout and tomato salad,
    marinated, 243
Bûche de Noël, 265–267
buffet menus, 93, 247
bunnies, minted pear, 47
butter cream frosting, 266–267
butters:
  Amaretto butter, 19
  curry butter, 24
  garlic butter, 24
  herb butter, 19
  lemon honey butter, 126
  whipped butter, 19
butterscotch chocolate sauce, 119
butterscotch-rum sauce, 10

cabbage casserole, 36
cakes:
  baby carriage apricot cake, 130–131
  chocolate cake, 140–141
  chocolate poppy seed torte, 70
  chocolate spice candle cake, 295
  dried fruit fruitcake, 294
  ginger spice cake with lemon
    glaze, 205
  pumpkin cheese roll, 224
  stars and stripes cake, 181–183
  pudding-mix type, 130
  yule log, 265–267
candied nuts, orange-flavored, 204
candies:
  chocolate-almond toffee, 206
  orange pecan truffles, 165
  raspberry almond truffles, 165
candy cane punch, 280
cappucino, 296
caramel chocolate bars, chewy, 191
caramel nut corn, 202

cardamom, 87
Carême, Antonin, 240
carrots:
  to cook unpeeled, 50
  creamed, 50
  Irish stew, 35
  marinated garden feast, 156–157
  orange-glazed, 9
  vegetables chartreuse, 240–241
cashews:
  avocado cashew wreath, 248
  green beans with, 221
  pea salad with bacon and, 195
cassis:
  cassis champagne with raspberry
    cubes, 9
  raspberry vacherin, 54–55
cauliflower:
  marinated garden feast, 156
  with purée of peas and watercress,
    100
  variation of asparagus au gratin,
    91
caviar, blini cups with, 5
champagne:
  cassis champagne with raspberry
    cubes, 9
  champagne rice pilaf, 153
  reception punch, 167
  variation of Mother's eye-opener,
    82
chartreuse of partridge, 240
Cheddar cheese:
  apple cheese muffins, 81
  asparagus au gratin, 91
  chutney frosted cheese spread, 149
  holiday fiesta chips, 255
  spinach quiche cups, 137
  turkey-sausage casserole, 228
cheese:
  casserole, vegetarian, 285
  filling for pumpkin roll, 224
  filling for Ritz crackers, 254
  and ham pâté, 44
  sauce, 7
  spreads, 4, 44, 149
  and tomato platter, 242
  trees, 233
  *See also* Brie; blue cheese; Boursin;
    Cheddar cheese; cottage
    cheese; cream cheese; Edam;
    Monterey Jack; mozzarella;
    Parmesan; ricotta; Rondelé;
    Swiss cheese
cheese crackers; crust for crunchy
    appetizer pie, 84
cheesecake, chocolate mocha, 198
cheesy spaghetti, 109
chestnut(s):
  double nut oyster stuffing, 218
  fresh, to peel, 234
  soufflé, cold, 269–270
  soup, 234
chewy chocolate caramel bars, 191
chicken:
  to barbecue, 174

chicken (cont'd)
  with barbecue sauce, 174–175
  breasts:
    in filo, 150–151, 152
    to poach, 125
    variation for ranch style turkey
      salad, 229
  livers:
    Bolognese sauce with pasta, 112
    currant-studded pâté, 148
  Madeira chicken and shrimp, 8
  pot pies, 196–197
  salad, chunky, 125
  wing drumsticks, 252
chilled cucumber and avocado soup,
  185
chocolate:
  bars, chewy caramel chocolate, 191
  basket, 56–59
  candies:
    chocolate-almond toffee, 206
    orange pecan truffles, 165
    raspberry almond truffles, 165
  cake, 140–141
    almond chocolate chip torte, 93
    chocolate poppy seed torte, 70–
      71
    chocolate spice candle cake, 295
  cheesecake, mocha chocolate, 198
  Easter egg, 51
  filling, for cream puff heart, 105
  frosting, 140–141
  glazes, 70–71, 105
  hearts, 160
  ice cream bombe, 129
  leaves, 271
  mousse Frangelico, 158–159
  sauces, 118, 119
chocolate wafer crust, 93, 198
chocolate-filled cream puff heart,
  104–105
chowder, tomato and scallop, 14
Christmas banquet menu, 232
Christmas cookies, 273
  almond, candy-decorated, 278–279
  almond dough for, 277
  brown sugar dough for, 274
  English currant tarts, 278
  holiday fruit bars, 280
  jam logs, 277
  Linzer cookies, 276
  marshmallow turtle cookies, 274
  thumbprints, 277
  wreath cookies, 275
  See also cookies
Christmas punch, 262
chuck roast, marinated, barbecued,
  175
chunky chicken salad, 125
chutney-frosted cheese spread, 149
cider, spiced, 207
cinnamon applesauce, 283
cinnamon French toast, 80
cinnamon syrup, 80
cinnamon Waldorf mold, 260
citrus iced tea, 192

clams, canned, seafood bisque, 12–13
classic pizza, 115
cocktails:
  pink stork cocktail, 122
  strawberry banana daiquiris, 23
coconut, to tint, 53
coconut-pineapple frappes, 134
coffee, Irish, 40
coffee can, cake baked in, 295
cold chestnut soufflé, 269–270
cold ham with tangy mustard, 256–
  257
cold steak salad, 187
confetti cheese spread, 4
cookies:
  almond, candy-decorated, 278–279
  almond dough for, 277
  baked on parchment paper, 273
  brown sugar dough for, 274
  chewy chocolate caramel bars, 191
  cookie menorah, 286–287
  dough, handling of, 273
  English currant tarts, 278
  Hanukkah cookies, 289
  holiday fruit bars, 280
  jam logs, 277
  Linzer cookies, 276
  marshmallow turtles, 274
  spice cookie goblins, 202–203
  thumbprints, 277
  wreath cookies, 275
coriander, 87
Cornish game hens:
  with apricot rice stuffing, 236–237
  to bone, 236, 238–239
cottage cheese:
  blini cups, 5
  mushroom ham quiche cups, 136
  spinach quiche cups, 137
country minestrone, 12
couscous, golden, 188
crabmeat; seafood bisque, 12–13
cranberry ice wreath, 262
cranberry pear tart, 225
cranberry raspberry relish, 221
cranberry sorbet, 222
cream, sour:
  blini cups with caviar, 5
  frosting for salmon soufflé torte,
    250
cream, whipped:
  apricot cake iced with, 130–131
  chocolate cream filling, 105
  creamy pineapple dip, 190
  frosting for stars and stripes cake,
    183
  ice cream bombe, 129
  strawberries Romanoff, 161
cream cheese:
  avocado-onion dip, 134
  bacon almond dip, 212
  chocolate mocha cheesecake, 198
  chutney-frosted cheese spread,
    149
  creamy potato puff, 90
  filling for pumpkin roll, 224

cream cheese (cont'd)
  salmon soufflé torte, 250–251
  salmon spread, 172
  smoked oyster roll, 251
  smoked salmon spread, 96
  tuna pâté, 4
cream of pimiento soup, 24
cream puff pastry, 104
cream puff heart, chocolate filled,
  104–105
creamed carrots, 50
creamy pineapple dip, 190
creamy potato puff, 90
crêpes, for quiche cups, 135
crown roast of lamb, 45
crunchy appetizer pie, 84
crusts:
  cheese cracker crumb, 84
  chocolate wafer, 93, 198
  cookie crumb, 141
  hazelnut, 158–159
  macaroon nut, 71
  pizza, 115
  sweet tart pastry, 225
cucumber(s):
  and avocado soup, chilled, 185
  Green Goddess cucumber cups, 32
  variation for marinated garden
    feast, 157
  yogurt cucumber sauce, 253
cucumber chips, sweet-and-sour, 127
currant jelly, spiced peaches with,
  103
currant tarts, 278
currant-studded pâté, 148
curry butter, 24

daiquiris, strawberry banana, 23
decorations:
  chocolate basket, 56–58
  corncob figure, 210–211
  filo bows, 151
  grapefruit baskets, 76
  hearts, chocolate, 160
  leaves, green chocolate, 271
  lemon peel rose, 164
  strawberries, white chocolate, 58–
    59
desserts:
  apple brown Betty, 250
  banana split pie, 141
  blueberry torte, 180
  butterscotch baked apples, 39
  chocolate cake, 140–141
  chocolate chip almond torte, 93
  chocolate Easter egg, 51
  chocolate mocha cheesecake, 198
  chocolate mousse Frangelico, 158–
    159
  chocolate poppy seed torte, 70
  chocolate-filled cream puff heart,
    104–105
  chestnut soufflé, 269–270
  cranberry pear tart, 225
  flaming fudge Alaska, 244–245
  fresh fruit with tropical dips, 190

desserts *(cont'd)*
  frozen strawberry meringue torte, 71
  holiday bread pudding, 268
  ice cream bombe, 129
  lemon Bavarian, 162–163
  lemon tarts, 264
  matzoh fruit kugel, 69
  pears in raspberry sauce, 28–29
  pumpkin cheese roll, 224
  raspberry vacherin, 54–55
  stars and stripes cake, 181–183
  strawberries Romanoff, 161
  toffee trifle bowl, 20
  vanilla mousse, 10
  yule log, 265–267
dill dip, 249
Dills, Elmer, 213
dinner menus:
  anniversary, 95
  Christmas banquet, 232
  day after Thanksgiving, 226
  Passover seder, 61
  Thanksgiving, 209
  Valentine's Day, 22
dips:
  avocado onion, 134
  bacon almond, 212
  blue cheese, 173
  dill, 249
  tropical, for fruit, 190
double mushroom timbales, 235
double nut oyster stuffing, 218
dressings:
  Amaretto bacon, 85
  basil vinaigrette, 261
  mustard vinaigrette, 187
  pesto, 186
  sweet-and-sour, 195
dried fruit fruitcake, 294

Easter nest bread, 52–53
Edam:
  confetti cheese spread, 4
  potted, 249
egg(s):
  Italian omelet gratiné, 78
  maple almond omelet soufflé, 78–79
  Mexican omelet, 77
  molded Easter egg spread, 44
egg poachers, chocolate melted in, 278
eggplant; vegetarian cheese casserole, 285
electric fry pan, rice cooked in, 153
English currant tarts, 278
entrees:
  brisket of beef with broccoli farfel stuffing, 66-67
  cheesy spaghetti, 109
  chicken breasts in filo, 150–152
  chicken pot pies, 196–197
  chicken with barbecue sauce, 174–175

entrees *(cont'd)*
  chuck roast, marinated, 175
  Cornish game hens with apricot rice stuffing, 236–237
  fillets of beef chasseur, 99
  fish, baked in lemon yogurt sauce, 87
  ham, cold, with tangy mustard, 256–257
  ham, pecan-stuffed, honey-glazed, 258–259
  Irish stew, 35
  lamb, crown roast of, 45
  lamb, roast leg of, 46
  Madeira chicken and shrimp, 8
  salmon Wellington, 26–27
  sole, fillet of, in parchment, 88–89
  turkey, roast, marinated, 214–215
  turkey-sausage casserole, 228
  veal au vin with quenelles, 154–155
  vegetarian cheese casserole, 285

farfel-broccoli stuffing, 66–67
feta shrimp triangles, 145
filet mignon chasseur, 99
fillings:
  cheese, for pumpkin roll, 224
  chocolate cream, 105
  strawberry, 183
filo artichoke pie, 123
filo pastry:
  bows, 151
  chicken breasts in, 150–152
  use of, 123
firecracker barbecue sauce, 175
fish:
  baked, in lemon yogurt sauce, 87
  fillet of sole in parchment, 88–89
  gefilte fish loaf, 63
  salmon Wellington, 26–27
  seafood brochettes, 86
flaky mushroom tartlets, 146–147
flaky pastry:
  for lemon tarts, 264
  for salmon Wellington, 26
flaming fudge Alaska, 244–245
forcemeat, 154
Frangelico, chocolate mousse, 158–159
frappe, pineapple-coconut, 134
freezing:
  of cookie dough, 273
  of potato pancakes, 282
French toast, cinnamon, 80
fresh cranberry sorbet, 222
fresh fruit salad, 77
frostings:
  butter cream, 266–267
  chocolate, 140–141
frozen desserts:
  banana split pie, 141
  bucket of frozen fruit, 128
  ice cream bombe, 129
  strawberry meringue torte, 71

frozen molds, decorative, for punch, 166, 167, 262
frozen salad; shamrock mint freeze, 38
fruit(s):
  apple brown Betty, 230
  bucket of frozen fruit, 128
  butterscotch baked apple, 39
  cranberry-pear tart, 225
  cranberry-raspberry relish, 221
  fresh, dips for, 190
  fresh fruit salad, 77
  fruited rice pilaf, 48
  haroset, 62
  matzoh fruit kugel, 69
  minted pear bunnies, 47
  pink cinnamon applesauce, 283
  poached pears in raspberry sauce, 28–29
  raspberry vacherin, 54–55
  spiced peaches with currant jelly, 103
  Waldorf cinnamon mold, 260
  white chocolate strawberries, 58–59
fruit bars, 280
fruitcake, dried fruit, 294
fruited rice pilaf, 48
fudge Alaska, flaming, 244–245
fudge cake, 244
fudgy fudge sauce, 118

garlic bread, herbed, 178
garlic butter, 24
gefilte fish loaf, 63
giblet gravy, traditional, 216
gift wrapping of fruitcakes, 294
gin fizz cooler, 173
ginger spice cake, 205
ginger strawberry dip, 190
glazes:
  chocolate, 70–71, 105
  honey-orange, 258
  lemon, 205
  sugar, 53
golden celebration punch, 109
golden couscous, 188
golden sausage rings, 144
granola, 292
grapefruit baskets, 76
gratin sauce, 91
gravy:
  giblet, traditional, 216
  minted, for roast lamb, 47
greatest granola, 292
green beer, 37
green chocolate leaves, 271
Green Goddess spread, 32
green onion marinade, 33
green peppercorn(s), 150
  pâté, ham, cheese and, 44
  and spinach stuffing, 150, 152
ground beef:
  cheesy spaghetti, 109

ground beef *(cont'd)*
  minted meatballs with cucumber
    yogurt sauce, 253
  quick deep-dish pizza, 114
ground meat; Bolognese sauce, 112

ham:
  biscuits, 6
  cheese, green peppercorn and,
    pâté, 44
  cold, with tangy mustard, 256–257
  and mushroom quiche cups, 136
  pasta salad with pesto and, 186
  pecan-stuffed, honey-glazed, 258–
    259
  prosciutto; Bolognese sauce, 112
Hanukkah cookies, 289
Hanukkah party menu, 281
haroset, 62
harvest vegetable patch, 210
hazelnut crust, 158–159
hazelnut fudge sauce, 93
hearts of palm:
  cold steak salad, 187
  lettuce and walnut salad, 102
herb butter, 19
herbed garlic bread, 178
herring salad spread, 284
holiday bread pudding, 268
holiday fiesta chips, 255
holiday fruit bars, 280
homemade pasta, 110–111
honey, to measure, 15
honey lemon butter, 126
honey wheat bread, 15
honey-glazed pecan-stuffed ham,
    258–259
honey-glazed pineapple bran muf-
    fins, 82
honey-orange glaze for ham, 258
hors d'oeuvres, *see* appetizers
hot mulled wine, 207
hot peanut butter topping, 118
hot sauces for ice cream, 117–119

ice cream bombe, 129
ice cream sundae bar, 117
ice cubes, raspberry, 9
Irish boiled potatoes, 37
Irish coffee, 40
Irish stew, 35
Italian omelet gratiné, 78

jalapeno jelly; holiday fiesta chips,
    255
jam logs, 277
Jell-O molds, 138
jelly and peanut butter muffins, 81

Kahlúa; toffee trifle bowl, 20

ladyfingers, lemon, 162
lamb:
  crown roast of, 45
  doneness of, 46

lamb *(cont'd)*
  gravy, 47
  ground; meatballs with cucumber
    yogurt sauce, 253
  leg of, roast, 46
latkes, 282
layered winter salad, 261
leftovers:
  ranch-style turkey salad, 229
  turkey-sausage casserole, 228
  turkey-vegetable soup, 227
leg of lamb, roast, 46
lemon Bavarian, 162–163
lemon beer marinade, 86
lemon glaze, 205
lemon honey butter, 126
lemon ladyfingers, 162
lemon matzoh sauce, 68
lemon pecan popovers, 126
lemon peel rose, 164
lemon tarts, 264
lemon yogurt sauce, 87
lettuce:
  spring peas with, 49
  and walnut salad, 102
lime tarts, variation of lemon tarts,
    264
linguini Alfredo con pesto, 113
Linzer cookies, 276
little porkers and beans, 178
liver, *see* chicken livers
luncheon menu, 133

macaroon nut crust, 71
Madeira chicken and shrimp, 8
mandarin oranges; bucket of frozen
    fruit, 128
maple almond omelet soufflé, 78–79
marinades:
  for chuck roast, 175
  green onion, for artichokes, 33
  lemon beer, 86
  orange, for fresh fruit salad, 77
  orange-flavored, 237
  for roast lamb, 46
  for shrimp, 194
  vinaigrette, 243
marinated artichokes, 33
marinated Brussels sprout and toma-
    to salad, 243
marinated chuck roast, 175
marinated garden feast, 156–157
marinated roast turkey, 214–215
marshmallow turtle cookies, 274
marshmallows; strawberry ginger
    dip, 190
matzoh balls, vegetable soup with,
    64
matzoh fruit kugel, 69
matzoh lemon sauce, 68
meatballs, minted, with cucumber
    yogurt sauce, 253
menorah cookies, 286–287
menus:
  banquet, 232

menus *(cont'd)*
  barbecue, 171
  breakfast, 75
  brunch, 121
  buffet, 43
  dinner, 22, 95, 226
    Thanksgiving, 209
  Halloween party, 201
  Hanukkah party, 281
  lap party, 193
  luncheon, 133
  open house, 247
  picnic, 184
  St. Patrick's Day party, 31
  seafood supper, 83
  seder, 61
  "soup bowl," 11
  supper, 3
  wedding reception, 143
meringue layers, 54
meringue torte, frozen, 71
Mexican omelet, 77
minestrone, 12
miniature Reubens, 34
mint freeze, 38
minted meatballs with cucumber yo-
    gurt sauce, 253
minted pear bunnies, 47
mixed-up salad, 138
mocha chocolate cheesecake, 198
molds:
  blueberry star mold, 288
  frozen, for punch, 166, 167, 262
  ice cream bombe, 129
  Jell-O, 138
  shamrock mint freeze, 38
  vanilla mousse with butterscotch-
    rum sauce, 10
  Waldorf cinnamon mold, 260
Monterey Jack:
  holiday fiesta chips, 255
  Mexican omelet, 77
  mushroom ham quiche cups, 136
Mother's eye-opener, 82
mozzarella:
  cheesy spaghetti, 109
  pizza, 114, 115
  vegetarian cheese casserole, 285
mousses:
  chocolate, Frangelico, 158–159
  vanilla, with butterscotch-rum
    sauce, 10
muffins:
  apple cheese, 81
  honey-glazed pineapple bran, 82
  peanut and jelly, 81
  sugar-and-spice yam, 223
mulled wine, 207
mushroom(s):
  and artichoke filling for salmon
    Wellington, 26
  and barley soup, 13
  currant-studded pâté, 148
  dried, 13
  and ham quiche cups, 136

mushroom(s) *(cont'd)*
 stuffed squash, 92
 tartlets, 146–147
 timbales, 235
 vegetarian cheese casserole, 285
mustard, jellied, cold ham with, 256–257
mustard vinaigrette dressing, 187

Nassikas, Jimmy, 253
Nelson, Richard, 126
nut caramel corn, 202
nut oyster stuffing, 218
nuts:
 orange candied, 204
 seasoned, 23

old-fashioned potato salad, 176
olives, black:
 antipasto salad, 116
 marinated garden feast, 156
 mixed-up salad, 138
olives, green; radish slaw, 177
omelets:
 Italian omelet gratine, 78
 maple almond omelet soufflé, 78–79
 Mexican, 77
on the Ritz, 254
onion poppy seed bread, 16–17
onion-avocado dip, 134
orange and watercress salad, 195
orange candied nuts, 204
orange pecan truffles, 165
orange praline yams, 219
orange-flavored marinade, 237
orange-glazed carrots, 9
oriental tuna salad, 124
overnight cinnamon French toast, 80
oyster nut stuffing, 218
oyster roll, 251

palm, hearts of:
 cold steak salad, 187
 lettuce and walnut salad, 102
pancakes, banana, 79
panhandle barbecue sauce, 174
parchment paper:
 cookies baked on, 273
 fish cooked in, 88
Parmesan:
 filo artichoke pie, 123
 Italian omelet gratiné, 78
 linguini Alfredo con pesto, 113
 mushroom ham quiche cups, 136
 pesto dressing, 186
 pumpernickel toast with, 194
 spinach quiche cups, 137
 vegetarian cheese casserole, 285
pasta:
 Bolognese sauce with, 112
 with broccoli sauce, 111
 homemade, 110–111
 linguini Alfredo con pesto, 113
pasta salad with ham and pesto, 186

pastry:
 for blueberry torte, 180
 cream puff, 104
 flaky, 264
 sweet, 225
pâtés:
 currant-studded, 148
 ham, cheese and green peppercorn, 44
 tuna, 4
peaches, spiced, 103
peanut butter and jelly muffins, 81
peanut butter topping, hot, 118
pear(s):
 cranberry-pear tart, 225
 matzah fruit kugel, 69
 minted pear bunnies, 47
 poached, in raspberry sauce, 28–29
pea(s):
 oriental tuna salad, 124
 pea salad with bacon and cashews, 195
 purée of, cauliflower with, 100
 spring, with lettuce, 49
pecan(s):
 double nut oyster stuffing, 218
 lemon pecan popovers, 126
 orange candied, 204
 orange pecan truffles, 165
 wild rice casserole, 101
pecan-stuffed honey-glazed ham, 258–259
pesto, 113
 pasta salad with ham and, 186
pickles:
 sweet-and-sour cucumber chips, 127
 vegetable jardiniere, 292–293
picnic menu, 184
pies:
 banana split pie, 141
 chicken pot pies, 196–197
pilaf, champagne, 153
pilaf, fruited rice, 48
pimiento soup, cream of, 24
pineapple, canned:
 bucket of frozen fruit, 128
 honey-glazed bran muffins, 82
 matzah fruit kugel, 69
 shamrock mint freeze, 38
pineapple, fresh:
 coconut-pineapple frappes, 134
 Mother's eye-opener, 82
 oriental tuna salad, 124
 pink stork cocktail, 122
pineapple juice; creamy dip, 190
pink cinnamon applesauce, 283
pink Madeira sauce, 151, 152
pink pastel punch, 166
pink stork cocktail, 122
pita bread:
 baked Brie with pita petals, 98
 feta shrimp triangles, 145
pizza:
 classic, 115
 quick, deep-dish, 114

platters, to carve on, 45
poached pears in raspberry sauce, 28
popcorn, caramel nut, 202
popovers, lemon pecan, 126
poppy seed chocolate torte, 70–71
poppy seed onion bread, 16–17
pot pies, chicken, 196–197
potato(es):
 creamy potato puff, 90
 Irish boiled, 37
 pancakes (latkes), 282
 salad, old-fashioned, 176
potted Edam cheese, 249
praline topping for yam casserole, 219
pudding, bread, 268
puff pastry, 146
 Brie en croûte, 96–97
 golden sausage rings, 144
pumpernickel toast with Parmesan, 194
pumpkin cheese roll, 224
pumpkin soup, purée of, 213
punch:
 candy cane, 280
 cassis champagne, 9
 champagne reception, 167
 Christmas, 262
 golden celebration, 109
 hot mulled wine, 207
 pink pastel, 166
 spirited punch bowl, 263
purée of pumpkin soup, 213

quenelles, veal stew with, 154–155
quiche cups, 135
 mushroom ham, 136
 spinach, 137
quick deep-dish pizza, 114

radish slaw, 177
ranch-style turkey salad, 229
raspberry(ies):
 almond raspberry truffles, 165
 candy cane punch, 280
 cranberry-raspberry relish, 221
 ice cubes, 9
 pink pastel punch, 166
 sauce, poached pears in, 28–29
 vacherin, 54–55
raspberry sherbet; ice cream bombe, 129
relish, cranberry-raspberry, 221
Reuben sandwiches, miniature, 34
rice:
 artichoke rice medley, 189
 champagne rice pilaf, 153
 fruited rice pilaf, 48
rice, wild, casserole, 101
ricotta:
 filo artichoke pie, 123
 on the Ritz, 254
Ritz crackers; on the Ritz, 254
Rondelé:
 Brie en croûte, 96–97
 molded Easter egg spread, 44

rum; Mother's eye-opener, 82
rum-butterscotch sauce, 10
rye beer bread, 18

salads:
    antipasto, 116
    Brussels sprout and tomato, 243
    chicken, chunky, 125
    cold steak, 187
    fresh fruit, 77
    golden couscous, 188
    layered winter, 261
    lettuce and walnut, 102
    marinated garden feast, 156–157
    mixed-up, 138
    oriental tuna, 124
    pasta, with ham and pesto, 186
    pea, with bacon and cashews, 195
    potato, old-fashioned, 176
    radish slaw, 177
    tomato and cheese platter, 242
    turkey, ranch style, 229
    spinach Amaretto, 85
    Waldorf cinnamon mold, 260
    watercress and orange, 195
salmon soufflé torte, 250–251
salmon spread, 96, 172
salmon Wellington, 26–27
sauces:
    barbecue, for chicken, 174–175
    bigarade, 237
    blueberry, 119
    Bolognese, 112
    brandy cream, 268
    broccoli, 111
    chocolate butterscotch, 119
    cucumber yogurt, 253
    fudgy fudge, 118
    gratin, for vegetables, 91
    hot peanut butter, 118
    for ice cream sundaes, 117
    pink Madeira, 151
    sour cream, 230
    spinach vinaigrette, 242
    strawberry, 71
saucy shrimp, 194
sausage, bulk:
    golden sausage rings, 144
    quick deep-dish pizza, 114
sausage-apple stuffing, 217
sausage-turkey casserole, 228
scallop and tomato chowder, 14
scaloppini squash, stuffed, 92
seafood bisque, 12–13
seafood brochettes, 86
seafood supper menu, 83
shamrock mint freeze, 38
Shefter, Alan and Barbara, 219
shrimp:
    feta triangles, 145
    Madeira chicken and, 8
    saucy (marinated), 194
    seafood bisque, 12–13
slaw, radish, 177
smoked oyster roll, 251
smoked salmon spread, 96

soda fountain Jell-O molds, 138
sole, fillet of, in parchment, 88–89
sorbet, fresh cranberry, 222
soufflé, chestnut, cold, 269–270
soufflé torte, salmon, 250–251
soups:
    chestnut, 234
    country minestrone, 12
    cream of pimiento, 24
    cucumber and avocado, chilled,
        185
    mushroom barley, 13
    purée of pumpkin, 213
    seafood bisque, 12–13
    tomato and scallop chowder, 14
    turkey vegetable, 227
    vegetable with matzoh balls, 64–65
sour cream sauce, 230
sour cream topping, 180
spaghetti, cheesy, 109
spice cake, ginger, 205
spice chocolate candle cake, 295
spice cookie goblins, 202–203
spiced peaches with currant jelly,
    103
spinach Amaretto salad, 85
spinach and green peppercorn stuff-
    ing, 150
spinach gratin, 7
spinach vinaigrette, 242
spinach quiche cups, 137
spirited punch bowl, 263
sponge cake layers, 182
spreads:
    chutney-frosted cheese spread, 149
    confetti cheese spread, 4
    Edam cheese, 249
    ham, cheese and green peppercorn
        pâté, 44
    herring salad spread, 284
    molded Easter egg spread, 44
    salmon spread, 96, 172
spring peas, 49
springform pan, to remove sides, 159
squash, summer, stuffed, 92
stars and stripes cake, 181–183
steak salad, cold, 187
stew, Irish, 35
strawberries:
    pink stork cocktail, 122
    Romanoff, 161
    white chocolate, 58–59
strawberry banana daiquiris, 23
strawberry filling, 183
strawberry ginger dip, 190
strawberry meringue torte, 71
stuffed brisket of beef, 66–67
stuffed squash, 92
stuffings:
    broccoli-farfel, 66–67
    double nut oyster, 218
    sausage apple, 217
sugar-and-spice yam muffins, 223
supper menus, 83, 193
sweet potatoes, apricot-glazed, 220
    See also yams

sweet-and-sour cucumber chips, 127
sweet-and-sour chicken wings, 252
sweet-and-sour dressing, 195
Swiss cheese:
    filo artichoke pie, 123
    pasta salad with ham and pesto,
        186
    radish slaw, 177
    spinach gratin, 7
    spinach quiche cups, 137
    stuffed squash, 92

tartlets, mushroom, 146–147
tarts:
    cranberry-pear, 225
    currant, 278
    lemon, 264
tea, citrus, iced, 192
Thanksgiving dinner menu, 209
thumbprints, 277
timbales, mushroom, 235
timetable for turkey roasting, 215
toast:
    curry, 24–25
    garlic, 24–25
    pumpernickel, with Parmesan, 194
toffee, chocolate-almond, 206
toffee trifle bowl, 20
tomato(es):
    Bolognese sauce, 112
    and Brussels sprout salad, 243
    and cheese platter, 242
    cheesy spaghetti, 109
    fillet of sole in parchment, 88
    Italian omelet gratiné, 78
    marinated garden feast, 156–157
    to peel, 242
    pizza, 114, 115
    and scallop chowder, 14
    vegetarian cheese casserole, 285
toppings:
    for classic pizza, 115
    for ice cream sundaes, 117–119
tortes:
    almond chocolate chip, 93
    blueberry, 180
    chocolate poppy seed, 70
    frozen strawberry meringue, 71
    salmon soufflé, 250–251
trifle, 20
    toffee trifle bowl, 20
tuna pâté, 4
tuna salad, oriental, 124
turkey, marinated roast, 214–215
turkey salad, ranch-style, 229
turkey vegetable soup, 227
turkey-sausage casserole, 228
turtle cookies, 274

vanilla mousse with butterscotch-
    rum sauce, 10
veal au vin with quenelles, 154–155
vegetable chartreuse, 240–241
vegetable jardiniere, 292–293
vegetable soup with matzah balls,
    64–65

vegetables:
asparagus au gratin, 91
asparagus with lemon matzah
sauce, 68
beans, green, with cashews, 221
blue cheese dip for, 173
broccoli bouquets, 25
broccoli sauce, pasta with, 111
Brussels sprout and tomato salad,
243
cabbage casserole, 36
carrots, creamed, 50
carrots, orange-glazed, 9
cauliflower with purée of peas and
watercress, 100
crunchy appetizer pie, 84
for dipping, 210
layered winter salad, 261
marinated garden feast, 156–157
peas, spring, with lettuce, 49
potato puff, creamy, 90
potatoes, boiled, 37
spinach gratin, 7
squash, stuffed, 92
sweet potatoes, apricot-glazed, 220
tomato and cheese platter, 242
turkey vegetable soup, 227
vegetarian cheese casserole, 285
yams, orange praline, 219

vinaigrette:
basil, 261
marinade, for vegetables, 243
mustard, 187
spinach, 242
vitamin C, in potato pancakes, 282

Waldorf cinnamon mold, 260
walnut oil dressing, 102
walnut and lettuce salad, 102
water chestnuts:
artichoke rice medley, 189
oriental tuna salad, 124
watercress:
and orange salad, 195
purée of peas and, with cauliflower, 100
wheat honey bread, 15
whipped butter, 19
whipped cream:
apricot cake iced with, 130–131
creamy pineapple dip, 190
servings of, 117
stars and stripes cake iced with, 83
strawberries Romanoff, 161
white chocolate:
green chocolate leaves, 271
strawberries, 58–59
white sauce, 91

white wine sauce, 26–27
wieners, cocktail-size; little porkers
and beans, 178
wild rice casserole, 101
wine, mulled, 207
wine sauce, white, 26–27
witches' brew, 207
wreath cookies, 275

yam(s):
casserole, 219
sugar-and-spice yam muffins, 223
vegetable chartreuse, 240–241
See also sweet potatoes
yogurt cucumber sauce, 253
yogurt lemon sauce, 87
yule log, 265–267

zucchini:
antipasto salad, 116
bread, 139
Brussels sprout and tomato salad,
243
golden couscous, 188
stuffed, 92
variation for marinated garden
feast, 157
vegetarian cheese casserole, 285